# COMPARATIVE GOVERNMENT AND POLITICS
Series Editor: Vincent Wright

*Published*

Rudy Andeweg and Galen A. Irwin
**Dutch Government and Politics**

Nigel Bowles
**The Government and Politics of the United States**

Robert Elgie
**Political Leadership in Liberal Democracies**

Rod Hague, Martin Harrop and Shaun Breslin
**Comparative Government and Politics (3rd edition)**

Paul Heywood
**The Government and Politics of Spain**

WITHDRAWN

Anne Stevens
**The Government and Politics of France**

Ramesh Thakur
**The Government and Politics of India**

Stephen White, John Gardner, George Schöpflin and Tony Saich
**Communist and Post-Communist Political Systems: An Introduction**
(3rd edition)

*Forthcoming*

Judy Batt
**Government and Politics in Eastern Europe**

Robert Leonardi
**Government and Politics in Italy**

Tony Saich
**The Government and Politics of China**

Douglas Webber
**The Government and Politics of Germany**

# Dutch Government and Politics

**Rudy B. Andeweg**

and

**Galen A. Irwin**

First published 1993 by
MACMILLAN PRESS LTD
Houndmills, Basingstoke, Hampshire RG21 6XS
and London
Companies and representatives
throughout the world

ISBN 0–333–47473–2 hardcover
ISBN 0–333–47474–0 paperback

A catalogue record for this book is available
from the British Library.

10   9   8   7   6   5   4   3   2
04  03  02  01  00  99  98  97  96

Printed in Hong Kong

*To Jan Andeweg and Arnold Irwin*
 *who inspired our interest in politics*

*and for Esther, David, Monica, and Mark*
 *whom we in turn perhaps may inspire*

# Contents

# List of Tables, Figures, Exhibits and Maps

## Tables

**Figures**

**Exhibits**

**Maps**

# Preface

The Dutch political system has long attracted the attention of political scientists outside the Netherlands, although the country ceased to be one of the world's great powers some centuries ago. It was put on the map of comparative politics largely through the writings of scholars such as Hans Daalder and Arend Lijphart, who used it as a theory-driven case-study to explain how deep social divisions need not preclude political stability. It has been not only as a consociational democracy that theoretical concerns prompted study of the Dutch polity: students of electoral systems were drawn by its extreme form of proportional representation; coalition theorists were puzzled by its stubborn deviation from the rule that governing combinations have to be minimal-winning; for those interested in the role of pressure groups, it was a showcase of neo-corporatist arrangements. Because so many aspects of Dutch politics featured in some debate in comparative politics, many papers, articles, and books were written for an audience wider than the relatively small but active band of Dutch political scientists. As a result, there is now a sizeable body of English-language literature on Dutch politics, but it is fragmented as each individual contribution is devoted to a single specific aspect. In English, or even in Dutch, there are few systematic treatments of the Dutch political system as a whole. This book is an attempt to redress that imbalance.

It would have been much easier, however, if we had set out to write this book some 25 years ago. Until the 1960s Dutch political culture, voting behaviour, the party system, and consociational and neo-corporatist policy-making arrangements all seemed impervious to change, as if they had reached the end-state of their respective developments. In the mid-1960s political life was full of change everywhere in Western Europe, but the changes seemed to be faster and more radical in the Netherlands. At the time of writing some features of Dutch politics, such as most of the institutional framework, appear to have escaped change altogether and some of the changes have subsided, (perhaps temporarily), while others are still going on. The dust has not yet settled, and maybe it never will. In our attempt to explain Dutch politics it is often not sufficient to provide a snap-shot of the present situation; we have to describe how it was before, and in what direction it has been developing.

The first two chapters provide an introduction to the country and the society that form the basis for the Dutch political system. Chapter 1 provides background information on the country, its historical development, its people, and its economy. It points to the political effects of factors such as the artificiality of the country's borders, the struggle against the water, and the openness of the economy. Chapter 2 describes the divisions in Dutch society and their political consequences. It does so by reviewing the theory of consociational democracy and the critique of that theory, to the extent that both apply to the Dutch case. It discusses the extent to which developments in society and politics have brought an end to the era of consociationalism in the Netherlands.

Chapters 3–7 examine the principal structures of the Dutch political process and the key actors therein. We begin with the input-side of the political system, and gradually work our way to the institutions that are central in the conversion of demands into policies.

Chapter 3 introduces the various Dutch political parties, their historical and ideological development, and their organisation. It continues by analysing the party system, often described as one of the most multi of multi-party systems. The Dutch electoral system has similarly been described as an extreme version of proportional representation. Chapter 4 explains the electoral system and its effects on parties and voters. It ends with an analysis of voting behaviour in the Netherlands and makes clear why elections fail to produce conclusive outcomes. The absence of an electoral or parliamentary majority in the Netherlands has led to coalition government. Chapter 5 describes how these coalitions come about and to what extent they deviate from the predictions of coalition theory. It goes on to show the impact of coalitions on decision-making in the Dutch Council of Ministers. Chapter 6 is devoted to the Parliament and to executive–legislative relations. Although a parliamentary system, Dutch constitutional documents and political culture still retain elements of a separation of powers. The chapter traces this ambivalence through

time and discusses its consequences. Chapter 7 rounds out this part
by examining decentralisation within the Dutch political system. It
looks at the roles played by local government, and in particular by
the Dutch bureaucracy and interest groups. Attention is given to the
incorporation of interest groups into the system, as the Netherlands is
often described as a classic example of neo-corporatist policy-making.

All these chapters take the impact of the important changes in
Dutch society and politics since the mid-1960s explicitly into
account.

Following the exploration of the policy-input and policy-conver-
sion mechanisms in the middle section, it seems only logical to turn
our attention to the policy outputs. This is easier said than done, as a
comprehensive analysis of policy outcomes in all fields is well beyond
our reach. We have, therefore, selected two policy fields, socio-
economic policy and foreign policy, to serve as examples. Chapter
8 discusses socio-economic policy primarily because it is an example
of a policy field that is well endowed with neo-corporatist arrangements. It describes the development of the Dutch welfare state (one
of the largest in the world), and the government's reactions to recent
socio-economic problems related to the size of the welfare state.
Chapter 9 is devoted to foreign policy, because it stands for those
policy fields that are relatively devoid of neo-corporatist organisations. Whereas domestic organisations are not very active in Dutch
foreign policy, the Dutch government is the second most active
country in the world when it comes to membership in international
organisations. Foreign policy is, therefore, discussed in relation to
three of these organisations: NATO, the EC, and the UN.

In addition to the contrast in the way policies are made, these two
fields have also been selected because they achieved some notoriety in
the form of two so-called 'Dutch diseases'. The socio-economic Dutch
disease is understood as the excessive reliance on temporary sources
of income (i.e, natural gas) to pay for permanent expenditure
programmes (i.e, the welfare state). In international relations
'Hollanditis' is the second Dutch disease, referring to a perceived
return to neutralism in the decade before the end of the Cold War.
Chapters 8 and 9 in this part examine the extent to which these two
diseases have been diagnosed correctly.

Chapter 10 concludes this book by discussing the political
fragmentation that has emerged as a common theme in the
preceding chapters: pillarisation, the multi-party system, propor-

tional representation (PR), coalition government, specialisation as a characteristic of elite recruitment, sectorisation and functional decentralisation. It places this fragmentation in its proper perspective by (re)introducing some of the integrating mechanisms that also exist in the form of an underlying consensus, the precedence of expert knowledge over ideological dogmas, the existence of tie-breakers such as the judiciary and scapegoats such as 'Brussels'. Chapter 10 ends by returning to a question posed at the end of Chapter 1 about the contribution of politics to the comparatively high level of life satisfaction in the Netherlands.

The aim of the book is to combine a detailed and up-to-date analysis of Dutch politics with a comparative perspective in a form accessible to both a Dutch and a non-Dutch speaking readership. Such a combination is difficult to achieve, even though it helps that one author is an American who has lived and worked in the Netherlands for 20 years, and the other is a Dutchman who studied and worked for some time in the USA and UK. We owe a great deal to the advice and assistance of others, not least to the foreign students and other visitors who led us to lecture them about Dutch politics and asked so many pertinent questions. We would like especially to express our gratitude to the Leyden colleagues who kindly read first drafts, pointed out mistakes and offered suggestions for improvements: Hans Daalder, Ron Hillebrand, Joop Van Holsteyn, Ruud Koole, Peter Mair, Hans Oversloot, Alfred Van Staden, Theo Toonen, and Jouke de Vries. We owe a special debt to Vincent Wright, who provided countless penetrating questions and critical comments, and to our publisher, Steven Kennedy, who cajoled us into finishing the book through many stern letters and faxes. In view of all this assistance and advice from others, it is merely out of respect for the time-honoured ritual that we acknowledge ourselves to be responsible for the remaining errors.

*Leyden*
*January 1993*

RUDY B. ANDEWEG
GALEN A. IRWIN

# Acknowledgements

The authors and publishers wish to thank the following for permission to reproduce copyright material:

Bohn, Stafleu, Van Loghum, for Table 2.2.
Kluwer (*European Journal for Political Research*), for Table 5.3.
University of California Press, for Figure 2.2.

Every effort has been made to contact all the copyright-holders, but if any have been inadvertently overlooked the publishers will be pleased to make the necessary arrangement at the earliest opportunity.

# 1

# The Country and the People

## A Small Country

The Netherlands comprises an area of land with a surface area of some 42 000 square kilometres located on the North Sea around the Rhine/Meuse estuary. By some standards this area is not particularly large, and the Netherlands is often referred to, even by the self-deprecating Dutch, as a 'small' country. Granted, the area is about twice the size of Wales or half of Scotland, and also equal to the size of the states of Massachusetts, Connecticut and Rhode Island combined. Yet a definition of size that relies only upon land mass is far too limited. Even though just over 4000 square kilometres of this area is uninhabitable, as it is covered by the water of rivers, canals, and lakes, the remaining space is utilised with great efficiency to provide homes for 15 million people. With an average of more than 400 people per square kilometre, it is one of the most densely populated countries of the world. In terms of inhabitants it has 1.5 times the population of Belgium or Sweden, twice that of Austria or Switzerland, and more than Norway, Denmark, and Finland combined.

In the past the Dutch controlled a colonial empire smaller only than that of France and Britain, and today the gross national product (GNP) of the Netherlands is among the highest in the world. Small is thus quite relative and on many scales it is one of the 'largest' countries of the world.

Whether one chooses to call the country large or small, it would have been smaller without the efforts of its population. Virtually no

1

discussion of the Netherlands is complete without reference to the well-known adage, 'God made the world but the Dutch made Holland.' Whoever made it, we have the problem of what to call it. The official name is 'The Kingdom of the Netherlands', but legally this also includes areas outside Europe (i.e., the Dutch Antilles). In colloquial speech it is often called Holland, but this is actually the name of its once most famous province (now the provinces of North and South Holland). The French *Pays-Bas* translates into the Low Countries in English, and is then usually meant to apply to Belgium as well. To avoid confusion we shall refer to the political system as the Netherlands. The twelve modern provinces are shown in capital letters on Map 1.1. Thus, although there are many themes that could be used to begin a discussion of the political system of the Netherlands, the interplay of geography and people may serve as well as any other. There is little doubt that, in their little corner of the world, the land contributed to shaping the people and the people have helped to shape the land. Understanding this relationship will help the reader to understand the society and politics of the country.

## The Struggle against the Water

Of course, the land area of the world began to take shape before people could have much influence upon it. In many places this shape has changed little since the prehistoric days that determined its form. In others, the interplay of factors such as earthquakes, volcanic eruption, and/or water have altered the land even during the period of recorded history. The area of land identified as the Netherlands falls under this category.

During the Ice Age, British and Scandinavian glaciers grew together, blocking the North Sea. The course of the Rhine and Meuse rivers was altered, although as the ice melted they partially returned to their old courses. The glaciers also brought the sand that began to form what became the higher, southern provinces of the country. As the climate warmed and the ice melted, peat bogs began to form, first in the western part of the country, later more towards the east. In places, the sea flooded areas that had once been above water (Van Valkenburg, 1943; Keuning, 1965).

When the sea broke through the connection between England and France, the force of the water in the Channel brought sand from the

**MAP 1.1**
**The Netherlands: provinces and major cities**

south and created the walls of sand dunes that still are characteristic of the Dutch coastline. Behind the dunes was a large lagoon that gradually began to fill with the sands and dirt that the rivers brought from higher ground. Peat bogs, swamps, and lakes characterised the land behind the dunes.

The earliest inhabitants of the low lands were tribes who came to the area to hunt reindeer. Gradually, the hunters and fisherman were joined by farmers and cattle herders. Sometime after 100 BC four waves of immigration took place, three Germanic ones from the north and a Celtic one from the south-east.

The Greeks had vague ideas of the existence of the lands of the Celts, but it was Caesar's expeditions that brought the first direct contact between the inhabitants of the great civilisations and those of the lowlands. With the Romans came also the first recorded history of the area in the works of Tacitus and Pliny. It was the former who wrote of the legendary Batavians. Caesar and his successors pushed northwards to the banks of the Rhine river, but to the Romans the area had little meaning other than the farthest extension of the Empire to the north.

The Rhine and Meuse rivers provided natural barriers for the Romans and, although the armies of Augustus crossed the rivers and included the Frisians in his Empire, the Romans later pulled back and never really subjected the inhabitants to the north. As Vlekke has written, 'the Romans set little store by the marshlands of the west and the north of the Low Countries which held no allure for them' (Vlekke, 1943).

Assaults by German tribes and by the sea finally drove the Romans from the area. The Franks gradually gained in power and pushed the Frisians back to the north, so that the Frankish kingdom of Charlemagne and his successors included much of the Low Countries. Frankish power brought with it the introduction of Christianity into the region. Frankish domination, however, did not greatly affect the social institutions of the people. The marshy areas of the south and west did not support the kind of large land ownership which was necessary to support feudalism so that this social system was never fully established in these areas. No nobility developed in what later became the provinces of Holland, Zeeland, and Utrecht. Instead, the low countries remained a territory of small land owners and free peasants. In remote areas of the north, free peasants were able to continue as democratic peasant republics for centuries.

Instead of the manorial system, the area was far more conducive to the development of cities, which sprang up at virtually every juncture of waters and at every harbour.

Three times in history the sea broke through the natural protective dunes to alter the landscape. About 300 BC the sea broke through via the estuaries of the Scheldt, Meuse, and Rhine to inundate areas in the south-west of the country. The second principal incursion of the sea occurred about 270 AD and was a key factor in driving the Romans from the area. The third period of incursion began in the tenth or eleventh century and resulted in the flooding of large areas, creating, for example, the islands in the current provinces of South Holland and Zeeland. In the North, areas of dunes were washed away; now only small islands formed by the remnants of these dunes indicate where the coast once was. Behind these islands, new seas (or bays) were created, the largest of which was the Zuiderzee; over a few centuries the Zuiderzee expanded to cover a substantial area of northern Holland.

This last incursion led the increased populations of the area to take protective measures, which were to alter the landscape. In about the eleventh century the first dikes were built to protect inhabited areas from flooding (Vlekke, 1943; Keuning, 1965). The threat of water came from three sources. In addition to the threat from the sea, there was the threat of periodic flooding from the great rivers. Moreover, the surplus of yearly rainfall had to be disposed of lest large areas revert at least seasonally into swamps. Thus, on the one hand, the systems of dikes were extended to cover increasingly large areas, and methods, including the use of windmills, were devised to drain off surplus water. By combining the use of dikes and drainage systems, areas of land could be reclaimed from the sea and from lakes.

From the very beginning, the battle against water was not something that could be left to an overlord (or to a little boy putting his finger in the dike), but required the combined efforts of the population. Since everyone behind the dike profited, maintenance could not justifiably be left only those whose land bordered the water. Water control boards were organised with the responsibility of maintaining the system. It is often claimed that these were the first democratic organisations in the country.

Nature has thus left those who inhabit the area with what may be justly described as the 'netherlands' or 'low lands'. Nowhere is it higher than about 30 metres above sea level. In the northern and western area of the country, most of the area varies between 0 and 2.5 metres below sea level. In some larger areas that have been drained the level is even lower; the area in which Amsterdam's Schiphol airport is located lies 4.2 metres below sea level and new areas have been created that once lay 6.9 metres under the Zuiderzee (Keuning, 1965).

Today, although windmills no longer play a role in the system, dikes and drainage systems must nevertheless be maintained. More than half of the country must be artificially protected against water from outside and more than half of the population lives in areas that would be under water at least at high tide if no protection were maintained. With the threat of global warming and the rise of the oceans, there is concern that the dikes must be heightened. Plans also continue to be made for land reclamation projects, and one of the country's current political question concerns whether to drain yet another portion of the former Zuiderzee. It is the long history of the struggle against the water through the building of dikes and land reclamation through drainage that gives rise to the expression that the 'Dutch built Holland'

## Boundaries

*Historical Boundaries*

So, both the people and nature have interacted to shape the land. However, the mere shape of the land is not the only factor of importance in understanding the relation between geography, social structure and politics. There are no mountains or natural boundaries separating the Dutch from their neighbours, and even modern satellite photographs will generally not reveal the important boundaries that separate peoples and have such an important impact upon them. In the area of the Rhine river delta, three boundaries divide the peoples of the low lands and even today influence the politics of both the Netherlands and its southern neighbour, Belgium.

*The Language Boundary*

In his discussion of the 'borders of the Netherlands', De Vrankrijker distinguishes 'structural borders', which he defines as natural borders or those resulting from geographical position, from 'historical borders', which simply through their long existence gain permanence and acceptance. The Rhine and Meuse rivers provided structural borders for the Romans, and although they never really subjected the inhabitants to the north, they did leave a lasting imprint by building a highway from Cologne through Aachen and Tongeren to Bavai in northern France and on to the sea coast.

The building of this highway and the Roman colonisation along its track was one of the most important events in the Netherlands history. It determined the farthest extent of Germanic influence in the northwestern corner of the European continent and fixed for thousands of years to come the dividing line between Romanic and Germanic peoples in this area (De Vrankrijker, 1946)

The Roman highway and the structural border of the rivers thus introduced two rough, but discernible, dividing lines between north and south. To the north Germanic influences prevailed; to the south the Romans imposed their authority and customs. The highway became the boundary between Germanic and Romanic languages. The rivers were to become the border between Rome and the Reformation. As neither of the two borders eventually became a boundary between two countries, both would later play a role of political significance. As the influence of the language demarcation is felt in the area of the Low Countries now known as Belgium, it will not be discussed further in this book. Any discussion of Dutch politics without mention of religion, however, is incomplete.

## Political and Religious Boundaries

At the end of the Middle Ages, the Low Countries were not excluded from the attempts to carve out larger entities which were to become the nation states of Europe. The politics of this period is quite complicated, involving war, marriage, and intrigue. As Vlekke writes, 'If death had struck left instead of right, the future of the Low Countries might have developed quite differently' . . . '(I)t is obvious that the federation of the Netherlands provinces was primarily due to accidental circumstances' (Vlekke, 1943, p. 74). The beneficiaries of these accidents were the dukes of Burgundy, who were temporarily able to carve out a buffer state between France and Germany. Yet, just as fate had brought Burgundy into existence it also brought its demise when the lands passed into the Habsburg dynasty through the marriage of Duchess Mary to Maximilian of Austria, son of the emperor of the Holy Roman Empire.

Charles V, as a descendent of the Habsburgs, combined the rule of the Low Countries with the thrones of Spain, Naples, and America, the princedom of Austria, and election as Emperor of the Holy

Roman Empire. He was the last of the 'natural' princes of the Low Countries, having been born in Ghent and speaking French as his mother tongue, but being well acquainted with Dutch (Vlekke, 1943). Upon his abdication in 1555, he passed the Low Countries and Spain to his son, Philip II. In this accidental union, Philip was far more interested in Spain. However, this might never have resulted in serious problem had not other events intervened (Schöffer, 1973). Philip never gained the loyalty his father had received, and the local authorities became more inclined to establish their independence. Revolt ensued when this flexing of local political muscle was combined with the forces of the Reformation.

Although the people of the Low Countries were known for their piety and devotion, they were aware of the excesses and faults of the Church, which were exposed and discussed by Erasmus and his followers. Even before Philip's ascension to the throne, religious reformers, largely inspired by Zwingli, had become popular. In 1552, Charles V crushed an Anabaptist revolt by expanding the powers of the Inquisition. The suppression of the Anabaptists was only a short-term success. Under these new powers, heretics could be prosecuted without regard for the traditional processes of law. Thus religion and politics became enmeshed, as the struggle for religious freedom became intertwined with the fight to protect traditional political freedoms. Remnants came into contact with John Calvin, and Calvinism quickly became the dominant force in the Protestantism of the Low Countries.

With the abdication of Charles V, the stage was set for the conflict between Lowlands Calvinism and Spanish Catholicism. There was considerable discontent at all levels within the Low Countries, but it was the Calvinists who provided the backbone of the revolt against Philip, opposing the new king on political as well as religious grounds. The Calvinists had the organisation and the discipline necessary to lead the revolt. In 1566 the churches in western Flanders were stormed; sculptured images were destroyed and all that was sacred to the Catholics was desecrated. The movement quickly spread from the south northward to Amsterdam, Leeuwarden, and Groningen. Just as quickly, however, this first revolt was suppressed; but, as one moved farther from Brussels, the influence of Calvinism continued. Despite this initial stabilisation of the situation, Philip chose not to attempt further pacification, but instead sent the Duke of Alva to centralise control. Never before had a Spaniard been appointed as governor of the Low Countries, and the zeal with which Alva attempted to carry out his orders made him and the king even more hated. Rather than bringing peace, Alva, through his ruthless enforcement of centralisation and heavier taxation, helped to unite the national opposition.

This opposition was led by William of Orange, a German count of Nassau by birth, who had inherited rich lands in the Low Countries as well as the principality of Orange in southern France. He was educated at the Court of Brussels and was a favourite of Charles V. He was a decent man, rather more intellectual than most of his rank, and sympathised with those who protested against the injustices of Spanish rule. Although he felt the initial Calvinist revolt to be inopportune, he became caught up in the events. After the suppression of the revolt by Alva, only he had the will and resources to continue. His attempt, with the help of French Huguenots and German Protestant princes, to invade the Low Countries in 1568 failed dismally. Although his own resources were eventually depleted, he continued to provide inspirational leadership.

When on 1 April 1572 the 'Sea Beggars' captured the town of Brill, the revolution spread rapidly. On 19 July representatives of the towns of Holland met in Dordrecht where William of Orange was proclaimed 'Stadtholder' of Holland and Zeeland. However, without personal resources, he was dependent upon the States-General. In January 1579 the rebel northern provinces met at Utrecht to form 'a closer union', in which they were to retain their sovereignty but would act as a single body in foreign policy.

Alva regrouped quickly in the south and, when the threat from France failed to materialise, headed north. Yet, even after his replacement, the Spanish were never able to crush the revolt. Hostilities dragged on for 80 years. William was murdered in 1584. His son Maurice succeeded to the leadership, successfully reorganised the army and reconquered Groningen and the towns in Overijssel and Gelderland. He also moved south and occupied some Flemish towns, thus securing a buffer zone to protect Zeeland.

With the domination of Spanish forces in the south, the Counter-Reformation was able to reestablish Catholicism, so that when Maurice recaptured parts of the area the inhabitants were firmly Catholic. The treaty of Münster in Westphalia in 1648 established a political border that was to the south of the religious border. To the south the Habsburg reign continued, with the new independent Republic of the Seven United Provinces to the north. This situation was to continue throughout the remainder of the seventeenth and the eighteenth centuries.

Upon the defeat of Napoleon, the Congress of Vienna was convened to redraw the map of Europe. In an effort to create a buffer state between the major powers, the southern provinces were once again united with the north. The Netherlands was raised to the status of a Kingdom, with William I as Monarch and Grand Duke of Luxemburg. Perhaps, with patience and understanding, William could have succeeded in undoing the effects of 250 years of separate development. Yet this was not William's manner, and in his haste to establish a modern, centralised state he quickly alienated many of his new subjects in the south. Catholics feared his Protestantism and his support of state over church schools. They also opposed him in his attempts to centralise authority at the expense of local interests. Liberals, on the other hand, supported him in his centralizing and anticlerical tendencies, but opposed his restrictions on the freedom of the press and his promotion of Dutch interests. The King favoured Dutch over Belgians in his appointments and had decreed that Dutch was to be the official language in the Flemish areas. After 20 years of 'Frenchification' during the Napoleonic occupation, the Flemish elite resented the imposition of Dutch as the official language. Despite their own differences, Catholics and Liberals joined in a 'union of oppositions' to rid the Belgians once again of 'foreign' oppression. On 23 November 1830 the National Congress declared an independent Belgium, and excluded the House of Orange from the possibility of ever ascending to the throne.

After only 15 years of unification, the Netherlands and Belgium were again separated. Hostilities continued for several years, but in 1839 King William accepted the terms of separation. Through the 'forces' of history, three boundaries had thus been drawn through the territory at the mouth of the Rhine. Yet none of these three – the political, religious, or linguistic – coincided. The political boundary which defined the two nation states left each with a boundary dividing it, thus forming the basis for an important source of political cleavage. Belgium, to the south, was relatively homogeneous religiously, but divided into French and Dutch speaking areas. The Netherlands, to the north, was linguistically homogeneous (with the exception of those areas in which Frisian continued to be spoken), but was divided into Protestant and Catholic areas. Exhibit 1.1 summarises the important events of Dutch history.

**EXHIBIT 1.1**

**Important dates in Dutch history**

| | |
|---|---|
| 1st century BC to 4th century AD | Romans occupy the southern portion of the low countries. |
| 7th century | Conversion to Christianity carried out largely in this period. |
| 12th and 13th centuries | Expansion of towns and granting of many city charters |
| 13th and 14th centuries | Foundation of the higher water control boards (*'hoogheemraadschappen'*) to coordinate control of water. |
| 1384–1579 | Burgundian and Habsburg rule. |
| 1566 | Revolt breaks out against Philip II of Spain. William (the Silent) of Orange eventually becomes leader of the revolt. |
| 1579 | Union of Utrecht; northern provinces first agree to cooperate. |
| 1648 | Treaty of Münster ends the Eighty Years War; Spain acknowledges the independence of the Netherlands. |
| 17th century | The 'Golden Age'. |
| 1795–1813 | Period of French Rule, from 1795 until 1806 as the Batavian Republic. |
| 1814 | Kingdom of the Netherlands founded at the Congress of Vienna. |
| 1830–9 | Belgians revolt, Belgium leaves the Kingdom. |
| 1848 | Introduction of ministerial responsibility. |
| 1914–18 | The Netherlands remains neutral during the First World War; Kaiser Wilhelm seeks refuge following the war. |
| 1917 | 'Great Pacification', resulting in universal male suffrage, proportional representation, and state financing of church schools. |
| 1940–5 | German forces occupy the Netherlands. |
| 1949 | Former Indonesian colonies gain independence. |
| 1952–8 | The Netherlands becomes founding member of the EC. |

## Recent History

This division between Protestant and Catholic forms one of the fundamental cleavages in Dutch politics. The dominant Protestants never forbade the Catholic religion, but did at times place restrictions upon its practice and relegate Catholics to second-class citizenship.

Resentment of this fact led to the establishment in the nineteenth century of Catholic emancipation movements that would provide equal status for Catholics.

Within the Protestant Dutch Reformed Church, groups of Orthodox Calvinists, known as *de kleine luyden* ('the little men'), such as small shopkeepers, artisans, and clerks, became unhappy with their position. Under the leadership of men such as G. Groen van Prinsterer and Abraham Kuyper, they broke away from the church and eventually formed the 'Rereformed', or *Gereformeerde*, churches.

A third mass movement of importance was the socialist workers' movement. Although somewhat late in arriving in the Netherlands, socialism did take hold towards the end of the century. The importance of these three movements for modern day politics and the current political party system is discussed in Chapters 2 and 3.

It was under William I that the Netherlands had its first experience with domestic authoritarian rule. His son, William II, attempted to continue this tradition, but is said to have been so frightened by the 1848 revolutions abroad that he almost literally became a liberal overnight. Under the leadership of the Liberal leader, Johan Rudolf Thorbecke, changes were introduced into the Constitution to provide for a modern constitutional democracy.

The primary political issues of the nineteenth century were the 'schools' question and the 'social' question. Once the Catholic hierarchy had been re-established in 1853, the Catholics began to join with the orthodox Calvinists in seeking state support for religious schools. The 'social' question involved the working and social conditions of the new industrial working class. An important element in this issue was the extension of suffrage to all adult citizens. The resolution of these issues in the 'Great Pacification' of 1917 and its subsequent importance for Dutch politics will be discussed at length in Chapter 2.

As the Netherlands entered the twentieth century, young Queen Wilhelmina had recently ascended to the throne. In addition to the major political issues just mentioned, the problem of the colonies began to develop. The islands of Indonesia were the most important Dutch colonial possessions, but there were also islands in the Caribbean and the small colony of Surinam on the coast of South America. Indonesia drew the greatest interest as concern began to develop for the treatment of the peoples of the islands and the need to develop policies that would provide education and better living standards. Such attempts, however, did not prevent the rise of nationalist groups and, after the Second World War, conflict broke out. The Dutch police actions of 1947 and 1948 resulted in protests by the UN Security Council. Sovereignty was granted to Indonesia in 1949.

During the First World War the Netherlands had maintained its policy of neutrality and even accepted Kaiser Wilhelm as a refugee after the war. Hopes of remaining neutral in the Second World War were dashed when Hitler invaded the country in May 1940. A traumatic five-year occupation ensued. Queen Wilhelmina and the government fled to England.

The Queen and government returned in 1945 to find a devastated country. Having grown old and wearied by the strain of the war, Queen Wilhelmina abdicated in 1948 in favour of her daughter, Juliana. Queen Juliana reigned over the period of economic recovery and herself abdicated in 1980. Her daughter, Beatrix, ascended to the throne. Thus the Netherlands has been ruled for over a century by a Queen, although the Constitution stubbornly refers only to the King.

## The People

*Religious Groups*

As we have seen above, and will see often in the following chapters, religion plays an important role in Dutch politics. The Eighty Years' War produced a situation in which religious groups were not scattered evenly around the country. The fact that the southern provinces of Brabant and Limburg were predominantly Catholic has already been mentioned. In contrast to this rather homogeneous area, the northern provinces have been more divided. Although the Protestants of the Dutch Reformed Church dominated, Catholic minorities continued to exist in the cities, and Catholic villages could be found in the countryside. Only about half of all Catholics live in the southern provinces; the other half are spread about the rest of the country.

In the nineteenth century major divisions within the Dutch Reformed Church took place. In 1834 and around 1880 groups of orthodox believers broke away and formed their own churches. Most of these were eventually united in the *Gereformeerde* churches.

These three groups – Dutch Reformed, Roman Catholic, and *Gereformeerden* – form by far the largest religious denominations in the country. In the 1879 census, a majority (54.5 per cent) of the population reported identification with the Dutch Reformed Church. The Catholics made up 35.9 per cent of the population and the *Gereformeerden*, who were only beginning to organise, comprised 3.5 per cent. Less than 1 per cent of the population reported no religious preference.

Somewhat more than 100 years later, the picture for Catholics and *Gereformeerden* has changed only moderately. In part because of a higher birth rate, the proportion of Catholics rose to 40.4 per cent in the final national census of 1971. Since then, survey figures show the percentage of the population identifying itself as Catholic has dropped to about 30–33 per cent. The *Gereformeerden* had unified about 8 per cent of the population by the 1889 census and stayed at this level (8–10 per cent) until the 1980s. Most recent surveys show a slight drop among this group to about 7 per cent of the population.

In contrast with the relatively stable percentages for Catholics and *Gereformeerden*, the position of the Dutch Reformed has changed dramatically. Even by 1889, the percentage reporting adherence to this church had dropped below 50 per cent. In the twentieth century, each decennial census showed a drop of between 3 and 5 per cent. By the last census in 1971, less than one-quarter (23.5 per cent) reported such identification. Subsequent survey figures show a continued drop to between 15 and 17 per cent.

All major religious groups thus show varying degrees of decline in the percentage of identifiers. The rise in the percentage of those claiming no religious identification is therefore substantial. Throughout the twentieth century this percentage has risen, and in 1971 it passed the percentage of Dutch Reformed identifiers (23.6 per cent to 23.5 per cent) for the first time. Over the past 20 years, the percentage has continued to rise rapidly. Depending upon how the question is posed in current surveys, between 37 and 43 per cent of the population report no religious identification.

Not only has change occurred in the numbers of persons expressing a religious identification, but those who still identify have changed in the degree to which they practise their faith. This is particularly clear among Catholics. Dutch Catholics were once among the most faithful in Europe. Surveys prior to 1960 showed that approximately 90 per cent of all Catholics attended mass regularly. Although many

Catholics have retained their identification with the Church, they no longer practise their faith to the same degree. In the 1960s about three-quarters of Catholics reported regular mass attendance; in the 1970s this figure was down to less than one-half. By the late 1980s and early 1990s, only slightly more than a quarter attended mass regularly.

The percentage of Dutch Reformed attending religious services regularly has traditionally varied between one-quarter and one-third. The percentage of believers attending services has not changed so dramatically, but since the size of the group has diminished the actual number of weekly attenders has dropped substantially. Even the most faithful, the *Gereformeerden*, have shown drops in levels of church attendance. Whereas once almost 90 per cent attended weekly, this number is now down to about two-thirds of identifiers.

An international comparative survey has estimated the percentage of Dutch who attend religious services at least once a month to be 40 per cent. This places the Netherlands considerably higher than Denmark (11 per cent), France (17 per cent), and Britain (23 per cent), and somewhat higher than Germany (35 per cent) and Belgium (38 per cent), but lower than Italy (48 per cent) and Spain (53 per cent) and considerably lower than the USA (60 per cent), Northern Ireland (67 per cent), and the Republic of Ireland (88 per cent). Close to 30 per cent of the Dutch report no belief in God. In the survey this figure was exceeded by the Danes and the French (37 and 35 per cent), but it is considerably higher than in Germany and Britain (approximately 20 per cent) and far above the levels of 2–7 per cent in countries such as the USA, Ireland and Canada (Inglehart, 1990, pp. 188–200).

*Social Class*

Changes in the structure of social class are more difficult to measure than the changes in religious preference. Yet it is clear that in this respect the Netherlands has also undergone changes, although more gradually than with respect to religion. The most dramatic changes are in the percentage of the population concerned with agricultural production and the rise of the service sector, as we shall discuss in more detail below.

The rise of the service sector has coincided with a rise in the levels of education. As late as the 1960 census, 56 per cent of the population had only a primary school education. Greatly increased educational opportunities for young people cut this figure to only 48 per cent at the subsequent census in 1971. Today perhaps slightly more than a quarter of the population has only an elementary school education. In contrast the percentage with a post-secondary education has risen from about 8 per cent in 1971 to 18 per cent or more.

Related to such changes are changes in the perception of social class identification. Beginning in 1971, Dutch academic surveys began asking to which social class people felt they belonged. In 1971 the classes were fairly evenly mixed; 40 per cent identified with the working class and 46 per cent saw themselves as middle class (throughout the years, about 2 per cent has considered itself upper class). In the most recent survey (1989), a considerable gap appeared; only 31 per cent of the population sees itself as working class, while 64 per cent considers itself middle class.

If we combine these two factors – religion and social class – we find that during the twentieth century the composition of the Dutch population has changed quite substantially. At the turn of the century, the population was basically working class, often employed in agriculture, and quite religious. The changes in both religious and class structure have produced a society at the end of the century in which the secular middle class makes up almost half of the population. How these changes have affected Dutch politics will be a theme that recurs frequently during the subsequent chapters.

## The Structure of the Dutch Economy

With its geographical location it is not so surprising that trade and commerce have for centuries been an important characteristic of the Dutch economy. The Dutch economy is what is called an 'open economy'; this implies that imports and exports play a major role and that it is particularly susceptible to influence from the international economic system. In recent years the value of both imports and exports have equalled between 50 and 60 per cent of the gross domestic product (GDP), figures approached only by Belgium among major economic powers. By comparison, the figures for Great Britain are about half these levels, and those for the USA are only about one-quarter to one-fifth as large.

The Dutch have for centuries been a nation of traders. Dutch farmers have long traded their products throughout Europe. Dutch merchants imported products to Amsterdam and then sold them elsewhere. In the seventeenth century the Dutch established colonies in North and South America and gained control over Indonesia. Except for some islands in the Caribbean, the colonies are now gone, but the importance of trade continues.

In the nineteenth century the Dutch trade position had diminished and the Netherlands had become primarily an agricultural society. The Industrial Revolution was relatively late in arriving in the country, a fact that has had importance for the development of political parties. Yet today the Netherlands is a major industrial power. Moreover, the country has passed into the 'post-industrial' era, since more than 50 per cent of employment is in the service sector.

Despite these changes, and the fact that only a minor portion of the population is employed in agriculture, agricultural and food products account for about 20 per cent of the export package of the Netherlands. In total volume, despite the small size of the country, the Netherlands ranks as the second or third largest food exporter in the world. It is the world's largest exporter of cocoa and dairy products, and in the potato industry it is the worldwide leader. Meat products, in particular poultry and pork, account for a volume equal to dairy products, according to the Ministry of Economic Affairs. In order to produce such products, the Netherlands is the world's largest importer of maize for fodder.

In addition to the famous bulb fields, natural gas allows huge greenhouses to produce flowers, potted plants, cucumbers, tomatoes, lettuce, onions, and mushrooms. Each day fresh flowers are sold at the computerised auction house in Aalsmeer, and are immediately sent out by jumbo jet to the USA, Japan, and the rest of the world.

There is, unfortunately, a dark side to such high agricultural production in such a small geographical area. Five million cows and twelve million pigs (in a country of only fifteen million people!) produce millions of tons of manure each year. Although much is used as fertilizer, disposal of the remainder has become a major environmental problem.

Despite its continued importance, agriculture now accounts for only about 4–5 per cent of the GDP. The Netherlands is home to three of the world's 25 largest multinationals: Royal Dutch/Shell, Unilever, and Philips. The huge petro-chemical industry is indicative of how raw materials are imported and turned into other products to be exported. Royal Dutch/Shell is the second-ranking oil producer in the world. In addition, other major producers, such as BP, Exxon, and Texaco, have refineries and petro-chemical operations in the Netherlands. Rotterdam has become the major storage depot for petroleum products for north-western Europe and is the home of the oil spot market. In addition to Shell, Akzo and DSM have become major international chemical producers, the latter having made the conversion to chemicals after the state mines were closed in the 1960s. Chemical products now account for approximately 19 per cent of Dutch exports.

More than 50 per cent of the labour force is now employed in the service sector, which generates almost half of the national income. An important component of this sector in the Netherlands is the transport industry. For centuries the Dutch have capitalised on their geographical position as controllers of the mouth of the Rhine river. The Rotterdam harbour is now the busiest in the world. From there and from other Dutch harbours, goods may be shipped to Germany and the rest of Europe by road, rail, or water. The Netherlands has the world's largest inland fleet and barges move up and down the Rhine and other inland waterways. In addition, Amsterdam's Schiphol Airport is one of the largest and most modern in Europe. The transportation network can easily reach the nearly 160 million inhabitants of Europe's most industrial areas that live within a 300-mile radius of Amsterdam. This helps to account for the fact that approximately 40 per cent of all Japanese goods imported into Europe pass through the Netherlands.

Table 1.1 indicates how the percentage of the population employed in the major sectors of the economy has shifted in the post-war period. Despite what has been said above about the importance of the Dutch agricultural industry, employment in this area has more than halved since 1950. Greater efficiency has contributed to the expansion of exports. In 1988, only 6 per cent of employment was in agriculture. Industrial employment has also declined. After expansion between 1950 and 1960, the number of jobs available in industry has declined in absolute numbers since then and by 1988 accounted for only 20 per cent of all employment. The greatest percentage growth has occurred in governmental employment. As the government took on new tasks,

**TABLE 1.1**

Employment in various sectors (in work years × 1000) 1950–88

| Year | Agriculture | % | Industry | % | Commercial services | % | Government | % |
|------|-------------|---|----------|---|---------------------|---|------------|---|
| 1950 | 582 | 15 | 1185 | 31 | 1614 | 43 | 392 | 10 |
| 1960 | 465 | 11 | 1336 | 32 | 1891 | 45 | 490 | 12 |
| 1970 | 329 | 7 | 1291 | 27 | 2517 | 53 | 572 | 12 |
| 1980 | 278 | 6 | 1047 | 22 | 2678 | 58 | 714 | 15 |
| 1988 | 266 | 6 | 974 | 20 | 2830 | 59 | 744 | 15 |

*Note:* Commercial services includes construction and installation companies; the values for 1988 were preliminary figures.
*Source:* Central Bureau of Statistics.

more employees were needed. During the 1980s, however, there was a general feeling that the size of government was too large. In Chapter 8 the attempts to reduce the size of government will be discussed; here we may note that the rate of increase of government has been slowed. In terms of numbers of new jobs created, the greatest growth in jobs has been in the service industries. Between 1960 and 1970 the Netherlands passed the level of 50 per cent that has been used to describe a post-industrial society. Since then, the service sector has continued to grow in both absolute and relative terms.

*Trade Relations*

Being dependent to such a great degree upon imports and exports, the Netherlands is particularly susceptible to influences from beyond its borders. Table 1.2 reports the percentages of trade related to the Netherlands' most important trading partners. These figures show that Germany is easily the most important Dutch trading partner. After the Second World War, the recovery in the Netherlands occurred in the slipstream of the Economic Miracle that restored (West) Germany as an economic power. The Dutch guilder is tied to – but worth slightly less than – the German mark, and when German interest rates rise or fall, Dutch rates are adjusted accordingly. One major Dutch newspaper recently referred to the Dutch Ministry of Finance in The Hague as a branch office of the German Federal Bank (*Volkskrant*, 21 September 1991). When German petrol taxes were raised in the summer of 1991 in order to help pay for the costs of unification, the Dutch parliament seized upon the opportunity to

**TABLE 1.2**

**Percentage of Dutch imports and exports by country (1988)**

| Country | Imports (%) | Exports (%) |
|---|---|---|
| France | 8 | 11 |
| Belgium/Luxemburg | 15 | 15 |
| W. Germany | 26 | 26 |
| Italy | 4 | 6 |
| UK | 8 | 11 |
| USA | 8 | 4 |
| Other Countries | 31 | 27 |
| Total | 100 | 100 |

*Source:* 'Investment in the Netherlands', Netherlands Foreign Investment Agency, June 1990.

generate new revenues and promptly increased Dutch petrol taxes by 25 Dutch cents, producing a 14 per cent rise in the price at the pump. German unification has already produced higher interest rates, and should German inflation rise, as seems likely, increased prices and inflation will result in the Netherlands. Similarly, higher wages in Germany produce wage demands by Dutch workers (Metze, 1990, p. 19).

In recent years, the Netherlands has supplied approximately 10 per cent of German imports. The unification of Germany will bring new opportunities and challenges to the Netherlands. The Central Planning Bureau estimated that an extra growth in exports of 1 per cent could be achieved in 1990, and 2.3 per cent in 1991. However, it was also feared that German needs would be in areas in which the Dutch have not been so strong and that competition from Eastern European countries would be great. Imports to the Netherlands might also increase, leading to a less favourable balance of trade (Metze, 1990, p. 59).

The importance of the EC is also seen from the figures above. Most Dutch trade occurs with countries of the Community where no customs duties are charged. Customs officials remain necessary, since excise duties and Value-Added Tax (VAT) have not yet been harmonised. After '1992' additional trade restrictions have fallen, providing an additional challenge to Dutch business.

In the past, it has been the agricultural industry that has profited most from the Community. The Community created larger markets for Dutch producers, allowing them to develop into an efficient and modern export-oriented industry. Certain areas, in particular the cattle and dairy industry, have been assisted by EC subsidies. However, after 1984, when the Community began to attempt to cut milk production, Dutch dairymen were able to increase their exports to non-EC countries and thus keep their incomes stable. Nevertheless, other areas of the dairy industry have stagnated (Metze, 1990, p. 41).

The figures of only 8 per cent of imports from the USA and 4 per cent of exports to that country belie the importance of the American economy for the Netherlands. Some countries of the world have tied their currencies to the dollar, so that fluctuations in that currency have an impact beyond trade with the USA itself. A large portion of world trade is pegged to the dollar; most importantly, perhaps, the price of oil. As reported above, the Netherlands has important oil-related industries. Recession in the USA and a drop in the value of the dollar produces price increases in the Netherlands. In 1989 the government Central Planning Bureau estimated that a fall in the value of the dollar from 1.80 guilders to 1.65 between 1990 and 1994 would cause growth predictions to be 0.5 per cent less each year and would lead to 35 000 additional unemployed (Centraal Planbureau, 1989). On the other hand, higher dollar rates would have an impact:

> To the Netherlands' economy, a more expensive dollar would raise the import prices and prompt a greater price increase of consumption, 0.75 per cent additional price increase in 1991 . . . Purchasing power would then turn out 0.75 per cent lower in 1991; in later years compensation would be found in additional wage increases. The improved competitive position would work out favourably for goods, exports, production, and employment . . . [There would be] increasing revenues from natural gas ensuing from a higher oil price in guilders. (Central Planning Bureau, 1991)

## Conclusion

We have now briefly introduced the geography, history, people, and economy of the Netherlands which should provide the reader with an outline that is sufficient as a basis for our exploration of Dutch government and politics. Today, the Dutch are among the most happy people in the world. More than 90 per cent reported that they are 'satisfied' or 'very satisfied' with life as a whole, a higher percentage than in any of the other 15 countries included in that particular survey. When reporting these results, Ronald Inglehart was even prompted to ask the question: 'But why are the Dutch so much happier than the Germans?' (Inglehart, 1990). In the following chapters we shall examine whether the government and politics of the country have contributed to keeping the pragmatic Dutch in their happy state.

# 2

# A Country of Minorities

## Three Threats to Stable Government

*Minorities*

The Netherlands is a country of minorities. This is without doubt the single most important characteristic of Dutch politics. From the introduction of universal suffrage to the present, no political party has ever succeeded in winning an electoral (or even a parliamentary) majority, and it is unlikely that we shall witness such a majority in the near future. In the 1989 Parliamentary elections the biggest party obtained only 35.3 per cent of the vote (a record nevertheless), and was still 22 (out of 150) seats short of an overall majority in the Second Chamber of Parliament.

With the exception of the Liberals, the political groups that make up the Dutch political landscape originated as minorities not only in a numerical but also in a social-psychological sense; they were underprivileged social groups. In the next chapter we shall discuss the peculiar meaning of the label 'Liberal' in Dutch politics, but here it suffices to say that it was used to denote a heterogeneous and loosely organised group of secular, or at least latitudinarian, relatively well-to-do citizens. Although a numerical minority in the population at large, the Liberals dominated Dutch politics for a long time during the nineteenth and early twentieth century. Prior to the introduction of universal suffrage in 1917, they at times even enjoyed a parliamentary majority. The explanation is a simple one; the Liberals' electoral importance was artificially enlarged by the *régime censitaire* that limited the franchise on the basis of property and income criteria. As economic growth and legislation enfranchised more and more citizens, the Liberals were gradually crowded out of political power.

Initially, however, the other minorities felt excluded and disadvantaged because of Liberal predominance. The Catholics formed the largest minority, comprising between 35 and 40 per cent of the population. To the extent that the Eighty Years' War of Independence can be perceived as a religious war, the Catholics were identified with the losing side. Under the Republic they could not publicly practise their religion; they were barred from holding public office, and the two predominantly Catholic provinces, Brabant and Limburg, were ruled by the central government as conquered territory. Gradually the discriminatory legal provisions were abolished, but Catholics remained wary of a Protestant backlash, and were slow to organise themselves openly. Hence it was only in 1926 that the Catholic party was founded.

Protestants constitute the second religious minority. The more orthodox Protestants felt the impact of Liberal dominance not only in politics, but also within the Dutch Reformed Church, the main Protestant denomination, where latitudinarians held power in synods and parish councils. In addition, many of the orthodox Protestants felt underprivileged in economic terms, calling themselves '*de kleine luyden*' (see Chapter 1). They were the first to organise themselves as an emancipation movement. While some orthodox Protestants remained within the Dutch Reformed Church, others eventually broke away to found several *Gereformeerde* Churches. Later these religious differences sustained, next to several very small parties, two major Protestant political parties: the Anti-Revolutionary Party (or ARP, supported primarily by *Gereformeerden*), and the Christian Historical Union, or CHU (backed largely by Dutch Reformed).

The Liberals had to face competition not only from these religious minorities, but also from the working-class movement and its political representatives. The Social Democrats entered the political arena relatively late. The Netherlands were slow to industrialise. Although there is some dispute about the exact timing of industrial 'take-off', it is safe to say that industrialisation did not really begin until the period between 1860 and 1880. Before the turn of the century there was hardly an economic basis for a working-class movement. When industrialisation rendered the ground fertile for Social Democracy, mobilisation of the masses was already well under way, however slowly and cautiously, along religious lines. The appeal of the denominational parties crossed the newly developing class divide and left the Social Democrats with only the secular manual workers to organise, a category that was far from a majority. As we shall see later, some Marxist commentators do not consider this to be a historical accident, but see religious mobilisation as a bourgeois strategy to weaken class consciousness: the famous 'opium for the people'. However, whether by accident or by design, the Social Democrats also had to reconcile themselves to minority status.

Our brief *tour d'horizon* of the most important political minorities in Dutch politics is now complete. The political situation is neatly summarised by the tree model of Figure 2.1, which also mentions the political parties that represent the social minorities. Although some of these parties carried different names before the Second World War, and although the Liberals were rarely able to confine themselves to just one party, these minorities found political expression during the gradual extension of the suffrage, and their political parties have dominated politics ever since the introduction of universal suffrage. Even today, these minorities basically still structure political conflict in the Netherlands.

*Two Cleavages*

Governing a country of minorities is no easy task, but the Dutch situation is further complicated by the fact that the parties cannot be ordered along a single ideological dimension. As Figure 2.1 shows, both religion and social class play an important role. After its

**FIGURE 2.1**
**Divisions within Dutch society**

fragmentation into several minorities, the second important characteristic of Dutch politics is, therefore, that it is a two-cleavage
society. As we shall see in more detail in Chapter 3, the resulting
ideological dimensions lead to different orderings of the political
parties. As in most other countries it is possible to position the parties
on a Left–Right socio-economic dimension. On this dimension 'Left'
stands for more, 'Right' for less, government intervention in the
economy and equality of income distribution, etc. Some non-
economic issues, such as defence, conform to the same party
ordering, where we find the Labour Party (PvdA) to the left, the
Liberals to the right, and the three Christian Democratic parties
somewhere in between. Depending on the issue and on the period, the
ARP could sometimes be discovered to the left of the KVP (Catholic
People's Party), and the CHU to the right, sometimes vice versa.

In addition to this dimension we have the religious dimension,
which has given rise to conflicts on numerous ethical or cultural issues
such as education and abortion. In fact, this dimension overshadowed
the socio-economic one during much of the first half of this century.
The 'anti-thesis', as the secular/religious cleavage was called, was
visible in Parliament, with MPs for secular parties being seated to the
left of the Speaker, and MPs from religious parties to his right.
Confusingly therefore, the terms left and right applied to the religious
as well as the class cleavage. On the left of the religious dimension we
find the Social Democrats and the Liberals in roughly the same
position. The Christian Democrats take position clearly right of
centre, outflanked only by the fundamentalist parties.

The salience of two ideological dimensions, each with a different
ordering of the major parties, creates special problems. In a country
of minorities, the only alternative to minority governments is
coalition government. Coalitions are usually formed by parties that
are ideological neighbours. But neighbours on which ideological
dimension? At the socio-economic level, coalitions of Christian
Democratic parties with either Liberals or Social Democrats seem
obvious possibilities. However, when it comes to ethical issues, the
secular party in either coalition is under constant temptation to
commit adultery with the secular party in opposition. Based on the
religious dimension, a coalition of Social Democrats and Liberals
seems most likely, but the opposition Christian Democrats would then
be in an ideal position to drive embarrassing wedges between both
coalition parties on socio-economic and related issues. Thus coalition

formation is complicated, and whatever coalition comes about has in the other dimension a built-in source of conflict between the governing parties.

## Pillarisation

The most notorious impediment to stable government in the Netherlands has yet to be mentioned. The minorities introduced above were not merely the constituencies for five major political parties: they were tightly organised social groups or subcultures that structured not just politics, but nearly every aspect of social life in the Netherlands. For example, let us take a look at the life of a hypothetical Catholic citizen during, say, the 1950s. As conversions were extremely rare our citizen's parents would probably also be Catholics. If he or she had been born in a hospital, it would have been in the 'Saint Elisabeth Hospital', or some other appropriately named Catholic hospital. It would not have been a 'Deaconesses Hospital', which is a common name for a Protestant hospital, and neither would it have been an 'Academic Hospital', which is where Socialist and Liberal babies were delivered. If birth took place at home, there would have been a midwife and maternity care from the 'White-and-Yellow Cross', the Catholic health care organisation, not from the Protestant 'Orange-and-Green Cross' or from the secular 'Green Cross'.

The father, if involved in manual labour, would have been a member of the Catholic Trade Union and not of its Protestant or Socialist rivals. If he had had some other occupation he would have belonged to the Catholic Farmers' Association, the Catholic Retailers' Organisation, the Catholic Teachers' Union, etc. The mother would probably not be a member of any of these organisations, as no other Western country had such a low percentage of married women in the work force (see Chapter 8). Perhaps she would sing in a choir, named after 'Saint Cecilia', for example. She would definitely not have joined the Protestant 'Cantate Deo Choir', let alone the Socialist (and mixed!) 'Voice of the People Choir'. The family would subscribe to a Catholic newspaper such as *De Volkskrant*, and would avoid reading the Protestant *Trouw*, the Socialist *Het Parool*, or the Liberal *Nieuwe Rotterdamsche Courant*. These are national newspapers, but a local paper for each subculture could also be found in most regions. As far as the other media are concerned, our young Catholic would grow up listening to, or watching, programmes aired by the Catholic Broadcasting Organisation (KRO). Radio stations and television channels are owned by the government, and broadcasting time is distributed to the KRO and its counterparts, the NCRV (Protestant), VARA (Socialist), and AVRO (Liberal). Each of these organisations published a radio/television guide with special features on its own programmes and those of its competitors hidden in small print. Originally there were only two radio stations, one shared by the religious broadcasting companies, and the other by the secular organisations. This facilitated social control; when priests made house-calls they were rumoured to 'check the dial' on the radio receiver!

Our young Catholic would attend Saint Bernadette Nursery School, Saint Joseph Primary School, or Saint Agnes Comprehensive, whilst his or her Protestant peers would enrol in a 'School with the Bible', or even a school admitting only children of one of the Protestant denominations. Socialist and Liberal children would attend a public (i.e. state-run) school. However, depending on the location in inner city or suburb, these schools would sometimes be populated predominantly by either Liberals or Socialists. In addition, Liberal children disproportionately attended private, non-denominational schools, such as Montessori schools. Upon completion of secondary school, our Catholic would perhaps enrol in one of the two Catholic universities (Nijmegen and Tilburg). Protestants could go to the Protestant Free University of Amsterdam, or to one of the theological Colleges. There was no Socialist university, unless one considers the Municipal University of Amsterdam as such, being administered by the Amsterdam municipal government which was dominated by the Left. The state universities (Leyden, Utrecht, and Groningen) attracted the remainder of the students, predominantly Liberals.

As far as leisure activities are concerned, our Catholic might have been a member of the Catholic Boy Scouts, and if he played football, he did so on Sunday, not on Saturday. To this very day Protestants play football on Saturday, and there are two separate amateur leagues. Of course, highlights from the Saturday matches are broadcast by NCRV, and whereas non-Protestant newspapers give only short reports of the Saturday results, *Trouw* provides extensive coverage, including articles and photographs, of Protestant football.

Marriage to another Catholic would be a matter of course. Intermarriage was extremely rare. There is even a Dutch proverb which translates (rather awkwardly) into English as 'two faiths on one pillow; between them sleeps the Devil'. In 1960, for example, a mere 5.3 per cent of all married Catholics had a non-Catholic spouse. Eventually, our Catholic might die in a Catholic home for the elderly, and be buried in the Catholic graveyard by a Catholic undertaker. Literally from cradle to grave, this Catholic would have lived his or her entire life within the confines of a homogeneously Catholic subculture and its organisational infrastructure. In Dutch these subcultures are known as *zuilen* (pillars), and the segmentation of Dutch society into these subcultures is called *verzuiling* (pillarisation).

The above life history of an imaginary Catholic may seem unimaginable, except for the obvious but troubling parallel with Northern Ireland. Indeed, to some extent our story presents a caricature of pillarisation. The choice of a Catholic as an illustrative example is, however, not entirely accidental, as the Catholics maintained the most extensive network of organisations. Lijphart (1971) has listed several criteria to measure the degree of pillarisation:

● the role of ideology or religion within the pillar;
● the size and density of the pillar's organisational network;
● the cohesiveness of that organisational network (coordination, interlocking directorates);
● the degree of social 'apartheid', or the absence of deviant (i.e., non-pillarised) social behaviour;
● the extent to which pillarised behaviour and loyalty was encouraged by the subcultural elite.

On each of these criteria the Catholic pillar scored very high. The Catholic pillar was to a large extent built and maintained by the Catholic clergy. The Church played an important role within the pillar. Each and every Catholic organisation, from the national trade union to the local bowling club, had a priest as 'spiritual adviser'. The organisational network was extremely tight, with separate Catholic organisations for nearly every form of social, economic and political activity (see Table 2.1). These organisations also enjoyed a monopoly; rival Catholic organisations would soon be 'persuaded' by the clergy to disband. The Catholic Church hierarchy provided guidance and coordination for this huge organisational

network, and interlocking directorates were numerous. Social apartheid was probably highest among Catholics, if only because half of
them lived in the two southern provinces, where non-Catholics were
rare. The other subcultures were much more dispersed, although
pillarised pockets could be found in particular villages or neighbour-
hoods. To say that pillarisation was encouraged by the Catholic elite
is something of an understatement; as late as 1954 the bishops issued
an episcopal letter condemning Socialism and Liberalism, and
forbidding such 'sins' as membership of the Socialist trade union or
listening to the Socialist broadcasting organisation.

The other pillars did not attain the same degree of pillarisation on
some or all of Lijphart's criteria. Protestant pillarisation differed from

### TABLE 2.1
### The structure of the Dutch pillars

|  | Catholics | Protestants | | Socialists | Liberals |
|---|---|---|---|---|---|
|  |  | Dutch Reformed | Calvinists |  |  |
| Party | KVP | CHU | ARP | PvdA | VVD |
| Trade union | NKV | CNV | | FNV | Some white-collar unions |
| Employers' organisations | NCW | | | — | VNO |
| Broadcasting | KRO | NCRV | | VARA | AVRO |
| Health care | White/Yellow Cross | Orange/Green Cross | | Green Cross | |
| Schools | Catholic schools | Schools 'with the bible' | | State schools | |
| Universities | Nijmegen, Tilburg | Free University, Amsterdam | | State and municipal universities | |
| Newspapers | *Volkskrant* | *Trouw* | | *(Parool), Vrije volk* | *Nieuwe Rotterdamsche Courant, Handelsblad* |

Catholic pillarisation in at least three respects. First of all, it is not clear whether one should speak of one or two Protestant pillars. For some activities there was only one organisation catering to all Protestants, (e.g., trade union activity and health care). For other activities there was more than one. We have already noted the existence of two major Protestant denominations. In addition, there was a wide array of smaller churches in various shades of religious orthodoxy, and these religious differences were reflected in some other areas of social life, most notably in politics. Second, the Protestant Churches did not provide the same leadership and coordination to their satellite organisations as the Catholic Church did. This is partly due to rivalry among the Protestant Churches, but also to the fact that the organisational culture of the Protestant Churches conferred considerably more autonomy on local church councils, compared with the more hierarchical Catholic Church. Third, the degree of social apartheid was less among Protestants. The *Gereformeerden* came closest to Catholic levels of pillarised loyalty. The Dutch Reformed, however, formed a 'broad church', encompassing a large group of fundamentalists, as well as several more latitudinarian currents. This religious heterogeneity resulted in a much lower degree of pillarised behaviour. The CHU, for example, was never able to attract a majority of Dutch Reformed voters.

The situation within the secular minority resembled that of the Protestants. Here, too, there is confusion concerning the number of pillars. Some authors speak of an *'algemene zuil'* (general pillar: virtually a contradiction in terms) and point to the fact that Social Democrats and Liberals often made use of the same school system, the same health care organisation, etc. Others refer to two pillars and emphasise the activities for which Social Democrats and Liberals had separate organisations, such as politics and broadcasting. Both minorities also lacked the central leadership that made the Catholic pillar such a cohesive one.

The confusion over the number of pillars is based partly on different definitions of the concept. One of the major authors on *verzuiling*, the sociologist Kruyt, emphasises the organisational infrastructure, based on a particular philosophy of life (Kruyt, 1959). On that basis he rejects the use of the word *'zuil'* for Social Democrats and Liberals. He argues that, before the Second World War, the Social Democrats perhaps could still have been classified as a 'pseudo-pillar', but after the war they lost all claims to that title because of de-ideologisation and the severing of formal links between organisations such as political party and trade union. In Kruyt's view the Liberals never qualified as a pillar. Many organisations commonly referred to as 'Liberal', such as the broadcasting organis-ation AVRO, rejected that label themselves. If the Liberals organised as such, they did so *à contre-coeur*, only to offer an alternative to the other pillars' organisations, or to defend their once dominant position.

Lijphart rejects such a narrow interpretation of pillarisation and defines a *zuil* primarily as a subculture. Although he concedes that the Social Democrats scored much lower on most of his criteria of pillarisation than *Gereformeerden* or Catholics, he maintains that they still formed an easily identifiable subculture within Dutch society. Finally, if we turn away from the supply-side of pillarisation to behaviour patterns, the secular working class was relatively loyal to the Social Democratic pillar; less than the *Gereformeerden*, but certainly more than the Dutch Reformed. The Liberals, however, form a pillar only by default, even in this respect.

Using our original example of an imaginary Catholic as an illustration is, therefore, somewhat misleading in that the Catholic minority was by far the most pillarised one. The *Gereformeerden* were a close second, followed by the Social Democrats. The Dutch Reformed take fourth place, with the Liberals providing more or less the exception to the rule of pillarisation.

To further qualify our description of pillarisation, it should be noted that there have always been isolated social activities that remained relatively untouched by pillarisation, or for which pillarised organisations faced non-pillarised competition. There were, for instance, no pillarised technical universities. Some professions (such as law and medicine) knew no pillarised associations. Large companies, and especially multi-nationals, were pillar-blind in their recruitment of personnel. The national newspaper with the largest circulation, *De Telegraaf*, was never affiliated with any pillar.

Such nuances and exceptions notwithstanding, there can be no understating the importance of *verzuiling* in structuring Dutch society up to the second half of the 1960s. Pillarisation had significant political consequences. As the minorities were not just political groupings the political parties were not autonomous political agents, but rather the subcultures' embassies in The Hague. Political strife was exacerbated by the depth of the subcultural cleavages, and

the animosity that existed between the pillars. The minorities were
introvert, isolated, and hostile towards one another. At times
emotions ran high. In 1911 unprecedentedly large Socialist demonstrations in favour of universal suffrage were considered too
dangerous to allow the Queen to come to The Hague for the
traditional opening of the parliamentary year. In 1913, referring to
the conflict about state-financing of religious schools, the Prime
Minister spoke of 'a wedge being driven into our population,
splitting the Dutch people in two'.

In later years such anxieties abated, but distrust between the pillars
remained. During the 1952 Cabinet formation, the Catholics claimed
the portfolio of Foreign Affairs, but the other parties feared a papist
Europe, as all the other Foreign Secretaries in the budding EC were
Catholics. As a compromise the Netherlands had *two* ministers of
Foreign Affairs from 1952 to 1956, a Catholic and a non-Catholic
(with the latter responsible for European affairs).

Pillarisation thus posed a further threat to stable government,
already jeopardised by the absence of a parliamentary majority and
by the existence of more than one ideological dimension. This was the
central problem confronting Dutch politicians, and the central puzzle
for analysts of Dutch politics. In the words of Robert A. Dahl,
reacting to a similar description of the situation by a Dutch colleague:
'Theoretically your country cannot exist' (Daalder, 1989a, p. 26).

## Consociational Democracy

Theoretically, Dahl had a point. The collapse of the eminently
democratic Weimar republic has profoundly influenced democratic
theory. In a renewed quest for 'stable democracy', post-war political
scientists were preoccupied with finding an alchemy for stability and
democracy. Stability is fostered by social homogeneity, by the
absence of division. Democracy, on the other hand, presupposes at
least a modicum of disagreement. The answer to the simultaneous
needs for homogeneity and heterogeneity was provided by the
pluralist theory of cross-pressures. Social cleavages are to be
rendered harmless by their cross-cutting each other; (i.e, social
groups that are homogeneous with respect to one social cleavage
are heterogeneous with respect to another). In his trade union, for
example, a church member would encounter secular working-class

comrades, and in his church he would encounter upper- and middle-class brethren. Thus the individual is pulled in different directions; he or she is *cross-pressured*, experiencing cross-cutting loyalties, which supposedly have a moderating effect on political views, and thus reduce the intensity of political conflicts. The puzzle of stable democracy is solved by having both centrifugal forces (social cleavages) and centripetal forces (cross-pressures) at the mass level.

Pillarisation, however, prevents such cross-pressures from arising at the mass level: the cleavages are not bridged by organisational overlap. Yet 'Dutch democracy is eminently stable and effective', as Lijphart asserted (1975, p. 19), albeit not entirely without exaggeration. The Dutch solution, and Lijphart's contribution to democratic theory, is to show that social heterogeneity need not be balanced at the same (mass) level; it can also be compensated for at the elite level. Since the masses can be either heterogeneous (segmented or pillarised) or homogeneous (or at least cross-pressured), and the elites can compete or cooperate, four situations are possible (see Figure 2.2).

The two situations in which no deep cleavages exist need not interest us here. In a segmented, or pillarised, society, competition among the elites exacerbates the divisions and inevitably leads to instability. Lijphart cites Weimar Germany, the French Third and Fourth Republics, and Italy as examples of such centrifugal democracies. When the threat to stability by social division is offset by a 'politics of accommodation' at the elite level, we have a consociational democracy. In addition to the Netherlands, Lijphart has listed Austria, Switzerland, and Belgium as European examples.

**FIGURE 2.2**
**Lijphart's typology of democracies**

|  |  | Mass level | |
|---|---|---|---|
|  |  | Cross-cutting cleavages | Segmented |
| Elite level | Cooperation | Depoliticised Democracy | Consociational Democracy |
| | Competition | Centripetal Democracy | Centrifugal Democracy |

*Source:*  A. Lijphart (1975), *The Politics of Accommodation: Pluralism and Democracy in The Netherlands*, 2nd rev. edn. Copyright © 1968 The Regents of the University of California.

The Dutch term *verzuiling* is very apposite in this light; the separate pillars were standing apart, only to be joined at the top, thus supporting the roof of the Dutch state.

Lijphart dates the beginning of consociational democracy in the Netherlands back to the 1913–17 period. Before those years disagreement on two major issues fuelled hostility between the minorities (see Chapter 1). One of those issues was the 'school struggle'. On the one hand the Liberals (and to some extent also the Social Democrats) defended the state school system, in which children of all creeds and classes went 'undivided' to the same school. On the other hand Protestants (and more hesitantly, Catholics) advocated state funding for their own parochial schools. The second issue at stake involved social issues in general, and the struggle for universal suffrage in particular, where the Social Democrats faced resistance from some Liberal groups and the denominational parties, especially the Christian Historicals. In 1913 two Parliamentary Commissions, in which the leaders of all major parties were represented, were charged with the task of finding a solution for the two conflicts. This proved no easy assignment, and it was not until 1916–17 that the recommendations of both Commissions were debated in Parliament. They were regarded as a single package deal in which both state-financing of religious schools and universal suffrage were agreed upon. The Liberal parties, which opposed both reforms, also received some satisfaction; the introduction of universal suffrage was to be accompanied by a change in the electoral system from single member district and absolute majority to nationwide proportional representation (see Chapter 4). This allowed the Liberals to survive, as the abolition of the *régime censitaire* would have rendered them a minority in virtually every district.

This package deal is known in Dutch history books as the 'Pacification of 1917', a term, as Lijphart noted, usually applied to international politics, as if the Dutch compromise was a peace treaty between sovereign nations. This parallel once again illustrates the precarious nature of the Dutch political system; it is seen not as a democracy based on a single society, but as a consociational democracy. Lijphart actually described Dutch politics in terms of international decision-making. He cites foreign policy prescriptions by Von Clausewitz and Woodrow Wilson in his discussion of the seven 'rules of the game' to which the Dutch elites apparently adhered to facilitate their cooperation:

- the business of politics (i.e.; politics is not a game, but a serious business)
- agreement to disagree;
- summit diplomacy;
- proportionality.
- depoliticisation;
- secrecy;
- the government's right to govern (without undue interference from Parliament or political parties).

Elsewhere, in more general analyses of consociational democracy, Lijphart has reduced his 'seven rules' to four basic principles: (1) executive power sharing or grand coalition, and (2) a high degree of autonomy for the segments as the two most important principles, the two secondary principles being (3) proportionality, and (4) minority veto (see Lijphart, 1977).

If we look at these seven rules of the game or at the four basic principles, they all seem to derive from the same simple precept; clear-cut, zero-sum game, yes/no decisions are to be avoided at all cost. Attempting to reach such decisions puts a system with permanent minorities under enormous stress. Even if it proves possible to reach decisions, they will result in clearly identifiable winners and losers, thus creating resentment among at least some of the minorities, and thereby mortgaging future decisions.

The first step in avoiding zero-sum decisions is the decentralisation of policy-making, not to local authorities but to the 'corporate' minorities (Lijphart's segmental autonomy). As Van Schendelen has pointed out:

> In the pillarised society the cleavages between the four main social groupings were such that 'the common government' could handle only a few issues and usually only in a procedural way, leaving as much substantial decision-making as possible to the pillars themselves. These pillars organised their own interference in socio-economic and private life. They created their own welfare organisations (for income, health, housing, education), industrial corporations, trade unions, services, banks and so on. (Van Schendelen, 1987, p. 65)

The functional decentralisation of government authority to socio-economic regulatory commissions, in which pillarised interest groups were heavily represented, provided one way to reduce the risk of overloading central political decision-making. We shall return to this relationship between consociational democracy and neo-corporatism in Chapter 7.

Such decentralisation has its limits, however. Issues that crossed the boundaries between policy areas, and in which several rival interest groups had a stake, remained within the government's domain. In handling such issues, political leaders generally did not seriously attempt to win outright, but rather sought to arrive at the best compromise possible. In later works Lijphart uses the term 'consensus democracy' to describe this elite style. Rules or characteristics – such as executive power sharing, minority veto, agreement to disagree, summit diplomacy, and secrecy – are illustrative of this quest for compromise. It even led one British observer to comment on 'the invertebrate character of coalition government' (Gladdish, 1972), but the word compromise has no such pejorative connotation in the Dutch context.

Unfortunately consensus or compromise cannot always be reached. In such situations, the rule of proportionality may bring relief. Lijphart argues that:

> The rule of proportionality is of fundamental importance to the success of the politics of accommodation in Holland. The establishment of the accommodation pattern of politics by the peaceful settlement of 1917 was intimately related to this rule: both the suffrage and the schools questions were settled on the basis of proportionality, The rule has been faithfully adhered to ever since. (Lijphart, 1975, p. 129)

Indeed, proportionality has become so engrained in Dutch political culture that it has become almost synonymous with fairness. The Dutch are appalled when they learn how majority electoral systems in other countries, such as the UK and the USA, 'distort' election outcomes. Not only are the seats in both Houses of Parliament, as well as in provincial and municipal councils, distributed to the parties in proportion to their share of the vote (see Chapter 4), but also portfolios in the Cabinet and in provincial and municipal governing bodies are similarly distributed among the parties in the ruling coalition. Broadcasting time on the state-owned networks is handed out in rough proportion to the size of the broadcasting associations' membership. Schools are financed on a proportional basis (i.e., according to the number of pupils enrolled). Mayors in all municipalities and the Governors of all provinces are appointed by the central government (see Chapter 7), and all major parties receive a share of these appointments more or less in line with their electoral strength. The same can be said for government subsidies to housing associations or health care organisations. The parties keep a keen eye on top civil service appointments, with the Catholics in the past, (and the Social Democrats at present) complaining of underrepresentation.

However important and successful such prophylactic measures have been, there are still stubborn issues left that cannot be delegated, compromised or proportionalised. It makes no sense to 'solve' the abortion question by distributing the number of abortions proportionally to Catholic, Protestant, and secular clinics. The problem of decolonisation could not be solved by distributing the islands of Indonesia among the pillars. Such issues, where yes/no decisions seem inescapable, are most dangerous to the Dutch political system. Faced with this type of problem, non-decision-making often seems less harmful than forcing a solution. Avoidance of such decisions takes three forms: postponement of the decision, defusion of the political dispute by technical arguments (depoliticisation), and removal of the responsibility from the government. The three tactics are often used in combination. Hence the appointment of an expert committee (preferably composed proportionally) to study the problem is a familiar feature of Dutch politics: 'putting hot potatoes in the refrigerator', as the jargon has it.

The Dutch chapter of the 'Lockheed Affair' may serve as an example of such a hot potato. In 1975, evidence from hearings by a US Senate Commission led to the suspicion that Prince Bernhard, the prince-consort to the then Queen Juliana, had accepted funds from the Lockheed aircraft company. At the time, the prince was inspector-general of the Dutch armed forces, and the money was intended to influence Dutch military procurement policy. This revelation placed the government in a difficult position, as the prince enjoyed personal popularity because of his role in the Second World War. The Labour Party, which led the government coalition at the time, was particularly hesitant to take on the issue because it has a reputation of being anti-monarchy, dating back to a half-hearted attempt at revolution in 1918. As a result a committee of three 'wise men' was appointed (a Christian Democrat, a Social

Democrat and a Liberal, even though his party was in opposition at the time). The Committee investigated the allegations, and published a verbose 240-page report half a year later, after the Lockheed Affair had ceased to be frontpage news. In this report the Committee concluded that the prince had acted most imprudently and unwisely. The Government immediately decided that there were insufficient grounds for a criminal indictment, and merely asked the prince to withdraw from all functions that could lead to a conflict of interests. In a sense the Lockheed affair was never solved: it faded away, and the Committee was instrumental in taking the heat away from the government.

More recently, successive governments have resorted to various tactics in ducking the thorny and divisive issue of euthanasia. In 1986 postponement seemed no longer possible after one opposition secular party had introduced an initiative bill, to a large extent decriminalising the actions of physicians in such cases. The Christian Democrats were vehemently opposed to revising the law, but were in the process of forming a government with the Liberals, who largely agreed with the initiators of the bill. The parties then agreed to ask for the advice of the Council of State, an advisory body made up primarily of elder statesmen. Being elder statesmen, they were aware of the value of non-decision-making. They recommended that legislation should not be considered until the courts had had the opportunity to decide a few more cases involving euthanasia, and thus clarify the nature of the problem (see Chapter 10). Although this advice ran clearly against constitutional law (the judiciary is to apply legislation, not make it), it provided a breathing space for the ruling coalition. In the 1989 coalition negotiations, this time between Social Democrats and Christian Democrats, the issue surfaced again. On this occasion, delay was achieved by appointment of a committee to conduct research on the current practice of euthanasia.

In some cases governments have been remarkably ingenious in avoiding decisions. In one such case, the entire population served as the refrigerator. In the late 1970s nuclear energy became an emotional issue, with large-scale demonstrations and human blockades of reactor plants. Of the political parties, the Social Democrats were opposed to nuclear energy, the Liberals in favour, with the Christian Democrats in between. Moreover, all parties were also internally divided on the issue. The government of Christian Democrats and Liberals then appointed a committee, charged with organising a 'Broad Social Discussion' on energy policy. The committee handed out subsidies to any organisation – from environmental activists to employers' associations – to study the problem and make recommendations. These recommendations were collected in a report, distributed freely to all interested citizens. In order to discuss the report, the committee convened public meetings in every community (1811 meetings in all). A questionnaire was distributed to the participants so that they could express their opinion on the energy issue. This procedure proved to be an ideal coolant. Few people took the trouble to read the report, and the 1811 local meetings attracted an average attendance of only about ten people. By the time the Committee reported on its activities – in 1983 – the issue had largely faded from the political agenda. Another example of taking decisions out of the hands of government and politicians will be discussed in Chapter 9; in that case the Dutch government avoided a decision on the positioning of cruise missiles on Dutch territory by placing the issue in the hands of the Kremlin!

## Alternative Interpretations

These illustrations conclude our outline of the theory of consociational democracy. So far we have followed Lijphart's interpretation of Dutch consociational democracy, albeit in our own words, giving our own examples and placing our own emphases. Lijphart's interpretation is appealingly simple; the Dutch faced a problem – the threat to political stability posed by social segmentation – and found a solution by replacing elite competition with elite cooperation.

However, both these elements of Lijphart's theory have been challenged. Although there has been a lively international debate on various empirical and normative aspects of consociational democracy, we shall confine our discussion to criticisms of the theory as applied by Lijphart to the Dutch case.

In the first place, Lijphart's very definition of the problem has come under attack. Pillarisation, it is argued, was not without its moderating cross-pressures. In a sense the class cleavage cross-cut the religious cleavage within the religious pillars, which had to accommodate both working-class and middle-class members. These cross-pressures were not to be found within individuals, but they did moderate political conflict. Lijphart has even been accused of finding a solution for a problem that did not exist. It is argued, for example, that pillarisation was not a problem to which elites had to respond, but a conscious strategy on the part of the elites to strengthen their own position. In this interpretation, pillarisation was a form of social control, rather than the result of emancipatory movements organising themselves to fight Liberal domination. (Neo-)Marxist authors assert that pillarisation was primarily a reaction by the ruling classes to the emergence of a working-class movement (e.g., Kieve, 1981). As we have seen earlier in this chapter, there can be no doubt that the mobilisation of citizens along religious lines prior to industrialisation took much wind out of red sails. However, it hardly seems plausible to suggest a conspiracy to retard industrialisation in order to pre-empt a Socialist surge. The strongest evidence in support of the Marxist interpretation of pillarisation is the fact that many religious organisations, apart from church and party, sprang up not before but after industrialisation took off. In the case of the trade union movement it is clear that religious organisations were often formed in direct response to attempts at Socialist unionisation. The case of the trade unions, however, stands relatively isolated, and the most erudite of Lijphart's Marxist critics, Stuurman (1983), is careful not to deny emancipatory aspects to pillarisation, next to aspects of social control. Lijphart complained that the Marxists seem unable to explain how the ruling classes have been able to manipulate and encapsulate the working class into this peculiar Dutch brand of false consciousness.

The historical development of pillarisation also plays a crucial role in the critique of those non-Marxist scholars who nevertheless espouse a social-control view of pillarisation. They point out that many pillarised organisations were formed not only after the advent of industrialisation, but also after the Pacification of 1917 itself. As we have seen, this episode plays a central role in Lijphart's interpretation because, in his view, it first established the cooperative mode of elite behaviour. If this Pacification is to be seen as the elites' successful solution to the problems posed by pillarisation, as Lijphart claims, is it not strange that the problem became aggravated only after the solution? Lijphart never denied that pillarisation reached its zenith only after the Pacification, but maintains that social divisions were already deep and potentially dangerous before the elites started to cooperate in 1913–17. That pillarisation increased (rather than decreased) after 1917 was all part of the elites' peace-making efforts: 'good fences make good neighbours'.

The second strand of criticism questions Lijphart's explanation of elite coalescence in the Netherlands as a 'self-denying prophecy', a conscious and courageous effort to offset the threat of the nation falling apart. In support of this 'self-denying prophecy' he emphasises the social turbulence accompanying the struggles for state-financed parochial schools, and for universal suffrage, and argues that the unrest was deemed so pernicious as to prompt the leaders into spontaneous cooperation. Others, however, doubt that the nation's survival was ever in any real danger, in part because pillarised mobilisation had not yet reached the level it would only attain after the Pacification. Indeed, with the benefit of hindsight, social unrest in the 1910s seems innocuous enough compared to what happened in the streets during the 1930s or 1960s. However, that is hardly the point. What is important is the danger, not as we perceive it now, but as the elites of the day perceived it then. Although some evidence can be found supporting Lijphart's view that the elites did fear for the worst – such as the Prime Minister's speech on a 'wedge' driving the nation apart- it is difficult to ascertain exactly how dangerous they thought the situation really was.

Perhaps we do not need to find out, because even if we assume that the leaders did see the nation on the verge of a civil war, the question still remains: what made the elites so courageous and sagacious as to put the nation's survival above their own tribal interests? Suspecting that Dutch leaders are not inherently more prudent than their counterparts in deeply divided countries such as Northern Ireland, Cyprus, or the former Yugoslavia, the self-denying prophecy merely gives us a description of *what* happened, not *why* it happened. In an attempt to answer that question, Daalder has drawn attention to the striking similarities between the rules of the game of consociational democracy and the way in which politics was conducted in the much earlier days of the Dutch Republic. The pillars replaced the provinces, but the emphasis on elite bargaining and compromise, and on the autonomy of the constituent parts, can be found both before 1795 and after 1917. The very term 'consociationalism' is borrowed from Althusius, one of the early writers on the political system of the Dutch Republic of the Seven United Provinces. Calling the package deal of 1917 a Pacification is an echo of 1576, when the (then still 17) provinces made a united front against the Spanish terror and agreed to respect their religious differences in the

Pacification of Ghent. Elite cooperation, Daalder argues, was no self-denying prophecy, but the continuation of traditional practices.

The weakness in Daalder's explanation is the miraculous and timely re-emergence of an elite culture that belonged to a political system of days long gone by. Even if this culture had survived among the ruling classes, why would the leaders of the new emancipatory movements adopt the ways of those they were trying to replace? Only adherents to a social-control theory of pillarisation have no difficulty explaining this anomaly: the leadership was taken largely from the ranks of the traditional elites; they mobilised the pillars to secure their own position and to defend their long-standing practice of consensual politics against the dangers of an extended franchise and industrialisation. It is true that the old 'regent classes' did provide leadership to some of the new emancipatory organisations, particularly in the Catholic pillar, where the 'notables' had been active as Liberals before the clergy decided to end the papo-liberal alliance, and in the Dutch Reformed part of the Protestant pillar. However, there seems to be considerably less evidence of continuity in elite recruitment when we look at the *Gereformeerden* and the Social Democrats. Yet they, too, conformed to the rules of consociational democracy. Why?

Perhaps the answer lies in the very first characteristic of Dutch politics mentioned in this chapter: the *zuilen* were *all* minorities. It does not seem too unreasonable to suppose that history might have taken a different course had one of the blocs been able to nurse any hope for an outright victory, as is the case in some other divided societies, such as Northern Ireland. The Social Democrats, for example, have occasionally left the fold of elite accommodation whenever they fell victim to the majoritarian illusion. This happened in 1918 when, on the eve of the first elections under universal manhood suffrage, Leftist hopes for a majority were high, and when the smell of revolution was in the air. The reality of minority status for all the pillars, however, meant that militant intransigence would reduce one's influence to that of a voice in the wilderness, whereas by sharing power at least something could be gained. We suggest that, rather than a noble defence of national unity or a revival of ancient elite customs, the self-denying prophecy was an act of rational behaviour on the part of political leaders with an eye for the interests of their respective subcultural constituencies. This interpretation is supported by the experience of other certified consociational democracies, with the exception of Austria. It is also borne out by later developments, to which we now turn.

## Depillarisation and its Consequences

If consociational democracy was designed to ensure political stability, it has not been without its vulnerable moments. Leaving aside external *force majeure* in the form of the Nazi occupation, the inter-war years in particular witnessed several challenges to stable democracy, starting with the half-hearted call for revolution by a Social Democratic leader, and ending with widespread criticism of parliamentary democracy and the rise of an indigenous National Socialist movement in the 1930s. Immediately after the Second World War, portions of the elite planned a renewal of Dutch politics rather than a return to pre-war practices. Five years of occupation, during which ancient political foes had become allies in the under-ground resistance and visions of a more harmonious and less segmented society had developed, resulted in an attempt to break through pillarisation. This 'breakthrough' failed eventually, largely because religious leaders, especially the Catholic clergy, were quick to rebuild their respective pillars. In many respects the post-war years even became the heyday of consociational democracy and of political stability. For example, in the 1948 parliamentary elections the net change consisted of four seats out of 100 in the Second Chamber.

This period came to an abrupt end in the second half of the 1960s. In the 1967 elections 15 (now out of 150) seats unexpectedly changed political hands. In both the 1971 and 1972 elections this figure rose to a record 20, earthshaking by Dutch standards. Increased electoral volatility is but one indicator of the changes; there were also large-scale demonstrations and riots in the big cities as old organisations merged, folded, or faced new competition. Depillarisation is the key word to describe the changes, and it can be measured by the same criteria that Lijphart has offered as measurements of pillarisation. First, the role of ideology or religion within the subcultures has declined. As we shall see in more detail in Chapter 4, religion has lost much of its predictive power with regard to voting behaviour. The newspaper *De Volkskrant* dropped its subtitle, 'Catholic paper for the Netherlands', and currently serves as the main left-of-centre daily.

Second, just as the size and density of the pillarised organisational infrastructure was a measure of pillarisation, so the number and size of non-pillarised organisations indicate depillarisation. In politics there has been a surge of small parties, often break-aways from the pillar-parties. The newcomers have not been very successful, as a Dutch commentary implies in a remarkable metaphor: 'New parties came and went like mushrooms in the autumn of Dutch politics' (Van den Berg and Molleman, 1975, p. 11). There was a Right-wing split from the Social Democrats; both Right-wing and Left-wing splits from the Christian Democrats; a Farmers' Party which sprouted its own splinter groups; and a Retailers' Party. None survived. The only newcomer that seems to have become a fixture in the party system is Democrats '66 (D66). In politics the pillarised organisations eventually recouped most of the ground lost initially, but in other areas, such as broadcasting, they have not been so fortunate. Today, the two largest broadcasting associations within the public broadcasting system are TROS and Veronica, both without any subcultural affiliation. In addition, the public system faces increasing competition from commercial satellite stations.

Third, the cohesiveness of the pillars has diminished. Most formal ties between organisations within one pillar have been severed. There are also fewer and fewer interlocking directorates. The parliamentary parties, for example, used to recruit many of their members directly from the leadership of other organisations belonging to the same pillar (see Chapter 6). This phenomenon has almost completely disappeared.

Fourth, social apartheid is waning. At the individual level this is shown by a transition from structured to open competition in elections, to be analysed more fully in Chapter 4. At the organisational level we may observe mergers of organisations formerly belonging to different subcultures. Instead of three health-care organisations, there is now only one 'Inter-Cross' in many communities; the Socialist and Catholic trade unions are now combined into the FNV trade union federation; and, last but not least, the three main Christian Democratic parties have fused into one party, the Christian Democratic Appeal (CDA).

Fifth, and finally, pillarisation is no longer encouraged by the elites. Whereas the bishops still threatened 'deviant' Catholics with exclusion from the holy sacraments in 1954, in 1967 a bishop announced on television that party choice was a matter for each Catholic's individual conscience. In summary, the life story of our imaginary early Catholic would have been quite different had he or she been born after the mid 1960s.

Just as the degree of pillarisation varied from one subculture to another, depillarisation did not affect all of them equally. The religious pillars were affected most, although we should differentiate between the *Gereformeerden*, who proved relatively impervious to change, and the Catholics who experienced the fastest and most far-reaching depillarisation. The strength of the Catholic pillar in the past, the central coordinating role of the church, now proved to be its weakness as well. The dramatic decline in attractiveness of the Catholic Church can be seen from Table 2.2.

Given its central role within the pillar, when the church swayed, so did the entire *zuil*. Again, the Liberals provide the exception to the rule: there was little for them to depillarise, and in many respects organisations that had been regarded as vaguely Liberal in the past were now in the best position to benefit from the changes.

One of the most intriguing puzzles of recent Dutch political history is what triggered this avalanche of change. There is no shortage of conjectures and hypotheses. Those who saw pillarisation as the byproduct of the emancipatory struggle of different minorities see depillarisation as the result of successful emancipation. Once the goals had been reached, discipline within the pillars relaxed, and the minorities were integrated into Dutch society at large. Those who interpreted pillarisation as a form of social control suggest that

**TABLE 2.2**
**Priests in the Catholic Church, 1960–70**

| Year | Priests leaving church | New priests ordained |
|------|------------------------|----------------------|
| 1960 | 11  | 318 |
| 1961 | 15  | 306 |
| 1962 | 14  | 279 |
| 1963 | 16  | 303 |
| 1964 | 18  | 271 |
| 1965 | 45  | 237 |
| 1966 | 74  | 227 |
| 1967 | 155 | 193 |
| 1968 | 202 | 143 |
| 1969 | 244 | 110 |
| 1970 | 243 | 48  |

*Source*: Thurlings (1978), p. 170.

depillarisation is a sign of insecurity or failure on the part of the elites. As Houska asserts:

> The organizations of the political subcultures of Western Europe grew and flourished because elites acted decisively to create and sustain them. They did so because they saw in organizations a way to achieve certain goals . . . More recently, subcultural organizations have declined and cohesion has been lost – in part because of a changed social and economic environment, but also in large measure because elites saw better or at least less costly means to achieve their goals. (Houska, 1985, pp. 149–50)

Other factors that are regularly mentioned in this context include the contention that pillarised loyalty was undercut by the homogenising message of television, or by increased mobility (be it social or geographic). A failure of socialisation is often suggested by authors who point to student protest, a generation gap, or the numerical prominence of youth in general. Such explanations sound rather plausible, and perhaps there is some truth in them. However, in so far as empirical evidence is available (in the 1960s survey research was still in its infancy in the Netherlands) none of the theories is supported by it (Andeweg, 1982).

Even more interesting than its explanation are the consequences of depillarisation. In terms of Lijphart's typology of democracies (see Figure 2.2) depillarisation has transferred Dutch society into another category. Now a more homogeneous society in combination with continued elite cooperation would classify Dutch politics as a 'depoliticised democracy'. However, this is not what most authors observed during the late 1960s and early 1970s. They noted that political competition seemed to intensify. This was partly the result of a change in electoral strategy by the political parties in an effort to win over depillarised voters. Some even speak of a tacit agreement by Social Democrats and Liberals to accelerate the demise of the religious pillars by mutual polarisation. Intensified competition was also partly the result of attempts at democratisation.

The elitist character of the politics of accommodation came under increasing attacks. The Netherlands was not the only country in which calls for direct democracy in universities and factories could be heard in the 1960s, and where political parties faced increasing competition from single-issue citizen action groups. In the Netherlands, however, the criticism was not only that representative democracy was not enough, but also that representative democracy itself was not fully operative. This gave rise to a number of proposals for constitutional reform, some of which we shall return to in Chapter 5. It was the combination of depillarisation and calls for democratisation that led Lijphart to speak of 'the breakdown of the politics of accommodation'. In his view the Dutch elites realised the dangers inherent in the disillusionment with the politics of accommodation. Once more, they showed their wisdom and prudence by resorting to a 'second self-denying prophecy': the conscious introduction of a measured amount of competition into the political system. This brings the Netherlands into the more familiar category of centripetal democracy, in the same league as countries such as the UK and the USA. The consequences of this transformation can be seen in Table 2.3, where we contrast Lijphart's seven rules of the game of consociationalism with what Daalder observed as the fashionable opinions in 1974 (Daalder, 1974).

Since 1974, however, even the new political style Daalder described seems to have evaporated. Some authors have even begun to talk of a 'restoration', or a 'silenced revolution'. If by 'restoration' they mean a halt to, or even a reversal of, pillarisation, they are mistaken; apart from an invigoration of fundamentalist Protestantism there are no signs in that direction. If, on the other hand, we look at political decision-making, Lijphart's old set of rules seem more

**TABLE 2.3**

**The changing rules of Dutch politics**

| Rules of the game observed by Lijphart, 1968 | Proclaimed rules of the game as observed by Daalder, 1974 |
|---|---|
| 1. The business of politics | 1. Exposure of 'Establishment ideology'; critical view of society |
| 2. Agreement to disagree | 2. Conflict |
| 3. Summit diplomacy | 3. Self-determination at the base |
| 4. Proportionality | 4. Polarisation |
| 5. Depoliticisation | 5. Politicisation |
| 6. Secrecy | 6. Open government |
| 7. The government's right to govern with little interference from Parliament | 7. A critique of 'the decline of Parliament', 'the Fourth Branch of government', etc. |

applicable than the claims of a new politics recorded by Daalder. It is not by accident that earlier in this chapter we presented several examples of (non-)decision-making from the post-pillarisation era, such as the Lockheed Affair, nuclear energy, and euthanasia. In recent writings Lijphart now admits that there have been few significant changes in elite culture since 1967. He attributes the original 'myopic and exaggerated interpretation of the degrees of difference and change' (Lijphart, 1989, p. 140) that led him to suggest a second self-denying prophecy to having been in the Netherlands at the time.

However, the problem may be more fundamental than the appropriate distance of the observer. There can be no gainsaying the depillarisation of Dutch society, however incomplete and unevenly distributed that process may be. *If it was pillarisation that necessitated the politics of accommodation, how may we explain the continuation of accommodationist practices now that the pillars have crumbled?* We suggest  that the importance of pillarisation has been overemphasised by most authors. It was this emphasis which led to the puzzle of increasing pillarisation after the Pacification of 1917, and it is this emphasis which now leads to the puzzle of continued consociationalism after depillarisation. Pillarisation, however, was only one of the threats to stable democracy, and probably not the most important one. We ended the preceding section by arguing that the minority position of all the subcultures may have been the crucial incentive for the elites  to cooperate instead of to compete. Whatever else has changed, all  political parties are still far removed from a parliamentary majority. This provides the explanation of continued accommodation without pillarisation. The political style Daalder observed in 1974 was a temporary aberration, brought about by the fact that depillarisation revived hopes, in particular within the Labour Party, of a majority. As soon as the dust had settled, the Social Democrats realised their mistake, abandoned their majoritarian strategy and calls for reform, and resumed traditional consensual practices. The Netherlands remains a country of minorities, which entertain no hope of becoming majorities.

# 3

# Political Parties and the Party System

## Historical Development of the Parties

*Christian Democrats*

The growth of political parties was integrally tied to the development of the pillars. For the Protestants, organisation was due in no small part to the efforts of the nineteenth-century leader, Abraham Kuyper. Kuyper was a master organiser and founded (or helped to found) many of the most important institutions within the pillar. He was in fact responsible for the organisation of those orthodox groups that had broken away, in part with his help, from the Dutch Reformed Church into the *Gereformeerde* Churches. He was responsible for setting up a newspaper to be the mouthpiece of the movement, and a university – the Free University of Amsterdam – to train an intellectual elite. In 1879 he founded the first mass political party of the Netherlands: the ARP.

The purpose of this movement, and the associated institutions, was the emancipation of those orthodox Calvinists known as the *kleine luyden*. Ideologically, these orthodox Calvinists were appalled by certain aspects of the liberal philosophy of the French Revolution, particularly the principle of popular sovereignty. 'Against the Revolution, the Gospel', wrote G. Groen van Prinsterer earlier in the nineteenth century. He argued also that sovereignty was given by God and could best be exercised through the Orangist monarchy. Opposition to the French Revolution led to the choice of the name Anti-Revolutionary Party.

Catholics had perhaps even more reason than the orthodox Calvinists to organise an emancipation movement. They had at times been denied political rights and the ability to practise their religion openly; in Amsterdam and other older cities, one can still visit such 'hidden churches'. The southern, and predominantly Catholic, provinces of North Brabant and Limburg had never been given equal status within the Republic, and were long governed as semi-colonies (*Generaliteitslanden*). Steps were taken in 1798 and 1848 to guarantee the freedom of religion, but the Catholics had to wait until 1853 before it became possible to re-establish the Church hierarchy.

Catholics were elected to Parliament in the nineteenth century, but it was only at the beginning of the twentieth century that the first Catholic political party appeared. The Roman Catholic State Party was established in 1926. With the support of the Church hierarchy, this party was able to become and remain virtually the only party for Catholics. It was supported by 85 per cent or more of all Catholic voters. After the Second World War, the party was refounded with a new name, the Catholic People's Party (KVP). The opportunity for membership was formally extended to non-Catholics, but it continued to be almost exclusively Catholic. In no small part due to the efforts of the Catholic clergy, the Roman Catholic State Party and its successor (the KVP) were essentially unchallenged within the Catholic pillar. Throughout their existence, these parties remained the political arm of the Catholic movement.

Protestants, however, have always been more prone to schism. Within the Protestant pillar there were two main religious groups, the Dutch Reformed and the *Gereformeerden*. Politically, it did not take long before a conflict within the ARP led to the establishment of a new party. At the end of the nineteenth century controversy arose within the ARP concerning the place of the Dutch Reformed Church. The problem was compounded by disagreement over one of the major political questions of the day, the extension of the franchise, as well as the question of the independence of parliamentary politicians from external party organisations. Those opposed to the expansion of suffrage left the party and eventually formed the Christian Historical Union (CHU). This party tended to draw its support from conservative elements within the Dutch Reformed Church, but was never as successful in mobilising as large a proportion of the believers of that Church as were the Catholic and Anti-Revolutionary parties within their related church groups, as will be shown in Chapter 4.

In the late 1960s and early 1970s electoral support for the KVP and the CHU declined rapidly (see Chapter 4). Stimulated at least in part by electoral losses, discussions concerning the formation of a unified Christian Democratic party were accelerated. Various forms of cooperation eventually led to the formation of a single parliamentary caucus and a combined list of candidates in 1977. The success of the combined list swept away any final reservations and in 1980, just slightly more than 100 years after the founding of the ARP, it merged with the CHU and the KVP to form the Christian Democratic Appeal (CDA).

Although these three parties were by far the most important of Dutch religious parties, numerous other such parties have been founded. Those that sprang up within the Catholic pillar were never of lasting duration, but this is not so for the Protestants. Small, usually orthodox Calvinist, parties have long had a place in Dutch politics. The oldest of these is the Political Reformed Party (SGP), which was founded in 1918 and has been represented in the Second Chamber of Parliament continuously since 1922. The party came about as a result of disagreements within the *Gereformeerde* movement (including a part within the Dutch Reformed Church) over the question of separation of church and state and the possibility of cooperation with the Catholics. The party remains ultraconservative in many of its positions, in particular on moral and ethical issues. It is perhaps most well known for its opposition to political activity for women.

Since the Second World War, other Protestant parties have emerged. Yet another disagreement over theology led to a walkout from the *Gereformeerde* church and the establishment of a new church with its own political party, the Reformed Political League (GPV). The party just missed achieving the electoral quotient in 1952 and ensuing elections; representation was finally achieved in 1963. Since then the party has continually held at least one seat in Parliament.

Two additional Protestant parties seemed more recently to have arisen less out of theological disputes and more because of political questions. Disapproval of the merger into the CDA and opposition to liberalisation of abortion seem to have been the main impetus for the founding, in 1975, of the Reformed Political Federation (RPF). Although less homogeneous than the other Protestant parties, it has managed to achieve representation in Parliament since 1981.

The merger of the ARP with the Catholics and the CHU produced a backlash not only on the Right, but on the Left as well. Some of the more Leftist-oriented members left the party to form the Evangelical People's Party (EVP) in 1980. However, the party won only a single seat at the 1982 election and has since become one of the partners in the Green Left.

Before moving to the next group, it is perhaps important here to mention the development of the Radical Party (PPR). This party was yet another product of the turbulent 1960s. In 1968, four MPs from the KVP bolted to found this new party. They were soon joined by Leftist oriented ex-members of the ARP and were led to their greatest electoral success in 1972 by one such ex-ARP person, Bas de Gaay Fortman. Although the party may be said to have had its origins in one Christian Democratic party and its most well-known leader from another Christian Democratic party, the PPR soon lost any clear religious identification and came to be considered as a secular Leftist party. In 1989 it became one of the partners in the Green Left party.

*Socialists*

'Socialism came too soon to the Netherlands', the historian Kossmann has written (Kossmann, 1978, p. 345). By this he meant that when the philosophy of socialism arrived via Germany, conditions were not ripe for a mass socialist movement. The economy, which had initially reached its height because of trade, was mainly based upon agricultural production in the middle to late nineteenth century. With late industrialisation, no large industrial proletariat existed in which socialism could take root. Instead, the first support for working-class movements was found among artisans, urban skilled workers, canal- and peat-diggers, economically depressed farmers, and agricultural labourers. In fact, it was a northern, rural district that sent the first socialist representative, Ferdinand Domela Nieuwenhuis, to Parliament in 1888.

When an industrial proletariat did begin to develop, the socialist movement found itself thwarted by the earlier efforts of Calvinists and Catholics. Workers who maintained their religious beliefs were organised into their respective organisations, including trade unions and political parties. The socialists could only appeal to the non-religious who, although growing in numbers, were still only a minority of the population. Nevertheless, socialists did produce organisations that paralleled and rivalled those of the religious groups, such as newspapers, trade unions, and youth organisations.

The first socialist political party was established in 1882 and adopted a programme that was modelled on the Gotha programme of its German counterpart. However, as a frustrated Domela Nieuwenhuis moved towards anarchism, a new party, the Social Democratic Workers' Party (SDAP), was established in 1894. It, too, took its ideological inspiration from the German socialists, but from the Erfurt programme. Although modest in its beginnings, it emerged as the dominant socialist party until it, together with all Dutch political parties (except for the National Socialists), was banned by the German occupiers during the Second World War.

After its futile attempt at revolution in 1918, the party gradually became less revolutionary and in the 1930s rejected revolutionary reactions to the Great Depression. It turned more towards Plan-Socialism and showed its desire and willingness to cooperate within the system with other parties in putting forward a national plan to deal with economic problems. In 1939, two Social Democratic ministers finally entered the government. Following the Occupation, the party reorganised, dropping the remainder of its Marxist trappings and changed its name to the Party of Work, or Labour Party (PvdA). Nevertheless, adherents of the party are still referred to as either Socialists or Social Democrats, as its attempt to break through the existing party lines failed. The long standing dream of reaching majority status proved illusory once more and the party generally attracts between one-quarter and one-third of the vote.

Socialists, like Protestants, have been troubled by schisms within their ranks. The earliest important break occurred at the beginning of the century when a group was expelled from the party and in 1909 organised what was to become the Communist Party in the Netherlands (CPN). This party first won representation in Parliament in 1918 and was represented thereafter continually until 1986. In that year, a conflict between 'reformers', who were particularly concerned about such issues as women's emancipation, and the more traditional members, who held to a stricter Marxist–Leninist line, led to a split in the party. Both groups failed to gain sufficient votes to achieve representation in Parliament. In 1989 the Communist Party joined with three other small Leftist parties to form the Green Left.

During the Cold War, protests against the militarism of both the East and West led in 1957 to the establishment of the Pacifist Socialist Party (PSP). The name clearly indicates its platform. It too suffered because of internal dissension in 1986 and joined the Green Left coalition in 1989.

In the 1960s a group calling itself 'New Left' and calling for closer adherence to socialist principles gained considerable influence in the Labour Party. In reaction, a group of more pragmatic members walked out and formed Democratic Socialists '70 (DS'70). The party had, however, only a short-lived success, gaining eight seats in Parliament and even participating in the governing coalition in 1971. It subsequently lost electoral support and has since been disbanded.

*Liberals*

From the founding of the Dutch Republic in the sixteenth century until the beginning of the nineteenth century, political conflict regularly centred on divisions between portions of the urban patriciate and the 'Orangists', the supporters of the House of Orange who could be found predominantly among the lower classes of society and among the more orthodox Protestants. However, with participation in politics limited, there was little need for organisations to mobilise and channel political activity, and within the urban elite various ideological trends could be identified. Nevertheless, this elite produced a social and political system that, at least by the standards of the time and the surrounding countries, could be considered quite tolerant. The revolutionary struggle for freedom of religion was not quickly forgotten, and although certain outward manifestations of Catholicism were restricted or forbidden, the individual's right to believe as he or she chose was generally respected. This open climate attracted many groups from abroad, including the French Huguenots and those who came from England to stay in Leiden for ten years before sailing to America to become the Pilgrim Fathers.

This liberal social and political climate was the breeding ground for the philosophy of liberalism that became increasingly important politically around the middle of the nineteenth century. Under the leadership of Johan Rudolf Thorbecke, a new constitution was drawn up in 1848 which provided for a directly elected chamber of Parliament and for ministers responsible to Parliament.

During the latter half of the nineteenth century Liberals were prominent both in politics and many areas of social life, such as the universities, the media, and in business. As was mentioned in Chapter 2, the Liberals were never highly organised and some authors have questioned whether one can speak of a liberal pillar. Nevertheless, they were sufficiently important politically and socially to provide a common foe against which the Protestants, Catholics, and Social Democrats could pit themselves in their struggle for equality.

Lacking a mass movement and mass organisation, the influence of the Liberals declined sharply with the introduction of universal suffrage and proportional representation (PR). Prior to the Second World War there were several Liberal parties, but together they seldom managed to receive more than 10 per cent of the vote. After the War, one of the Liberal parties re-emerged as the Party of Freedom, while another joined the new Labour Party. However, P.J. Oud and his followers soon left the PvdA, and together with the Party of Freedom formed a new party, the People's Party for Freedom and Democracy (VVD) in 1948.

Until 1972 the image of the party remained associated with the 'regents' of the past and support for the party continued to hover around the 10 per cent figure that had been traditional for Liberals before the war. However, under the leadership of Hans Wiegel the party began to change its image. Wiegel did not make an intellectual liberal appeal, but attempted to broaden the base of the party. He fought against the bigness of government brought about by the welfare state. Although perhaps still inspired by nineteenth-century liberal principles of *laissez-faire* and still viewed as liberal in many social matters, in twentieth century economic terms the party had become the most conservative of the major Dutch parties.

*Other Parties*

In addition to those political parties that were associated with the pillars or which grew out of parties associated with the pillars, there have always been many other political parties in the Netherlands. In the following section, we shall deal with the question of the number of parties in the Netherlands and its supposed effects upon political stability. Most additional parties never receive sufficient votes to gain representation in Parliament and, of those that do, many have been of only passing importance. A small number have, however, had sufficient lasting importance in Dutch politics to warrant mention here.

Parties of the extreme Right have seldom been of any importance in the Netherlands. In 1931, admirers of Mussolini and Hitler founded the National Socialist Movement (NSB). Under the leadership of A.A. Mussert, the party achieved its peak of electoral success in 1935 when it gained 8 per cent of the vote at the provincial elections. One can only speculate what might have happened to the party if the Germans had not invaded. During the Occupation, the NSB was the only political party not banned by the Germans. It was banned by the government in exile in London, after having been declared guilty of treasonous activities. After the War the party did not return and many of its former members were prosecuted.

In the 1960s a party emerged that often was referred to, even by its leader, as a Rightist party. The Farmers' Party (*Boerenpartij*) had its roots in the dissatisfaction of farmers. Ideologically the party is somewhat difficult to locate; its opposition to governmental intervention, especially in agriculture, and commitment to law and order and traditional principles undoubtedly justify a Rightist placement. Its electoral success, however, may have been more related to dissatisfaction with the pillarised system than to sympathy with its Poujadist position. The leader of the party, the laughable 'Farmer Koekoek', appealed to voters who were fed up with the system and with the dominant political parties. The party reached its electoral summit in 1967 with seven parliamentary seats, but was beset by internal divisions and departed from Parliament in 1981.

Most recently, small groups on the Right have attempted to play upon fears and hatred directed at the immigrant workers who had originally been imported to support the economic boom of the 1960s. The size of such radical groups has in general been smaller in the Netherlands than in some other European countries but, because of the low electoral threshold, on two occasions such groups have succeeded in electing a representative to Parliament. In 1982, the so-called Centre Party elected J.G.H. Janmaat to Parliament. After internal party conflicts, Janmaat was thrown out of the party in 1984, but retained his seat in Parliament. He founded a new party, the Centre Democrats, but neither party was able to achieve representation in 1986. In 1989, with less than 1 per cent of the vote, Janmaat returned to Parliament where he is ignored and ostracised by the other members.

Away from the extreme Right, dissatisfaction with the dominant parties of the pillars also led to the founding of a party in 1966 whose express purpose was to 'explode' the existing party system. The party was begun by a group of Amsterdam intellectuals, who called their party Democrats '66, or D66. The party pushed for constitutional reforms that would produce a more 'democratic' political system, such as direct election of the Prime Minister and a district system of election to Parliament (see Chapter 5). Although none of these changes (with the exception of abolition of compulsory voting) has been implemented, and despite quite varying electoral results, the party has gained an important position within the Dutch party system. It is often regarded as a progressive-liberal party (as opposed to the conservative-liberal VVD). In the European Parliament it has joined the VVD in the Liberal parliamentary group. Despite its yoyo electoral performance during the past 25 years, it now enjoys a status as the 'fourth' party in the Netherlands.

The last party to be mentioned here is the Green Left, which has already been referred to several times above. Although Dutch political parties have more often been the victims of splits and defections, the Green Left and the CDA provide examples of successful attempts at merging political parties. A primary impetus for this merger (as well as that of the CDA) was electoral losses. The Pacifist Socialists, Communists, the EVP and, to a lesser extent, also the PPR, suffered heavily at the 1986 election. The need to do something dramatic and a desire to capitalise upon the popularity of the 'green' concept led to the new combined party. Exhibit 3.1 gives a brief outline of Dutch political parties.

## Party Organisation

*Party Structure*

One of the distinctive elements of modern political parties is organisation. Organisation became necessary during the nineteenth-century in order to mobilise the expanding electorate. Mobilising the electorate for support, writing a party programme and offering candidates are perhaps the three main purposes of political parties. For all three, organisation remains a necessity.

Despite the fact that there is no legislation with regard to political parties and despite the diversity of political parties in the Netherlands, there is considerable uniformity in their organisational structure. Rather than attempt to provide extensive detail about each of the political parties, a general outline can be given which fits most of the parties reasonably well.

The organisation of Dutch political parties parallels the territorial structure of the Dutch state. The Netherlands is organised somewhat hierarchically in some 700 municipalities, 12 provinces, and the national state (see Chapter 7). At each of these levels, representatives are chosen for legislative bodies, such as municipal councils, provincial legislatures, and the Second Chamber of Parliament. Since candidates must be selected at each of these levels it is not surprising that party organisations exist at each of these levels. The election for the Second Chamber tends to complicate matters, however. As we shall see in Chapter 4, the election to the Second Chamber is carried out formally in 19 electoral districts. This means that boundaries for the electoral districts do not coincide with the boundaries for the provinces, so that some provinces have more than one electoral district. Parties tend, therefore, to have local divisions at both the provincial level and the level of the electoral district, the latter being important only because of its national significance.

The lowest level in the party organisation is formed by the local branches at the municipal level. If a municipality is small, a single local branch may be sufficient. Within the cities, more local units are necessary, as well as a municipal organisation to coordinate the activities within the town or city. Local branches generally elect representatives to the Party Congress (or General Assembly); for the largest parties, between 800 and 2000 delegates to a party congress may be chosen. A Party Congress is the highest decision-making body in a party. In general, it is concerned with the position of the party in the long term. It meets once a year or once every two years, although special meetings may be called in order to ratify a new electoral manifesto or to make the final determination of the list of candidates.

Other, smaller bodies are elected to carry out the more day-to-day activities of the party. The smallest group is the Party Executive, consisting of the party chairman, deputy party chairman, party secretary, and between four and nine additional members. In the larger parties, some of these will be full-time salaried positions.

**EXHIBIT 3.1**

**Dutch Political Parties at a Glance**

| | Full (English) Name | Dates | Description |
|---|---|---|---|
| *Christian Democrats* | | | |
| ARP | Anti-Revolutionary Party | 1879–1980 | First national mass political party. Associated with the *Gereformeerde* Churches. |
| CHU | Christian-Historical Union | 1908–80 | Second major party in Protestant pillar. Supported primarily by members of Dutch Reformed Church. |
| KVP | Catholic People's Party | 1926–80 | Post-war successor to Roman Catholic State Party. Associated with Catholic Church. |
| CDA | Christian Democratic Appeal | 1980– | Formed as a merger of ARP, CHU and KVP. Major Christian Democratic party. |
| SGP | Political Reformed Party | 1918– | Extreme orthodox Calvinist party. Opposes separation of church and state, and female suffrage. |
| GPV | Reformed Political League | 1948– | Calvinist party organised after split within *Gereformeerde* Churches. |
| PPR | Radical Party | 1970–89 | Formed by breakaway members of KVP parliamentary party. Became secular Leftist party. Merged into Green Left in 1989. |
| RKPN | Roman Catholic | 1972–81(?) | Formed to oppose liberal policies in matters of morals of KVP. |
| RPF | Reformed Political Federation | 1975– | Less homogeneous Calvinist party, formed in opposition to Leftist tendencies of ARP. Opposed merger into CDA. |
| EVP | Evangelical People's Party | 1980–89 | Formed as Left-wing response of merger of ARP into CDA. Became part of Green Left in 1989. |
| *Socialists* | | | |
| PvdA | Labour Party | 1946– | Successor to Social Democratic Workers Party. Major social democratic party. |

**Exhibit 3.1** *cont.*

|  | Full (English) Name | Dates | Description |
|---|---|---|---|
| CPN | Communist Party of the Netherlands | 1909–89 | Split off from Social Democratic Workers Party. Suffered from internal division in 1980s. Merged into Green Left in 1989. |
| PSP | Pacifist Socialist Party | 1957–89 | Formed as reaction to Cold War. Suffered from internal dissension in 1980s over course of party. Merged into Green Left in 1989. |
| DS'70 | Democratic Socialists '70 | 1970–83 | Founded by group leaving PvdA because of dissatisfaction with New Left radicalism. Held rather centre-Right views on economic and social policies. |
|  | Green Left | 1989– | Formed in 1989 as merger of CPN, PSP, PPR and EVP. Strong support for environment and for Leftist social policies. |
| *Liberals* |  |  |  |
| VVD | Liberal Party | 1948– | Successor to various pre-war liberal parties. Now major conservative liberal party. |
| *Other* |  |  |  |
| D66 | Democrats '66 (name no longer used) | 1966– | Organised in 1966 to 'explode' party system. Proposed numerous political reforms. Now 'progressive-liberal' of 'Left-liberal' party. |
| BP | Farmers' Party | 1958–81 | Populist, sometimes called Poujadist, anti-system, anti-government party. Strongly conservative. |
| CP/CD | Centre Party/ Centre Democrats | 1980– | Party and successor under leadership of J.G.H. Janmaat. Most prominent in its opposition to foreigners. Often called extreme Rightist or racist. |

Somewhat larger is the Party Committee, consisting generally of between 25 and 50 members. These may include MPs, representatives from regional party organisations, chairpersons of important party committees, and representatives chosen by the Party Congress or Party Council. The size of the Party Committee is intended to be such that it can meet regularly (at least six times a year) and can give policy guidelines to the Party Executive.

If political matters are sufficiently controversial that the Party Executive or Party Committee feels that broader consideration or support is needed, a meeting of the Party Council may be called if such a body exists. This body is generally composed of delegates from the provincial or electoral district organisations and from other organisations within the party. In the major parties the Party Council consists of between 130 and 300 members, and is the highest decision-making body in the party in the period between meetings of the Party Congress. In the CDA, which has the largest Party Council, this body has in practice assumed the position of highest decision-making body, making the function of the Party Congress primarily ceremonial.

Such an overview of party organisation cannot, of course, do justice to the differences between the parties. Each party determines the manner in which it chooses to administer itself, and reasonably important differences can be found. For example, the orthodox Protestant parties (SGP, GPV, and RPF) have a more federal than hierarchical structure. Formally, they are comprised of autonomous local or regional political clubs or associations that are united at the national level. D66, on the other hand, has some elements of a direct democracy. Each member of the party has the right to attend and vote at the Party Congress. Selection of candidates occurs by a postal vote in which all members may take part. Among the larger parties, there are also differences in the importance that the regional organisations have in the process of electoral manifesto composition and candidate selection.

In addition to these subunits within the party, which are based upon geographical representation and are arranged hierarchically, parties have committees or organisations for particular groups within the party. All parties have semi-independent organisations for young people, and most have an organisation for women members. Most also have a special organisation for those party members who represent the party on municipal councils or in provincial legislatures, or who hold executive positions at these levels. In some parties these internal party organisations have direct representation in the Party Council and/or the Party Executive.

Finally, most parties have two organisations that do not formally belong to the party organisation but which are closely associated to it: a Research Foundation and an Institute for Political Education. The former serves as the intellectual satellite for the party, producing books and other documents to provoke discussion of the party ideology. The latter is concerned with producing better and more informed citizens and was set up in some parties only when a law was passed that made it possible for such organisations to obtain governmental subsidies for such activities.

## Party Membership

As a consequence of the close relationship between the major political parties and the societal pillars, it is perhaps rather surprising to note that actual dues-paying membership in political parties in the Netherlands has never been particularly high. Even during the 1950s, when pillarisation may be said to have reached its zenith, membership in the KVP was seldom more than one-fifth of its vote, and the figures for the Anti-Revolutionaries hovered just over 15 per cent. The Social Democrats have never had membership that equalled 10 per cent of the number of votes cast for the party. Part of the explanation for low membership may lie in the definition itself. During the period of pillarisation, large numbers of voters in these groups clearly identified themselves with the pillar and the associated party. In a 1954 survey, fully 27 per cent of the population claimed party membership, whereas informed estimates put membership at about 15 per cent. There may be many reasons for overreporting, but one surely must have been that people 'felt' themselves to be members, even though they did not pay dues.

Figures on party membership are themselves not particularly reliable until about 1970. Before that, national party headquarters did not have complete or accurate information concerning membership. Only after parties became more centralised (and membership lists more computerised) did the figures become more than rough estimates. There is, however, no argument that the number of party members has dropped. In 1989, only 8 per cent of the population even claimed membership, and figures from the parties show the actual figure to be closer to 3 per cent, (a substantial decline from the 15 per cent of the 1950s). Table 3.1 gives the size of party membership in 1992 and shows how party membership was related to the size of the vote for each party in 1989.

**TABLE 3.1**

**Party membership and membership as a percentage of the party vote**

|  | Membership 1992 | 1989 membership as percentage of 1989 vote |
|---|---|---|
| CDA | 120 000 (approx.) | 4.0 |
| PvdA | 79 059 | 3.4 |
| VVD | 56 200 | 5.0 |
| D66 | 11 325 | 1.4 |
| Green Left | 14 971 | 4.3 |
| SGP | 23 062 | 13.9 |
| GPV | 13 000 (approx.) | 11.9 |
| RPF | 8 586 | 9.8 |
| Centre Democrats | 3 000 (estimated) | 3.7 (estimated) |

*Source*:   Documentation Centre for Dutch Political Parties, Groningen.

The drops in membership figures are dramatic, even in recent years. When the three constituent parties merged into the CDA in 1980, the new party could claim about 150 000 members. This was already far below the figures that the three had held at their height – KVP (300 000–400 000), ARP (just under 100 000), CHU (almost 50 000) – but since its founding the party has again declined by almost 30 000 members. Figures for the PvdA were almost always above 100 000 until recent years, and a drop of approximately 12 000 members in 1991 alone has been nothing short of catastrophic for the party. Although membership in the Liberal Party took a dramatic jump under the leadership of Hans Wiegel after 1972, the current figure is well below the peak of more than 100 000 in 1982. CDA and PvdA are at post-war lows, whereas the VVD is almost back to pre-1972 levels.

A declining vote may have been more important than declining membership in convincing the Green Left parties to merge, but the two are certainly related. The current membership of just under 15 000 is less than the CPN itself had as late as 1980. In the 1970s the Radicals also had well over 10 000 members, a level also approached by the Pacifist Socialists in 1979.

D66 has had the greatest roller-coaster ride in party membership of any party in post-war history. In the year of its founding it could claim 1500 members. However, initial success waned and in 1974 it had dropped to only 300 members and seriously considered disbanding itself. Recovery came, however, and in 1981 it reached a peak of over 17 000 members. Given this history, its current level is quite healthy.

The small, fundamentalist Calvinist parties are not so small if one looks at their membership figures. The SGP has a membership that is fourth in total size, and almost half that of the Liberals. The GPV has more members than D66, and the relatively new RPF has just under 9 000. The success of these parties in mobilising their voters is seen by looking at the column showing membership as a percentage of the vote. Ten per cent, or more, of the voters for these parties are paying members. This is more than twice the percentages for the major parties, who in 1989 had memberships that were no more than 5 per cent of their electorates in that year. Worst of all was D66. This party has often held the sympathy of substantial numbers of voters and has, as in 1989, done well at the polls, but it has had difficulty in building up a body of members with a long-standing commitment.

*Party Finances*

Katz and Mair have argued that it is a characteristic feature of modern political parties that they are less concerned about the size of party membership (Katz and Mair, 1992). The claim can, however, hardly be made for Dutch parties. Even if no other reason were to exist, Dutch parties are concerned about membership because members supply the main source of funds for the party.

In most parties dues are assessed according to the income of the member. Exceptions are found among the smaller religious parties which maintain a flat rate, and the Liberal party which bases its dues on age. Recent figures for the major parties show that Labour Party members pay the highest dues, about 85 guilders on average, followed by members of the Liberal Party (58 guilders) and the Christian Democrats (47 guilders). About 80 per cent of the income of the major parties comes from contributions paid by party members.

The remaining 20 per cent of party income may come from various sources. Traditionally, parties of the Left have levied a 'tax' upon their party representatives who are elected to salaried positions. The Communist Party once allowed party representatives to keep only the equivalent of the salary of a skilled worker, and the Pacifist Socialists asked 25 per cent. In comparison, the 2 per cent requested by the Social Democrats is quite modest.

Gifts make up a relatively small portion of party income, certainly in comparison with parties in other countries. Only for the Liberals has the total amount been of any real importance in recent years, and much of this has been from a single foundation. Parties do not generally receive gifts from business enterprises. This absence of business gifts is not the result of legal limitations, since enterprises may receive tax benefits for donations of up to 6 per cent of their profits to non-profit organisations (such as political parties). It is the parties themselves that have placed restrictions upon the acceptance of such gifts. When on occasion such gifts have received publicity, as in 1989 when a provincial division of the CDA accepted gifts in ignorance of party guidelines, the public outcry was so great that parties deem it unwise to accept donations. Such events are generally treated as 'scandals' by the media. Whilst public pressure seems to have been sufficient to make parties hesitant to accept gifts, it has been suggested that the neo-corporatist nature of the Dutch political system (see Chapter 7) may make it unnecessary for business to 'purchase' access. Moreover, the Dutch system of worker participation would make it difficult for a business to favour one party over another.

Parties do at times receive assistance indirectly from organisations sympathetic to the party's cause. Since the broadcasting organisations once belonged to the 'pillars' that included the parties, there is still sympathy among the broadcasting organisations for particular parties. They may air broadcasts, especially at election time, that provide additional exposure for the party. Also, during election campaigns, organisations such as the employers' association or the trade unions may make appeals to the voters. Direct links between such organisations and political parties have been severed during the period of 'depillarisation', but the information they provide voters certainly indicates a sympathy for a particular party. In 1986, the FNV trade union federation spent about 3 million guilders 'to inform the voters about the socio-economic paragraphs of the manifestos of the three major parties'. This may have backfired and may not soon recur.

The Labour Party and the CDA have financial reserves that were built up during the period of pillarisation. The Labour Party has a capital reserve of more than 7 million guilders and has almost 3 million invested in stocks. The Christian Democrats have approximately 2.5 million guilders capital reserve and also receive income from investments. Interest and dividends thus supply these two parties with additional income. Paradoxically the Liberals, with more business and middle-class supporters, lack such capital reserves. The party has turned to special appeals to members and has begun fundraising campaigns, albeit still on a small scale, in an attempt to increase its income.

Parties have never received subsidies from the government in the form of direct grants, but various assistance is provided indirectly. Parties represented in Parliament are provided with free access to radio and television. Each party is allotted ten minutes' radio time every two weeks and ten minutes of television time every three months. Parties also receive between 100 000 and 150 000 guilders to cover the production costs of such programmes. During an election campaign, all parties that are offering candidates in each of the 19 electoral districts receive radio and television time.

Additionally, since the early 1970s, government subsidies have been available for the affiliated foundations that carry out the research, education, training and youth work of the parties. Subsidies are now temporarily available for parties helping to educate new leaders in central and eastern Europe, and EC subsidies are available which cover most of the costs for campaigns for the European Parliament in the Netherlands. Since at least some of this work was done before the subsidies were available, such funds, even though they are not received directly by the parties, relieve the financial pressures. The law stipulates that funds raised by these organisations will be matched, up to a maximum amount based upon the size of the party in Parliament. The maximum amounts that may be claimed by the parties vary between somewhat more than 125 000 guilders for the small parties to between 600 000 and 700 000 guilders for the largest parties.

These are still modest figures. However, the reliance on membership dues has created financial difficulties for the parties because of the sudden drop in membership figures. This, in turn, has led to increased demands on the government to provide adequate funding for the parties. A recent Royal Commission, appointed to study the question, unanimously advised against direct subsidies. It was felt that direct subsidies would make the parties dependent upon the government, or might lead the government to attempt to manipulate parties. In order to insure independence, any subsidies should be indirect. The Commission also emphasised that reliance upon membership dues was a means of guaranteeing that the parties would remain responsive to the members.

Some of the funds raised by membership dues are returned to the local and regional branches of the party. The percentages for the three largest parties vary from 25 per cent for CDA and 30 per cent for the Labour Party to 47 per cent for the Liberal Party. This high percentage for the VVD emphasises the power and importance of these bodies within the party.

A substantial proportion of party expenditures is spent on the maintenance of the national party bureaucracy. The Labour Party has the largest bureaucracy, employing some 50 persons at its national headquarters. Drops in income have, however, forced the party executive to make recommendations to decrease this number. The amount spent on the party bureaucracy amongst the main parties is lowest for the Liberal Party, which has been in financial difficulties in recent years.

The parties also spend substantial amounts on the affiliated organisations of the party. However, as was just mentioned, not only do these organisations carry out important activities for the party, these expenditures generate additional matching funds from the government. Finally, funds are necessary for the publication of party journals that are distributed free to party members. And, of course, funds are set aside for use at election campaigns.

All in all, the size of the budget for Dutch political parties remains quite modest. The Christian Democrat and Labour budgets are approximately 7 million guilders per year each, and those for the Liberals and D66 are only about 2 and 1 million guilders respectively.

## A Decline of Parties?

During the period of pillarisation, the role of the political party was well-defined. Political parties were tied directly into the network of newspapers, broadcasting, trade unions, employers' organisations, and other organisations that made up the pillar. The political party was not a separate organisation but the political arm of the pillar, defending its interests in politics.

With the disintegration of the pillars, the role of political parties became less clear. As in many other countries, observers began to question the importance of political parties. The loss of members is often taken as a sign that political parties no longer play an important role in people's lives. Only a small minority are members of a political party, and even fewer participate in the activities of the parties. Single-issue action groups can at times mobilise far more persons than political parties are able to do on a more permanent basis.

In the Netherlands, Tromp has pointed to other indicators of the decline of party. More and more political positions, including membership in the Second Chamber of Parliament, have become 'professionalised', (i.e., it is no longer possible to combine the position with other employment). This, he argues, has isolated politicians and parties from the voters. Moreover, the role of parties in facilitating communication between voters and their representatives has been largely taken over by radio and television. Professional public opinion polling organisations often provide quick, but reasonably accurate, indications of how the public views a particular question or issue. Election campaigns are increasingly media, rather than grass-roots, events (Tromp, 1985). Tromp is equally critical of parties in their exercise of the aggregation function. No longer do parties have a clear political ideology. Instead of a clear set of political principles, party manifestos have become a pot-pourri of hundreds of statements on all possible issues, but lacking any unity. 'The only thing holding party programmes together', he complains, 'is the staple.' Others have also accused Dutch parties of becoming more 'catch-all' parties.

Yet it would be far too soon to speak of the 'end of party' in the Netherlands. In one sense, parties are only beginning to come into their own. During pillarisation, the parties acted merely as the subculture's embassy to the national government, and only recently have they become the independent organisations that one generally defines as a political party.

One such defining quality is that parties nominate candidates at elections, and the Dutch parties have tightened rather than loosened their control over the pathways to political office. During the period of pillarisation, some parties reserved positions on the candidate list for the representatives of other organisations within the pillar (see Chapter 6). The candidate selection process itself was largely in the hands of the party elite. In the interest of providing balance, persons without a long record of party service could be placed on the list. Cabinet Ministers were frequently recruited from outside Parliament, and at times lists even included persons with no party affiliation (see Chapter 5). Since the 1960s, however, the grip of parties has become stronger. Internal party democratisation and decentralisation has put candidate selection somewhat more in the hands of the membership. This has made lateral entry more difficult, as the party members stress service within the party in making their selection. All in all, the possibilities for a career in politics is now completely in control of the parties.

The parties may also have increased their control over the political agenda. In recent years, parliamentary parties have attempted to bind governments to the accords reached during the Cabinet formation process (see Chapter 5). Parties and party leaders also continue to dominate the political discussions. Although broadcasting and polling organisations occasionally are successful in placing an issue on the political agenda, the discussion will die without the participation of the parties. More often it is the parties who either generate or sustain political discussions. The research foundations of the parties can play a role in either internal political discussions or public debates.

In 1991–2, a group within the Labour Party expressed disenchantment with both the direction that their party was taking and the way the political system was functioning. They threatened to leave the party and form a 'movement'. They quickly realised, however, that a movement without representation in Parliament could hardly expect to be taken seriously for too long. Thus it would be necessary to nominate candidates for office. That they at least temporarily abandoned their plans attests to the continuing importance of party control of both the political agenda and candidate selection.

## Political Party System

### The Numerical Criterion

From our description of the individual parties, it is clear that there are a large number of political parties in the Netherlands. Based to a considerable extent upon the unfortunate experiences in the German

Weimar Republic and French Fourth Republic, political observers have often expressed a fear that having too many political parties can pose a threat to a stable democracy. The concern has been that too many parties make the achievement of majority consensus virtually impossible. Moreover, in such systems it was feared that almost inevitably extremist 'anti-system' parties would arise which would tend to polarise political conflict. Such parties would pull votes away from the centre, and the political system would fly apart through centrifugal force.

The simplest classification of party systems is in terms of numbers: one-, two-, or multi-party systems. This is a very rough means of counting, and Sartori has expanded the classification by denoting three types of one-party system, and three types of multi-party systems: 'limited pluralism', 'extreme pluralism' and 'atomised' (Sartori, 1976).

From the discussion above of the historical development of parties, it is quite clear that the Netherlands has a multi-party system. An important fact to note is that the Netherlands provides a clear exception to the commonly held proposition that the electoral system is a major cause of the type of party system. This proposition holds that single member district systems produce two-party systems, whereas PR produces multi-party systems. Prior to the Pacification of 1917, which introduced universal male suffrage and PR, election to the Second Chamber of Parliament was by single-member district. The system required a majority vote, so that if no candidate received an absolute majority in the first round, a second vote was taken. Nevertheless, the system was clearly multi-party. The major five parties that were to dominate politics in the twentieth century all had their roots in the nineteenth-century with its single-member district system. At the turn of the century, between seven and eleven political parties (or political groupings) could be found in Parliament.

Introduction of PR only made it easier for even more parties to take part. Table 3.2 shows that at the first election (in 1918) with proportional representation and universal (male) suffrage, fully 32 parties submitted lists. Of these, 17 exceeded the electoral threshold and gained seats in Parliament. The number of lists increased at the following election, but an increase in the electoral threshold (from 0.5 to 0.75 per cent) reduced the number of successful parties to 10. The peak number of lists submitted (54) was in 1933, when 14 parties were successful. After that election, parties were required to make a

**TABLE 3.2**

**Number of parties contesting the elections and number
of parties achieving representation, 1918–1989**

| Year | Number of lists competing | Number of parties achieving representation in Parliament | Percentage of vote won by five (after 1977 three) major parties | Number of seats won by five (after 1977 three) major parties |
|------|------|------|------|------|
| 1918 | 32 | 17 | 87.2 | 87/100 |
| 1922 | 48 | 10 | 87.8 | 94/100 |
| 1925 | 32 | 11 | 88.4 | 94/100 |
| 1929 | 36 | 12 | 89.1 | 92/100 |
| 1933 | 54 | 14 | 83.9 | 87/100 |
| 1937 | 20 | 10 | 84.6 | 89/100 |
| 1946 | 10 | 7 | 86.2 | 88/100 |
| 1948 | 12 | 8 | 87.0 | 89/100 |
| 1952 | 13 | 8 | 86.7 | 90/100 |
| 1956 | 10 | 7 | 91.5 | 94/100 |
| 1959 | 13 | 8 | 91.6 | 142/150 |
| 1963 | 18 | 10 | 87.5 | 135/150 |
| 1967 | 23 | 11 | 78.9 | 123/150 |
| 1971 | 28 | 14 | 71.7 | 113/150 |
| 1972 | 23 | 14 | 73.1 | 113/150 |
| 1977 | 24 | 11 | 83.7 | 130/150 |
| 1981 | 28 | 10 | 76 | 118/150 |
| 1982 | 20 | 12 | 83 | 128/150 |
| 1986 | 27 | 9 | 85 | 133/150 |
| 1989 | 25 | 9 | 81.8 | 125/150 |

deposit of fl.250 which was only returned if a specified percentage (but less than the electoral threshold) of votes was achieved. This reduced the number of lists presented at the last election before the Second World War to only 20, of which 10 were successful.

At the first post-war elections, the number of lists presented tended to be less than previously, in part because of attempts to restructure the party system. The number of parties in Parliament was also less than before, with only seven or eight represented. However, in the mid-1960s, when the system of pillarisation began to weaken, the numbers began to increase again. Since 1967, in any given election, 20 or more parties have generally submitted lists at the elections and up to 14 parties have been successful in getting candidates elected.

Just counting parties, however, does not prove to be particularly satisfactory in describing a party system. Some parties are really quite inconsequential and hardly deserving of being counted. Sartori therefore added a criterion of 'relevancy' to the counting operation. A party is relevant if it participates in governing coalitions or has the 'power of intimidation' or 'blackmail potential'. In the Netherlands, certainly not all the parties can fulfil one of these criteria. Since 1918 five parties have dominated Dutch politics. The Catholics, Anti-Revolutionaries, and Christian-Historicals were, with few exceptions, in all Cabinets between 1918 and 1939. Until 1939, Social Democrats were excluded from the government coalition, but it would be strange not to count them as a relevant party. The Liberals were not particularly strong in this period and were dispersed over more than a single party. Counting them as a single group brings the number to five parties.

After the Second World War, five parties (KVP, ARP, CHU, PvdA, and VVD) dominated. The figures in Table 3.2 show the extent of this domination. From 1918 until 1963, the Big Five gained between 84 and 92 per cent of the vote cast and held no less than 87 per cent of the seats in Parliament. In fact, between 1918 and 1967, the three confessional parties always held 50 per cent or more of the parliamentary seats so that, if considered as a single bloc, one could fashion an argument that the Dutch party system was one-party hegemonic. Such an argument has never been made, however, so the system is called a five-party system.

It is just this fact that five parties are relevant that brought Sartori problems with his classification system. Although he at times drew the line between 'moderate pluralism' and 'polarised pluralism' at four, the five Dutch parties presented an anomaly. Thus, at least to an extent because of the Dutch case, he usually drew the dividing line between five and six.

The situation since 1967 has not become easier for someone trying to count parties in the Netherlands. After 1967 the stranglehold of the major five parties began to loosen, at least temporarily. In 1971, they dropped to an all-time low of only 72 per cent of the vote and 75 per cent of the seats in Parliament. The three Christian Democratic parties held only 58 of the 150 seats in the Second Chamber. In order to form a Cabinet, a new party (DS'70) was brought into the coalition. The following year, new elections changed little in the balance of power, and two more new parties (D66 and the Radicals) joined a coalition with the Social Democrats, Catholics, and Anti-Revolutionaries.

Such expansion would have necessarily led to a classification as 'polarised pluralism' if the merger of the confessional parties had not taken place. Since 1980, only four parties have participated in government: CDA, PvdA, VVD, and D66. Yet it is not clear that the other parties should be considered irrelevant. There is no particular reason to assume that Green Left is excluded from government by the other parties, although its inclusion may be far from the first choice. Whether or not the orthodox Calvinist parties could ever participate in a coalition is still open. Clearly this also is far from a first choice but, in 1986, when there was a question as to whether the Christian Democratic/Liberal coalition could gain the necessary seats to continue in government, there was speculation that the smaller religious parties might be called upon to provide support. This would have given them something close to blackmail potential, and thus rendered them relevant.

What the Dutch case shows is that the numerical criterion is not the only factor affecting the effective functioning of a democratic system. In the previous chapter we have shown how the Dutch have derived means for dealing with reasonably severe segmentation without a threat arising to the continuance of the democratic system.

*Dimensionality*

A second feature of political party systems that has attracted considerable attention is the question of dimensionality. Most observers of politics, from voters to professional journalists or political scientists, employ shorthand to describe the relationships between political parties. Such shorthand typically consists of some sort of ideological dimension along which the parties can be arrayed. Perhaps the most popular such dimension is the idea of 'Left' and 'Right'.

The use of the Left–Right dimension has become common in both the political discussions of most European countries and in treatments of party systems by political scientists. Klingemann has shown that Dutch voters rank high when compared to voters in several other countries in recognition of the Left–Right dimension, and fairly high in levels of ideological conceptualisation (Klingemann, 1979). In recent research, he reasserted that 'there is wide-spread familiarity with the left-right schema both among educational elites and within the mass public' (Fuchs and Klingemann, 1989, p. 209).

Exactly where parties are to be placed in terms of Left and Right is a matter not easily resolved. Positions will always depend to an extent upon who one asks and what definitions they employ. In order to illustrate the dimensionality of the Dutch party system, we have chosen here to report the results from a major study of political party members. In 1986 all persons who declared themselves a candidate for one of the political parties then represented in Parliament were asked to place themselves on a ten-point Left–Right scale. Their average placement gives at least some idea of where prominent persons with each of the parties stand and thus roughly how the parties may be ordered across the dimension (see Figure 3.1).

**FIGURE 3.1**

**Average positions of party candidates on a Left–Right scale**

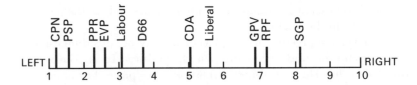

Figure 3.1 shows clusters of smaller parties at both ends of the scale. At the left are the candidates of the Communist, Pacifist Socialist, Radical, and Evangelical People's parties. Seeing their positions, it is not difficult to understand why these parties could forge a merger into a single party in 1989. At the right of the scale one finds the three small Protestant parties. Although the SGP is farthest to the right, the other two also clearly place themselves to the right of the scale. Were any of these parties anti-system parties, one might be concerned about 'centrifugal' competition as a threat to democracy. But none is anti-democratic and, in almost a century of competition, they have hardly grown in size. Nevertheless, they must be taken into account by the parties more towards the centre as these map out their electoral strategies.

The candidates of the four large parties are placed more in the centre of the political spectrum. Being larger, they are almost by definition less homogeneous and thus more inclined to have an average position somewhere nearer the centre. Yet, to an extent, these placements also represent the sum or combination of placements based upon different definitions of Left and Right. Since by any definition the Social Democrats should be to the Left, the average position taken by the Labour candidates is about what could be expected.

For the remaining three, D66 candidates have placed themselves clearly to the Left of centre, reflecting the trend of the party to perceive itself as a progressive-liberal party. The Christian Democrats and the Liberals place themselves on average very close to the centre of the ten-point scale, but with the latter clearly to the Right of the former. This position of the Christian Democrats will surprise no observer. Discussion of the party generally treats it as a centre party, although this position has recently been questioned with regard to coalition formation (see Chapter 5). The Liberals have also placed themselves close to the centre. Such a placement might, however, be disputed by respondents from other parties, who tend to emphasise the party's conservative stand on economic issues and see the party as being more to the Right.

Whatever the precise correct placement may be, this dimension is quite useful in understanding Dutch politics. It is along this dimension that Dutch Cabinet formation takes place. For almost 40 years, the Labour and Liberal parties have excluded cooperation in government. Thus, the Christian Democrats at the centre dominate, as no coalition can be formed without them. Traditionally they have by choice or by necessity shared power with one of the parties to their left or right.

Exactly when the concepts of 'Left' and 'Right' entered political jargon may be disputed. In any case, by the nineteenth-century they had become concepts with strong emotional attachments. The terms themselves, however, are essentially devoid of political meaning. Thus, some interpretation of the terms must be given if participants are to be able to utilise them as a shorthand.

In the Dutch case, at least two different usages of the terms have been predominant (see Chapter 2). The older usage, in the nineteenth-century, referred to the differences between religious and secular elements in the population. 'Right' was associated with parties based upon religious principles, whereas 'Left' referred to non-religious or anti-confessional elements and included Liberals, Socialists, and Communists. This interpretation has not disappeared entirely from the Dutch political scene. In the twentieth century the terms have more often been employed with respect to the question of the role of the government in economic and social affairs, where 'Right' was opposed to governmental intervention and 'Left' positively inclined (or at least less fearful).

In attempting to employ 'Left' and 'Right' as a shorthand, no problems are encountered for some parties. Whichever definition of the terms is employed, for example, the Social Democrats are on the Left. However, for the Christian Democrats and the Liberals the position on the scale may alter according to the definition used. If the definition refers to the difference between secular and religious, the Christian Democrats are clearly on the Right. However, if the terms refer to the role of government, or other definitions such as 'progressive' and 'conservative', they may be placed more towards the centre. The position of the Liberals also shifts, depending upon which definition is to be used. Their *laissez-faire* attitudes, which were liberal in the nineteenth-century, now lead them to reject governmental regulation and intervention. Thus, as the 'social' question and economic affairs have to a large extent replaced the religious–secular conflicts of the previous century, the Dutch Liberals are now seen as being on the Right.

These two dimensions can be illustrated by presenting results from the same survey of party candidates (see Figure 3.2). The social-economic Left–Right dimension is illustrated by the position taken with regard to proper levels of income differences. The respondents in this survey were asked to place themselves on a seven-point scale. The religious–secular dimension is illustrated by the positions taken with respect to euthanasia, also measured on a seven-point scale.

These positions, based upon specific ideological issues, reveal quite different orderings of the parties from those found for the less specific Left–Right scale. In a statistical sense, the positioning on euthanasia is slightly closer to that on the general Left–Right scale than those on the income differences question. Closer examination of the differences shows where tensions may result when parties try to reach agreements.

The four parties that became Green Left and the Labour Party are clearly on the Left on the question of reduction of income differences, as they are on the issue of euthanasia. As we saw above, any definition of terms places such parties on the Left. It is on the 'Right' that differences occur, and for which the placements differ considerably.

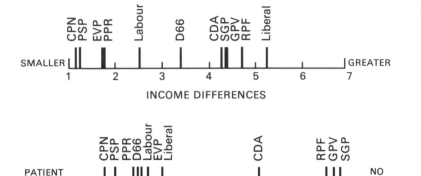

**FIGURE 3.2**
**Average positions of party candidates with**
**regard to income differences and euthanasia**

On the question of euthanasia we find the fundamentalist Calvinist parties to the Right, as we would expect given their Biblical inspiration. Somewhat less strongly opposed, but clearly to the Right, are the candidates for the CDA. However, the Liberals are found in a position quite similar to that of the Labour Party and D66. Such ordering of the parties contrasts considerably with that found on the question of reduction of income differences. Now all the religious parties are just to the right of centre, whereas the Liberals occupy the most extreme position.

Whether one chooses to treat the Dutch party system as uni-dimensional or two-dimensional depends to an extent upon the context employed. For some purposes, such as understanding Cabinet formation or in some models of voting behaviour, a single dimension may be sufficient. But if one is to understand more fully the bases for divisions between the parties, which can lead to difficulties in forging legislative coalitions, at least two dimensions are needed. As we shall see in the next chapter, both dimensions are also needed for a full understanding of electoral competition and voting behaviour in the Netherlands.

# 4

# Elections

Although elections are a fundamental, necessary characteristic of any democratic system, nations differ substantially in which officials are chosen via elections and in the electoral rules by which they are chosen. Even behind such general terms as single-member district system or PR, there hides a rich variety of possibilities. The first part of this chapter is thus devoted to various aspects of the electoral system in the Netherlands. We discuss which Dutch officials are elected by ballot, how the names of candidates get on the ballot, how a vote is cast (and how many people choose to do so), and how votes are counted and parliamentary seats distributed.

Aside from legal differences, countries develop their own traditions concerning how parties present their candidates to the electorate. In the Netherlands, the frequency with which one hears the cry that election campaigns are becoming 'Americanised' indicates that these traditions are, on the one hand, different from those in the USA, but on the other hand under pressure to change. In the second part of this chapter we therefore discuss briefly campaigns and campaigning in the Dutch context.

Finally, in the previous chapters the support for political parties has been discussed only implicitly in relation to *verzuiling*. The time has come in this chapter to examine more directly the bases of support for the various parties. Since we have already discussed in earlier chapters how the pillarised system has changed, it is hardly surprising that we must examine how these changes have affected the decisions of voters to choose particular parties. How voters make their choices thus rounds out this chapter.

## Characteristics of the Electoral System

*Few Shall be Chosen*

Although there is no disagreement about the principle that the power of the people to choose their leaders in free elections is essential in a democratic system, there are considerable differences among democracies in the degree to which the principle is applied. For example, the USA seems to apply what might be called an 'elective principle', i.e., leaders should be elected directly by the people unless there is some good reason not to do so. Thus there are numerous elective offices at the local, state, and national levels, and for all three branches of government: legislative, executive, and judicial. The Netherlands, on the other hand, applies an 'appointive principle' (i.e., offices are filled by appointment unless there is reason not to do so). Only representatives to legislative bodies are elected by the people, and even then the First Chamber of Parliament is still elected indirectly by the provincial legislatures. No positions within the executive branch of government are elected. As described in Chapter 5, it is the parliamentary parties who select the members of the government, who are then formally installed by the Queen. Mayors of all cities and towns are also formally appointed by the Queen, but in fact it is the Home Office and the Cabinet who decide. This is also true for the provincial governors, who are still called 'Queen's Commissioners'. For most Dutch it is therefore hardly even thinkable that judges might be elected rather than appointed.

With this limitation of election to the legislative branch, Dutch voters are asked to cast votes for four legislative bodies: the municipal council, the provincial legislature, the Second Chamber of Parliament, and the European Parliament. Interestingly, even this level of involvement seems at times to have been viewed as a considerable burden upon the electorate. In 1986 the fulfilment of legal requirements would have led to the holding of municipal, provincial, and national elections in the same year. Rather than ask the voter to go to the polls three times in a single year, special arrangements were made to postpone the provincial elections for a year and to ensure that such a coincidence would not occur again in the future. No consideration has ever been given to holding elections on the same day, the assumption being that this would not lead to independent considerations in casting a vote for the different bodies.

*The Simple Act of Voting*

Casting a vote is not too complicated, since the ballot presented to the Dutch voter is relatively simple. At any election, only one choice has to be made. Since the list system of PR is employed, the candidates are listed in a column under the name of the party, as shown in Exhibit 4.1 (before 1956 the party names were not listed on the ballot, making the situation somewhat more complicated for the voter). A party may list up to 30 names on the ballot, or twice the number of its incumbent representatives in Parliament, with a maximum of 80.

Voting may be done by paper ballot or by voting machine. In either case, with between 15 and 25 parties participating in parliamentary elections, the ballot may be quite large. This complicates the task for the voter only slightly, however, since the parties are ordered on the ballot by the size of their current representation in Parliament. For parties having no parliamentary representation, the ordering is determined by lot. The voter casts her or his vote by filling in a single circle, corresponding to the candidate of choice, with a red pencil. Where voting is done by machine, the lever next to the candidate is pulled down. This single, simple act completes the voting process.

The number of persons taking part in this simple process has always been quite high. However, this is not due only to the simplicity and infrequency of the act. Voters are presented with few barriers to exercising their right. Registration is done automatically by the municipality in which one lives. Shortly before the election, each eligible voter is sent a card listing the nearest voting station. The voter need only appear with this card on the appointed day to obtain a ballot and cast a vote. Since only one choice is to be made, the time needed to complete the procedure is short and waiting times are generally negligible.

An additional factor that certainly has contributed to the high level of voter turnout in the Netherlands was the form of 'compulsory voting' that was in effect for many years. When, after decades of slow expansion of the electorate, all males were granted the franchise in 1917 (females acquired this right in 1919), it was also decided to switch from a system of election of parliamentary representatives by district to a system of proportional representation. If all citizens were to have the vote, then each vote should carry equal weight; yet if

## EXHIBIT 4.1

### What a Dutch ballot-paper looks like
### (*one-eighth* of total ballot paper)

| 1<br>CDA | 2<br>Partij<br>van de Arbeid | 3<br>V.V.D. |
|---|---|---|
| Lubbers, R.F.M.<br>Rotterdam | Kok, W. (Wim)<br>Amsterdam | Voorhoeve, J.J.C.<br>Noordwijk aan Zee |
| de Vries, B.<br>Bergschenhoek | van Otterloo, Gerrit<br>Jan p.<br>'s-Gravenhage | Jorritsma geb.<br>Lebbink, Annemarie<br>Bolsward |
| van den Broek, H.<br>Wassenaar | Kukler, Nelly<br>Zoetermeer | Linschoten, R.L.O.<br>Dronten |
| Braks, G.J.M.<br>Sint Michielsgestel | Kalsbeek geb<br>Jasperse, N.A. (Ella)<br>Zoetermeer | Nijhuis, G.B. (Ad)<br>Noordwijkerhout |
| van Rooy (v), Y.M.C.T.<br>'s-Gravenhage | Faber, Mient Jan<br>s-Gravenhage | Blauw, P.M. (Piet)<br>Veendam |
| Deetman, W.J.<br>Gouda | Chandoe, I. (Johan)<br>'s-Gravenhage | Korthals, A.H.<br>Rotterdam |
| Brinkman, L.C.<br>Leiden | Plemper geb. Veltman,<br>W.S.M. (Wobbie)<br>Huizwn | van Erp, A.A.M.E.<br>(Broos)<br>Best |
| Bukman, P.<br>Voorschoten | Klink, G.P. (Paul)<br>'s-Gravenhage | Kamp (v), M.M.H.<br>(Margreet)<br>Vianen |
| baron van Voorst tot<br>Voorst, B.J.<br>'s-Gravenhage | Kruizinga, H. (Piet)<br>Nieuwegein | Blaauw, J.D. (Jan Dirk)<br>Zeist |
| de Jong, G.<br>Voorburg | Ruygrok, H.G.W.<br>(Willemien)<br>Amsterdam | Rempt geb. Halmmans<br>de Jongh, N. (Len)<br>Wassenaar |
| van Iersel, J.P.<br>'s-Gravenhage | Huurman, J.W.G. (Jaap)<br>'s-Gravenhage | van Rey, J.F.B. (Jos)<br>Roemond |
| de Leeuw, J.F.<br>Krimpen<br>aan den IJssel | van Nieuwenhoven,<br>Jeltje<br>Amsterdam | Lauxtermann, H.Th.M.<br>(Herman)<br>'s-Hertogenbosch |
| de Hoop Scheffer, J.G.<br>'s-Gravenhage | Jagersma, H. (Henk)<br>'s-Gravenhage | Remkes, J.W. (Johan)<br>Groningen |
| Gualthérie van<br>Weezwl, J.S.L.<br>'s-Gravenhage | Pronk, J.P. (Jan)<br>Maastricht | Labohm, P.H. (Paul)<br>Voorburg |
| van de Camp, W.G.J.M.<br>'s-Gravenhage | Vermeend, W.A.F.G.<br>(Willem)<br>Leiden | van Hoof, H.A.L.<br>Alkmaar |
| Krajenbrink, J.G.H.<br>Bleiswijk | Moor, Frans<br>Hoek van Holland | Verbugt (v), P.J.L.<br>Helden |
| Biesheuvel, P.J.<br>'s-Gravenhage | Jurgens, E.C.M. (Erik)<br>Amsterdam | Luchtenveld, R. (Ruud)<br>Amersfoort |
| Vreugdenhil, Th.O.<br>Koudekerk<br>aan den Rijn | ter Veld, Elske<br>Leiden | Klein, Norbert, P.M.<br>Nijmegen |
| Hagendoorn, J.<br>'s-Gravenhage | | Muntinga, J.K.<br>Deventer |

## 4
## D66

- van Mierlo, H.A.F.M.O. (Hans) Amsterdam
- Wolffensperger, G.J. (Gerrit Jan) Amsterdam
- Kohnstamm, J. (Jacob) Amsterdam
- Groenman, L.S. (Louise) Maarssen
- Tommel, D.K.J. (Dick) Norg
- Nuis, A. (Aad) 's-Gravenhage
- Eisma, D. (Doeke) 's-Gravenhage
- Scheltema geb. de Nie, O. (Olga) Haren
- Schimmel, A. (Arthie) Leiden
- ter Veer, P.K. (Pieter) Woltersum
- Versnel geb. Schimitz, M.J. (Machteld) Utrecht
- Ybema, G. (Gerrit) Leeuwarden
- Langenberg, P.J. (Pex) Leiden
- de Graaf, Th. C. (Thom) Leiden
- van 't Riet, N.G. (Nicky) Utrecht
- Bakker, E.C. (Ernst) Amsterdam
- Combee geb. van Geuns, J.W. (Hanneke) Hoofddorp
- de Nijs geb. van den Berg, M.A.J. (Marjolijn) Os

## 5
## Staatkundig Gereformeerde Partij
### (gecombineerd met 7 en 8)

- van der Vlies, ir. B.J. Maartensdijk
- van Dis, C.N. 's-Gravenhage
- van den Berg, mr. dr. J.T. Nunspeet
- Scholten, L.M.P. Capelle aan den IJssel
- Holdijk, mr. G. Apeldoom
- van Ree, drs. P.H.D. Lunteren
- van den Berg, G. Veenendaal
- Barendregt, H.G. Barendrecht
- Boonzaaijer, drs. G. Capelle aan den IJssel
- Wolterink, J.H. Rijssen
- Janse, dr. C.S.L. Vaassen
- Bolier, mr. L. Elspeet
- Dankers, J. Waddinxveen
- van der Waal, ir. L. Ridderkerk
- de Jong, S. Staphorst
- Hovius, drs. W. Chr. Katwijk aan Zee
- Bron, W. Staphorst
- Pieters, W. Genemuiden
- Verdouw, N. Gouda

## 6
## Groen Links

- Beckers geb. de Bruijn (v), M.B.C. (Ria) Wadenoyen
- van Es (v), A.C. (Andrée) Amsterdam
- Rosenmöller (m), P. (Paul) Rotterdam
- Lankhorst (m), P.A. (Peter) Amsterdam
- Willems (m), W.J. (Wilbert) Tilburg
- van Ojik (m), A. (Bram) Amsterdam
- Ernsting (m), M. (Marius) Amsterdam
- Robles (v), E.M.A. (Ellin) Amsterdam
- Sipkes geb. van Zijl (v), L. (Leonie) Apeldoorn
- Ofman (m), C.J.P. (Cor) Winkel
- de Boer (m), W.T. (Wim) Amsterdam
- Oedayraj Singh Varma (v), T. (Tara) Amsterdam
- van Poelgeest (m), M. (Maarten) Amsterdam
- van Leeuwen (v), M.J.W. (Marion) Rotterdam
- van Schijndel (m), B. (Bob) Amsterdam
- Lameris (m), G.H. (Geert) Groningen
- Roemer (v), A.H. (Astrid) 's-Gravenhage
- Platvoet (m), L.H.G. (Leo) Amsterdam

some citizens chose not to vote, one could hardly determine what the proper proportions were to be. Thus it seemed only logical to require citizens to exercise this right, and a form of 'compulsory voting' was introduced. Voters were not actually forced to vote, but were required by law to present themselves at the polling station on election day. Virtually all voters complied, and once there they also tended to cast a vote. At eleven national elections, from 1925 until 1967, the average percentage of votes cast (based upon eligible voters) was 94.1 percent. From 1945 to 1966, in municipal elections the average turnout was 92.7 percent.

The legal compulsion for voting was discussed on numerous occasions in Parliament, and in 1970 the law was finally repealed. The impact was far greater than had been anticipated; turnout at the first non-compulsory election (for provincial legislatures) was only 68.1 percent. At the municipal elections the same year, an even lower figure was achieved, 67.2 percent. Turnout at the first parliamentary election without compulsion in 1971 was 79.1 percent.

Figure 4.1 shows the changes in turnout from 1966 to 1991. For parliamentary elections, 1971 remains the low point and turnout has been generally quite high (i.e., between 80 and 90 percent). Whereas under compulsory voting there was little difference in turnout between the types of elections, without the legal stimulus turnout for provincial and municipal elections has consistently been lower than for parliamentary elections. In the most recent cases, substantial dips have occurred. Elections for the European Parliament have not ignited the enthusiasm of voters, and turnout has been generally lower. We can conclude that interest in national parliamentary elections remains high, but that voters now differentiate in the importance they attach to elections, at least in so far as they indicate that importance by taking the trouble to vote.

*Absence of Geographical Representation*

During the nineteenth century, elections to the Second Chamber of Parliament always involved geographical representation. Immediately prior to the introduction of universal suffrage in 1917, there were 100 single-member districts. The law required that the winning candidate in the district receive an absolute majority of the vote, in a system very similar to the one currently used for French presidential elections. If no candidate received a majority in the first round, the

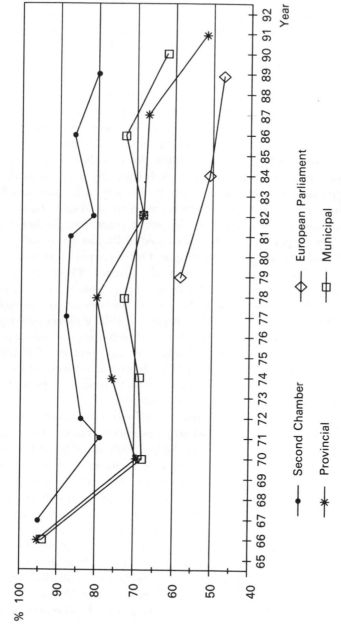

**FIGURE 4.1**
**Voter turnout 1966–91**

*Source:* All elections except 1989 CBS, *Statistiek der Verkiezingen*; 1989, *Volkskrant*, 7 September 1989.

top two candidates were voted on in a second round. It is important to note that numerous parties and groups participated in these elections and that single-member districts did not prohibit the development of a multi-party system, (see Chapter 3). Even under the district system, up to eight parties or groups were represented in Parliament.

With the introduction of proportional representation, geographical representation was abandoned. Eighteen (now nineteen) electoral districts were created, but, for the determination of the size of the parliamentary delegations, the country is treated as a single electoral district. The districts are important only for administrative reasons. Parties that wish to appear on the ballot of a district must submit a list of candidates in that district. Although any party of significance will participate nationwide in all 19 districts, it is quite possible to submit a list in fewer districts or even a single district. The importance of the districts has in recent years been further reduced by allowing parties already represented in Parliament to submit their list for all 19 districts in The Hague. Other parties must submit their lists at a designated place within the district. These lists must be supported by written declarations of support from ten eligible voters, who must have signed the declaration in the presence of the mayor of their municipality. Previously a deposit of 1000 guilders was required for each district in which a party wished to participate; now a deposit of 25 000 guilders is required whatever the number of districts in which the party submits a list. The deposit is returned if the party receives 75 percent of the national electoral quotient, which amounts to roughly 0.5 percent of the total vote.

A party may submit the same or different list of candidates in each of the electoral districts. Most larger parties will have some degree of overlap, especially at the top of the list. Since the 1950s it has become standard for parties to place the same name at the top of the list in each district. This top candidate is the electoral leader of the party and is known as the 'list puller'. His or her job is to pull the party to victory, and with the growing role of the media in campaigning, the importance of the 'list puller' has increased, becoming in many respects the personification of the party (at least for the duration of the campaign). At lower positions on the list, there may be various reasons not to have the same list of candidates in all 19 districts.

The possibility of submitting different lists should nevertheless not lead to the conclusion that some sort of geographical representation is present. There is no legal requirement that any name on the list have

any relationship with any particular district. What regional representation does occur is the result of the geographical organisation of
the political parties. In the major parties there is strong regional
pressure to include local candidates. Some parties, notably the
Labour Party, have also at times attempted to stimulate a relationship between MPs and the district in which they were formally
chosen. However, both are internal party matters and not a part of
the electoral system.

The districts again come into play in determining which individuals within a party are elected to Parliament. If the party has
submitted the same list in each district or has formally linked the lists
in a specified procedure, this potential impact is effectively negated.
Otherwise, the actual selection is carried out within the districts in a
quite complicated procedure. Nevertheless, geographical representation exists only in so far as the parties deem it important in their
nominating procedures.

*Extreme Proportionality*

In the Netherlands there is no special electoral threshold that a party
must cross in order to achieve representation in Parliament. The only
threshold is the electoral quotient formed by dividing the number of
votes cast at an election by the number of seats in Parliament (see
Exhibit 4.2). This amounts to only 0.667 percent of the vote. Since
the electoral districts play no role in determining the number of seats
allocated to each party, this means that, depending on the turnout,
approximately 60 000 votes nationwide are sufficient to gain a seat.

Each multiple of the electoral quotient entitles a party to an
additional seat. However, when each party has received the seats to
which it is entitled in this manner, it is generally found that not all
seats have been allotted. The votes for parties under the electoral
threshold and the votes a party has above one multiple of the
threshold, but less than the next multiple, have been lost in the
process. The seats that remain after parties have been allotted their
multiples of the electoral quotient are the so-called 'remainder seats'.
These seats are then distributed among the parties that have
exceeded the electoral quotient, according to the method of largest
average (the so-called d'Hondt method).

Use of the d'Hondt method gives an advantage to larger parties. A
feature of the electoral law introduced in the 1970s helps the smaller

**EXHIBIT 4.2**

**Distributing Parliamentary Seats, 1989**

| | |
|---|---|
| Number of eligible voters | 11 131 972 |
| Number of votes cast | 9 919 787 |
| Turnout | 80.1% |
| Number of valid votes | 8 893 202 |
| Number of votes needed to secure seat | |
| (valid votes/150 seats = 'electoral quotient') | 59 289 |

**Determining the distribution of seats in Parliament**

| Party | A<br>Number<br>of votes | B<br>Multiples<br>of electoral<br>quotient | C<br>Number<br>of seats<br>plus one | D<br>Average<br>votes<br>per seat | E<br>Average after<br>assignment of<br>first remainder<br>seat |
|---|---|---|---|---|---|
| CDA | 3 140 502 | 52 | 53 | 59 255 | 58 157 |
| SGP | 166 082 | 2 | 3 | 55 361 | unchanged |
| PvdA | 2 835 251 | 47 | 48 | 59 068 | unchanged |
| VVD | 1 295 402 | 21 | 22 | 58 881 | unchanged |
| GPV | 109 637 | 1 | 2 | 54 819 | unchanged |
| D66 | 701 934 | 11 | 12 | 58 495 | unchanged |
| RPF | 85 231 | 1 | 2 | 42 616 | unchanged |
| CD | 81 427 | 1 | 2 | 40 714 | unchanged |
| Green Left | 362 304 | 6 | 7 | 51 758 | unchanged |
| Other parties | 115 532 | 0 | | | |
| Total | 8 893 302 | 142 | | | |

**Step 1.** The 'electoral quotient' is determined by dividing the total number of valid votes by the 150 seats in the Second Chamber. In 1989 the electoral quotient was 59 289.

**Step 2.** For each multiple of the electoral quotient, a party receives one seat. These numbers are listed in column B. Since only 142 of the 150 seats have been allocated, there are eight 'remainder seats' still to be allocated.

**Step 3.** One seat is added to the number in column B. This value, in column C, is then divided into the number of votes in column A to determine what the average number of votes per seat would be if the first remainder seat were to be allocated to this party. This average value is listed in column D.

**Step 4.** The party with the largest average, in this case the CDA, is assigned the first 'remainder seat'.

**Step 5.** The average number of votes per seat is recalculated for the party receiving the remainder seat; the value for all other parties remains unchanged.

**Step 6.** The party with the highest average is assigned the second remainder seat. In this case it will go to the PvdA.

Steps 5 and 6 are repeated until all remainder seats have been distributed.

parties by allowing any parties to request that their lists be combined both within districts and across districts. This combination is announced on the ballot and the parties are treated as a single unit for the purpose of the initial distribution of parliamentary seats. Once this distribution has been determined, the law provides additional procedures for determining how the seats are to be divided proportionally between the partners. In recent elections the three orthodox Calvinist parties have requested to be treated as a unit for the initial counting.

With the absence of a special threshold other than the electoral quotient and the treatment of the entire country as a single 150-member district, the Dutch electoral system is one of the most proportional systems in the world (Taagepera and Shugart, 1989, p. 196). The proportional distribution of seats is as close as possible to the proportion of the vote that the parties have achieved. As one of the 'rules of the game', proportionality has become an important feature of Dutch political culture (see Chapter 2). It is one of the few aspects of the electoral system that is enshrined in the Constitution itself. Attempts to reduce the political complexity in Parliament by erecting a higher threshold, thus eliminating some of the smaller parties, have always failed.

The absence of geographical representation is less ingrained in political culture. In the early 1970s a parliamentary majority emerged in favour of the introduction of multi-member districts, only to fall apart when the PvdA and D66 made their support conditional on the simultaneous introduction of an elected Prime Minister. In the 1990s the creation of multi-member districts, or even the introduction of the German system in which single-member districts are combined with PR is being seriously debated. However, such debate proceeds only under the strict condition that no change in the electoral system is allowed to impinge upon the principle of proportionality.

## Parties and Campaigning

*Candidate Selection*

As has just been seen, the role of the voter in the Netherlands is to determine how many seats each party will receive in Parliament. It is the party, and not the electorate, that determines which individuals fill these seats. Parties submit lists of candidates, and the votes for any name on the list accrue to the list for the purpose of the distribution of the seats. There is only one possibility for voters to attempt to influence who is chosen. A voter does choose an individual candidate. Generally, however, at least 90 percent of the voters simply vote for the first name on the list. A vote for any other name on the list is called a 'preference vote', i.e., this person is preferred to the candidates above her or him. If a candidate receives at least half the number of votes required to meet the electoral quotient, he or she is declared elected, whatever the position on the list. Previous rules required that these votes be gained in a single electoral district, and since the Second World War only three persons have been elected under those rules. The number of preference votes has risen slightly in recent years, reaching a post-war high of 17.4 percent in 1986, so it is possible that under the new regulations the number so elected may increase. Yet parties generally discourage the casting of preference votes and in some cases have gone so far as to require candidates to sign agreements that they would refuse election in this manner. Parties thus exercise almost complete control over candidate selection and the determination of which individuals will sit in Parliament.

There are virtually no legal restrictions or regulations concerning how parties must select candidates. Political parties in the Netherlands are considered to be voluntary associations and are covered only by the laws that relate to such organisations in general. The law merely requires party names to be registered with the Electoral Council.

Since the parties are free to determine their own internal procedure for candidate selection, considerable diversity is found (Hillebrand, 1992). On just one point are all parties agreed: only party members participate in the process of selection of candidates (see Chapter 3). In establishing rules for candidate selection, the parties attempt to pursue two goals. On the one hand, there is the desire to present a strong, balanced list of candidates. This attempt at balance means at the very least that the parliamentary group should have knowledge and expertise across the various areas of government activity (e.g., finance, education, agriculture), but may also mean balance in terms of the percentage of female candidates, minority group candidates, or other relevant characteristics. On the other hand, since candidate selection is one of the most important party activities, parties wish to make the procedures as democratic as possible, (i.e., allow the membership influence in the decisions). In practice, these goals seem to conflict.

It is hardly surprising, given its commitment to change in party politics and procedures, that D66 is the party which has given the greatest weight to internal democracy. Any party member can nominate herself or himself as a potential candidate. All such candidates are then presented to the party members in a postal ballot. With the exception of the first place on the electoral list, the ordering of candidates is determined by the number of votes received in this party balloting. This procedure maximises member participation, but provides no possibility for ensuring a balanced list. Despite the objections of the national party board that it would restrict the influence of the party members, a motion was passed in 1985 creating an independent party committee to prepare a suggested list for the members. This committee could better seek a proper balance in the distribution of men and women and the representation of various areas of expertise. Allowance of a recommended list quickly shifted the balance of power within the party. Of the 15 persons on the recommended list in 1986, only one did not end up in the first 15 positions on the list of candidates.

No other party has ever allowed the direct influence of the membership that D66 has through the postal ballot. All other major parties employ procedures that make use of the geographical organisation of the party (see Chapter 3). The Labour Party has had the most decentralised procedure, with the regional party organisations controlling the selection of candidates (with the exception of the 'list-puller') for the electoral districts. Criticism of lack of balance has led to the adoption of new rules in 1992 by which for future elections a single list of candidates will be prepared centrally.

The Liberal Party has attempted to provide democratic input by allowing the local party branches to begin the process by suggesting names of possible candidates. Moreover, the regional party leaders were given influence both in the evaluation of these proposals and, most importantly, in the determination of the final list. However, the result seemed to be more of a battle for regional interests than a concern for a balanced list. New procedures, adopted in 1990, will allow the national executive to prepare a proposed list, which will then be debated in the local and regional branches. Based upon the outcome of this debate, a revised list will be presented to a general assembly of the party.

Since the 1977 merger producing the CDA, the procedure for candidate selection in this party has been rather centralised. Although on paper the procedure appears to give important influence to the local party organisation, by allowing them to vote on the final order of candidates, their actual influence is limited. The real influence is wielded by the national party leaders. One reason for this centralisation may be the continuing necessity to produce a balance between Catholic, Dutch Reformed, and *Gereformeerde* candidates on the list.

Thus the trend in the larger parties seems to be away from direct democracy and towards centralisation as a means of producing a balance on the list. With the exception of the CDA, whose procedure already allowed considerable influence from the national leadership, the major parties have all made changes in recent years towards greater influence from the top. This shift in influence occurs at the cost of loss of influence by individual party members and local party branches. At the moment, the goal of balance seems to have a slight edge over the goal of party democracy.

*Campaigning*

During the period of pillarisation (i.e., until approximately 1967), there were not too many votes to be won during an election campaign. Voters belonging to a particular pillar tended to vote for the associated party, and were not greatly inclined to switch to a party of another pillar. The KVP, for example, was not going to win the votes of non-Catholics whatever programme it adopted or electoral strategy it followed. Campaigns were aimed more at mobilising the faithful and retaining their support than converting and obtaining new votes. The strategies may be described more as defensive than offensive, although this may have applied more to the religious parties than the secular parties.

The attitude towards campaigning can at least now be described as quite conservative. A survey conducted in 1954 showed that 55 percent of the voters were opposed to the idea that 'candidates at the elections attempt to visit as many people as possible in order to clarify in a personal conversation what they will do if they are elected'. The primary reasons mentioned for such opposition was that the voter might be influenced or bought off(!), or that easy promises might be made that could not be kept.

The organisation of the campaign was also reasonably simple. Campaigns were generally run by the party organisation: 'A number of well-meaning amateurs gathered after office hours to discuss the question of political propaganda for their party' (Hoogendijk, 1971, p. 207). No special research was carried out and no marketing strategy was formulated. (Brants, Kok and Van Praag 1982) The campaign consisted mainly of organising speakers to appear at meetings of party supporters. Since within each pillar there was also at least one newspaper and a radio/television organisation that supported the party, there was little need to work to attract media attention.

The 1960s brought changes that would have a major impact upon election campaigns. First, there was a change in the electorate. Fewer people voted along traditional lines (see Table 4.2 below), and more people became floating voters. The Christian Democratic parties, who were losing votes most heavily, adopted even more defensive strategies, whereas the Labour and Liberal parties, (together with several new parties) employed strategies that attempted to woo new voters.

Second, the pillars began to crumble. Organisations that had been a part of the pillar became more independent, or fully independent. The newspaper *Volkskrant*, for example, dropped the Catholic identification in its heading. The independence of the editorial staffs meant that they could no longer be counted on to support the party in campaigns.

Third, technological developments, such as the introduction of television and the rise of public opinion polling organisations, both reinforced the first two changes and provided new opportunities for the parties to communicate with the voters. As a party committed to political change, D66 was also instrumental in leading the way in introducing new elements into election campaigns. Since the 1960s, foes have decried and friends have lauded the 'Americanisation' of campaigning.

Most modern campaign techniques will be familiar to the reader and need not be discussed at length here. Two aspects – television and campaign financing – have sufficient uniquely Dutch aspects to warrant some special treatment.

*Television and the election campaign.*   The aim of any election campaign is to get the party message on television as often as possible in the most positive fashion possible. Since there are no opportunities to purchase television time, parties must obtain coverage by other means. We mentioned in Chapter 3 that minimal access is granted by law to each party presenting a list of candidates in each of the 19 electoral districts. These parties are all granted two blocks of 10 minutes of television time (and also 20 minutes of radio time) during the campaign, together with technical support to produce their programmes. The amount of time is equal for all such parties, regardless of their size. Certainly, for the more important parties, this is woefully inadequate: such parties must seek other means to obtain coverage.

First, there is the evening news. There is nothing particularly Dutch about this type of coverage. Parties attempt to gain coverage by making important campaign statements or through newsworthy campaign 'incidents'. In principle coverage is evenly distributed among the major parties. However, both the evening news and the news analysis programme, 'The Hague Today', also devote attention to the smaller parties. Even though the amount of coverage will be smaller than that given the major parties, any coverage whatsoever is often disproportionate to their size. Finally, since coverage must also be given to current affairs of state, the coalition parties have an advantage.

A second source of coverage is the current affairs programming of the various broadcasting organisations. The evening news programmes are produced by an independent organisation, but the broadcast organisations have their own news teams and programmes. These programmes are considerably longer than the news broadcasts and are intended to provide background information. During a campaign, a considerable portion of such programmes is devoted to the most recent developments and analysis thereof. More than the newspapers, the television coverage tends to concentrate on the major parties. The broadcasting organisations are under no obligation to be neutral or to provide equal time for all parties. None would dream of devoting all its coverage to a single party, but preferences do emerge. This is hardly surprising, since these organisations were once part of the tight network of pillars. Thus, the socialist broadcasting organisation VARA, for example, may provide a disproportionate amount of time to coverage, including critical coverage, of the

Labour Party. The organisations, however, never give endorsements or advice to the voter.

Finally, parties get coverage through organised election debates. In principle, any of the broadcasting organisations can organise a debate. They choose the participants and the format. For example, in 1986, one of the small religious broadcasters organised a debate between the leaders of the various religious parties. (This gave the leader of the CDA an advantage over the other major parties, since he was the only major party representative invited.) The most important debate has become the debate generally held on the eve of an election. In recent years, the various broadcasting organisations have negotiated among themselves for the right to organise this debate. The debate is limited to the major parties, as determined by the organisers, who also pretty much dictate the other conditions of the debate.

*Campaign expenditures.*   It has just been mentioned that it is not possible to purchase time on the Dutch public broadcasting channels. For the parties this is just as well, since a second feature of Dutch campaigns that must be mentioned is the lack of funding. In 1981 the total amount spent by all parties on the election campaign was only just over 8 million guilders. When new elections were necessary only a year later, the parties were able to spend less than 5 million guilders. This works out to about 1 guilder per voter in 1981 and only 0.6 guilders in 1982. Koole points out that comparable figures for Belgium, Canada, and the USA are seven times higher, and for West Germany twenty times greater (Koole, 1989). Recent research has shown that, at least for the larger parties, local party branches also spend on parliamentary campaigns. The exact amounts are undocumented but may be as much as half the amount spent by the national party. Even then, the total amount spent is comparatively small (Van Praag, 1987).

As was seen in Chapter 3, political party income is derived almost exclusively from party members. Each year the parties set aside a portion of this income to be used for campaign expenditures. These funds may be supplemented by special election appeals during the campaign. Very little is supplied by outsiders, of which almost nothing comes from businesses.

There are several factors that may help to account for the low expenditures. First of all, there has simply been little need to spend more. Even with the development of a more volatile electorate, the balance of strength between the parties has been reasonably stable. The system of PR ensures that minor shifts in the vote lead to only minor shifts in the number of seats in Parliament, as contrasted with the 'winner takes all' system in which minor changes can produce major shifts. Moreover, since no party ever receives a majority of the vote, the crucial question of who will obtain control of the government is left to the Cabinet formation process and is thus beyond the influence of campaign efforts. Second, there is little evidence that increased expenditures will ensure better results. In 1989 it was rumoured that the Socialist Party, a small splinter party which failed to gain a single seat in Parliament, spent more on its election campaign than the Liberals, who won 22 seats. Many factors influence voting behaviour, only some of which can be affected by the level of campaign expenditures. Third, social pressure against business contributions and a lack of clarity concerning what influence might be gained have kept such corporate gifts virtually non-existent (see Chapter 3). Finally, because of the total domination of the candidate selection process by the parties and their discouragement of casting preference votes, there is no incentive or reason for individual candidates to spend on their own behalf.

All this might change if it became possible for the political parties to purchase television time. Now that commercial television is gradually gaining importance, this possibility is beginning to open up. In a recent election, it was rumoured that two parties had taken options for the purchase of broadcast time, but these were never exercised. It is difficult to predict how public opinion might react to commercial advertising. As was noted above, the Dutch have been very conservative in their attitudes towards campaigning. However, if one political party is able to purchase television time and is successful at the election, major changes in both patterns of campaign expenditure and in campaigning itself will most definitely ensue.

## Electoral Behaviour

*From a Structured to an Open Model*

Despite the plethora of parties, Dutch voters were not accustomed to listening to the appeals of various parties or shopping around for the most appealing party, but to a considerable extent voted according to their social position. In fact, between the introduction of proportional representation and some point in the mid-1960s the Netherlands fitted almost perfectly into what Rose and McAllister have described as a 'structured' system: the Netherlands 'has been a classic example of a structured system of multi-party competition, because the electorate has been determined along two dimensions, religion and class, each sustaining separate political parties'. Further, when the electorate is *determined*, voting reflects the persisting structure of society' and not the 'voluntaristic choice of individuals, or transitory influences of a particular election, such as the personality of a party leader' (Rose and McAllister, 1986, p. 12 and p. 8).

The structure of voting during this period did indeed follow the lines of class and religion. In Chapters 2 and 3 we have seen how these divisions produced five major political parties, each more or less associated with one of the 'pillars'. These parties (KVP, ARP, CHU, PvdA, and VVD, or their predecessors) dominated the electoral process by generally capturing 90 percent of the vote. The KVP gained the votes of about 85 percent of all Catholics. About 80 percent of all those from the *Gereformeerde* churches supported the ARP, and half of the rest voted for one of the minor orthodox Calvinist parties. Members of the Dutch Reformed Church were not so uniform in their voting behaviour. The CHU was never able to capture more than about one-third of this group, although the party was indeed made up almost exclusively of regular church-going Dutch Reformed members. The more nominal members tended to vote along class lines for Labour or Liberal. This was also true for those who professed no religion; the working class voted Labour, the middle class Liberal. Not only could voting behaviour be explained to a considerable extent by this simple model (see also Table 4.2 below), but voters were quite consistent in their choices. If one treats the two Protestant parties as part of a single bloc, voter consistency during this period has been estimated as high as 85–90 percent (Houska, 1985). Only slightly more than 10 percent of the seats in Parliament changed hands after elections.

All this began to change in the 1960s. Religious affiliation and church attendance declined. The pillars weakened and mass media began to change society. The impact of religious and class changes can be seen from Table 4.1, which compares the composition of the electorate over roughly ten-year intervals between 1956 and 1986,

**TABLE 4.1**

**Distribution of the population according to the structured model of voting behaviour**

| Percentage of: | 1956 | 1968 | 1977 | 1986 | 1989 |
|---|---|---|---|---|---|
| Catholics (practising) | 30 | 30 | 24 | 16 | 14 |
| Dutch Reformed (practising) | 12 | 16 | 9 | 8 | 8 |
| *Gereformeerd* (practising) | 10 | 12 | 9 | 5 | 8 |
| Secular working class | 33 | 25 | 28 | 26 | 22 |
| Secular middle class | 15 | 18 | 30 | 45 | 48 |
| Total | 100 | 101 | 100 | 100 | 100 |
| *N* | 982 | 1491 | 1199 | 1192 | 1370 |

*Sources:* For 1956 and 1968 Lijphart, (1974), p. 258; for 1977, 1986 and 1989 the Dutch National Election Study.

and for 1989. The first three rows of the table indicate the proportion of the electorate that indicated active participation (i.e., regular church or mass attendance) in one of the three major religious groups. Whereas in 1956 these groups comprised a majority of the population, by 1986 they made up less than one-third of the population. The size of the secular (i.e. non-church going) working class also declined in this period, while the percentage identifying itself as secular middle class trebled.

Even if no changes had occurred in the voting preferences of these groups, such shifts in the composition of the population would have produced major alterations in the balance of support for the associated political parties. Table 4.2, however, indicates that even within these groups, major changes in voter preferences have taken place.

In Table 4.2 the proportion of the group actually voting for the associated party is indicated. For Protestants the vote for the ARP and the CHU has been combined, and for all three religious groups after 1977 the associated party is the CDA. The extraordinary ability of the KVP and the ARP, during the period of pillarisation, to mobilise voters from their respective religious groups is seen in the more than 90 percent casting such a vote. By 1968, however, these percentages had dropped sharply to between 70 and 80 percent, and in 1977 and in 1986 they were lower still. For the secular groups, the percentages choosing the associated party have not changed

**TABLE 4.2**

**Electoral choice according to the structured model of voting behaviour**

| Percentage of: | 1956 | 1968 | 1977 | 1986 | 1989 |
|---|---|---|---|---|---|
| Practising Catholic voting KVP/CDA | 95 | 72 | 66 | 66 | 72 |
| Practising Dutch Reformed voting ARP, CHU/CDA | 63 | 55 | 52 | 58 | 53 |
| Practising *Gereformeerd* voting ARP, CHU/CDA | 93 | 78 | 75 | 58 | 59 |
| Secular working class voting Labour Party (PvdA) | 68 | 65 | 67 | 60 | 63 |
| Secular middle class voting Liberal Party (VVD) | 32 | 25 | 30 | 28 | 23 |

*Sources*: For 1956 and 1968 Lijphart (1974), p. 258; for 1977, 1986 and 1989 the Dutch National Election Study.

substantially. Of course, since the working class was shrinking and the middle class was growing, even a steady percentage had an impact on the share of the vote these parties received.

The obvious conclusion from such figures is that the 'structured model' of voting behaviour is no longer as powerful as it once was. In 1956, 72 percent of the electorate voted according to this model. However, by 1989, this figure had dropped to only 44 percent.

One side-effect of the demise of the 'structured model' has been a significant increase in electoral volatility. There was a time, during the 1950s, when the number of voters changing their choice between two elections was no higher than perhaps 10–15 percent; now as many as one-third of all voters may switch choices between elections. The number of parliamentary seats changing hands has increased accordingly. With far more votes 'up for grabs' parties must now compete more for the votes they receive. By the 1990s the Netherlands has moved toward a more open model of electoral competition. In order to explain the choices of voters we must now also look to other factors. The following sections examine the current impact of three possible explanatory variables:

● party identification;
● ideology and issues;
● candidates.

*Party Identification*

The party identification model of voting behaviour assumes that voters develop a psychological identification with a political party and that this identification is a primary motivating force in the decision concerning which party to vote for. In individual elections short-term factors may pull the voter away from the party, but the identification is more stable and results in a 'homing' tendency.

This model may be disposed of rather quickly in the Dutch case. As we have seen above, political parties in the Netherlands traditionally were closely allied with social groups. In fact, they may be seen as the political arms of such groups. Although research during the heyday of pillarisation is lacking, it seems reasonable to assume that the identification of individuals was with the group and not the political party. Perhaps little distinction was made between the two. Voting for the appropriate party was merely part of belonging to a group. Leaving the group, particularly in the case of those abandoning their religious affiliation, often meant turning away from the party as well.

If party identification was to provide an explanation in the open model of competition, we would have to assume that identification with parties had developed as the group identification declined. However, recent research does not indicate this to be the case. Responses to party identification questions in the Netherlands lack the stability that the model requires. In panel surveys, the percentage stating the same identification over time was lower than in comparable cases for the USA, Canada, and Great Britain (LeDuc, 1981). In fact, voting itself proved to be more stable than identification. Thomassen has shown that, in contradiction to the model, a change in the vote tended to produce a change in identification (Thomassen, 1976).

Finally, Van der Eijk and Niemöller (1982) demonstrated that voters had an 'identification' with various parties, rather than the single party which the model requires. Such multiple identifications were found even among those who were operationalised as 'strong party identifiers'. It would seem, therefore, that the standard party identification questions tap a sympathy towards one or more parties at a particular moment, but not a long-lasting and stable identifica- tion with a party. Failing this, party identification does not provide assistance in understanding current voter choice.

*Ideology and Issues*

In the quest for explanation of the less structured voting behaviour, attention has turned to party ideology and political issues. The problem of the dimensionality of the Dutch party system (see Chapter 3) has led to considerable discussion among analysts of voting behaviour. Van der Eijk and Niemöller have argued that a single Left–Right ideological dimension is dominant and sufficient for understanding voting behaviour. They have shown that most voters are able to place themselves and the political parties on a seven-point or ten-point Left–Right scale. Moreover, a large number of persons vote for the party closest to them on such a dimension. According to Van der Eijk and Niemöller, identification with an ideological position has replaced identification with the social group, so that Left–Right turns out to be the most important determinant of voter choice (Van der Eijk and Niemöller, 1982, 1987).

Other observers are less convinced that a single dimension provides a satisfactory representation of the Dutch ideological issue space. Luyten and Middendorp have shown that voters do not employ a single definition of Left–Right. Instead, they argue that both for placing themselves, and for placing the political parties, voters seem to employ a two-dimensional structure (Luyten and Middendorp, 1990; see also Middendorp, 1991).

We agree that a single Left–Right dimension is insufficient to describe the ideological issue space. There is no argument that the socio-economic Left–Right dimension is of great importance in Dutch politics. Some of the most important political issues – such as unemployment policy, budgetary policy, social welfare policy, and income policy – are fought out along such a dimension (see Chapter 8). Yet the religious–secular dimension remains of sufficient importance to make it necessary to include it in any analysis of Dutch politics in general and Dutch voting behaviour in particular. This dimension becomes important when such issues as abortion, euthanasia, or equal treatment for homosexuals enter the political arena.

In Figure 4.2, questions drawn from the 1989 National Election Study have been used to operationalise these two ideological dimensions. The issue selected as most indicative of the socio-economic dimension is the position on the question of how great differences between high incomes and low incomes should be. Other than in Chapter 3, the issue selected to exemplify the religious–secular dimension is whether abortion should be forbidden or whether the woman should have a choice. The two questions combined produce the results shown in Figure 4.2.

**FIGURE 4.2**
**Distribution of the electorate over the parties'**
**ideological heartlands and battlefield, 1989**

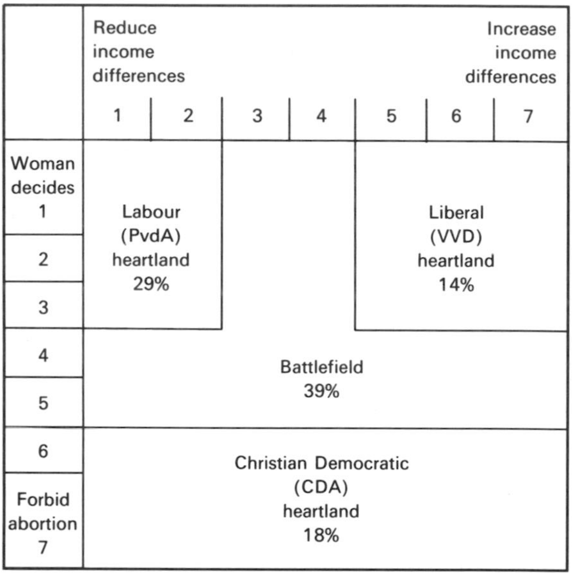

|  | Reduce income differences | | | | | Increase income differences |  |
|---|---|---|---|---|---|---|---|
|  | 1 | 2 | 3 | 4 | 5 | 6 | 7 |
| Woman decides 1 | Labour (PvdA) heartland 29% | | | | Liberal (VVD) heartland 14% | | |
| 2 | | | | | | | |
| 3 | | | | | | | |
| 4 | Battlefield 39% | | | | | | |
| 5 | | | | | | | |
| 6 | Christian Democratic (CDA) heartland 18% | | | | | | |
| Forbid abortion 7 | | | | | | | |

In Chapter 3 we discussed the alignment of the political parties on such dimensions. Based upon our analysis there, it is possible to define areas within this figure that correspond to the positions of the three major parties. For example, the Labour Party favours both the reduction of income differences and allowing women choice over abortion. The Liberals would also give women the right to choose, but favour no reduction in income differences or find that these differences have even become too small. The Christian Democrats have traditionally opposed abortion, but because they attempt to draw from all classes in the population they tend to take a broad centrist position on the question of income differences. For each of these major parties, it is thus possible to block out an area that corresponds roughly to its ideological issue positions. We have called these the 'heartlands' and it may be expected that persons with opinions that place them in one of the heartlands will vote for the corresponding party.

The relative size of these heartlands is not even. The largest heartland is that of the Labour Party, 29 per cent; the CDA heartland (18 per cent) and Liberal heartland (14 per cent) are considerably smaller. These heartlands have been drawn so that there is a clear boundary between them. Between the heartlands, an area has been left undefined with respect to these parties (i.e., this portion of the ideological issue space does not clearly belong to one of these parties). In practice, of course, these boundaries are undoubtedly too distinct and the areas intermingle and overlap with one another. Voters in this middle ground do not belong so clearly within the heartland of one of the parties. Their vote should be much less certain and it should be worthwhile for the parties to compete with each other for such voters. Thus this area has been called the 'battlefield'. The figure demonstrates that the largest number of voters (39 per cent) are found in this area, so there are plenty of votes to compete for.

In this model we have included only the three largest parties. Clearly if we had more space and could give full consideration to the smaller parties, we would find that we have not modelled all of the electoral competition in the Netherlands. The smaller religious parties compete to some extent within the CDA heartland, but such votes are determined more by one's religious denomination than by other factors. Within the Labour heartland this party also has competition from the Green Left; how a voter in this area determines his or her vote is not considered here. D66 is a party that is more difficult to locate within this ideological space and thus provides competition within more of the areas.

Table 4.3 gives the electoral choice of those individuals in each of the four areas. In each of the three heartlands we find that the largest percentage is for the associated party. Only the Liberals (in an election in which they did not do well) fell below a majority in their own heartland. If the Green Left vote is added to the Labour percentage and the small religious parties to the CDA percentage, we find as many as two-thirds to three-quarters of the voters in these areas voting along expected ideological issue lines.

As expected, the vote in the 'battlefield' area is more evenly distributed. However, with a percentage only 12 points lower than in its own heartland, the CDA has done surprisingly well here.

**TABLE 4.3**

**Vote distribution within ideological heartlands and battlefield, 1989**

| Party | Labour heartland | Liberal heartland | Christian Democratic heartland | Battlefield |
|---|---|---|---|---|
| PvdA | 59 | 17 | 17 | 26 |
| CDA | 14 | 22 | 53 | 41 |
| VVD | 6 | 45 | 3 | 15 |
| D66 | 10 | 11 | 3 | 15 |
| Green Left | 11 | 3 | 0 | 4 |
| Orthodox Calvinist parties (SGP, GPV, RPF) | 0 | 1 | 23 | 0 |
| Centre Democrats | 0 | 1 | 0 | 0 |
| Total (%) | 100 | 100 | 99 | 101 |
| $N$ | 395 | 184 | 244 | 527 |

Interestingly, there is no competition from the orthodox Calvinist parties in this area. It would therefore appear that we have either restricted the Christian Democratic heartland too greatly or that the party has simply competed quite well in recent elections, aided by its centrist position.

The D66 vote follows the expected pattern. It gained 15 percent of the vote in the battlefield area, but did only slightly less well in the Labour and Liberal heartlands. Only in the Christian Democratic heartland has it achieved a far lower share of the vote.

Although this simple model explains a substantial portion of electoral choice, clearly not all votes can be accounted for by these two ideological dimensions. Ideological factors may be viewed as long-term factors predisposing voters to a particular party. Every election, however, brings with it short-term factors, including political issues less fundamentally related to the ideological dimensions (see Exhibit 4.3, which shows the percentage of votes cast per party since 1946). For example, research has shown that attitudes towards nuclear weapons and nuclear energy have had an influence upon voting behaviour, helping to explain the vote within the battlefield and deviations within the heartlands (Irwin *et al.*, 1987; Irwin and Van Holsteyn, 1989b).

# EXHIBIT 4.3

## Election results since 1945 (% of vote obtained)

| Party | 1946 | 1948 | 1952 | 1956 | 1959 | 1963 | 1967 | 1971 | 1972 | 1977 | 1981 | 1982 | 1986 | 1989 |
|---|---|---|---|---|---|---|---|---|---|---|---|---|---|---|
| Catholic People's Party (KVP) | 30.8 | 31.0 | 28.7 | 31.7 | 31.6 | 31.9 | 26.5 | 21.8 | 17.7 | | | | | |
| Anti-Revolutionary Party (ARP) | 12.9 | 13.2 | 11.3 | 9.9 | 9.4 | 8.7 | 9.9 | 8.6 | 8.8 | | | | | |
| Christian Historical Union (CHU) | 7.8 | 9.2 | 8.9 | 8.4 | 8.1 | 8.6 | 8.1 | 6.3 | 4.8 | | | | | |
| Christian Democratic Appeal (CDA) | | | | | | | | | | 31.9 | 30.8 | 29.4 | 34.6 | 35.3 |
| Political Reformed Party (SGP) | 2.1 | 2.4 | 2.4 | 2.3 | 2.2 | 2.3 | 2.0 | 2.3 | 2.2 | 2.1 | 2.0 | 1.9 | 1.7 | 1.9 |
| Labour Party (PvdA) | 28.3 | 25.6 | 29.0 | 32.7 | 30.4 | 28.0 | 23.6 | 24.6 | 27.3 | 33.8 | 28.3 | 30.4 | 33.3 | 31.9 |
| Communist Party (CPN) | 10.6 | 7.7 | 6.2 | 4.7 | 2.4 | 2.8 | 3.6 | 3.9 | 4.7 | 1.7 | 2.1 | 1.8 | 0.6 | |
| Party of Freedom (PvdV) | 6.4 | | | | | | | | | | | | | |
| Liberal Party (VVD) | | 7.9 | 8.8 | 8.8 | 12.2 | 10.3 | 10.7 | 10.3 | 14.4 | 17.9 | 17.3 | 23.1 | 17.4 | 14.6 |
| Catholic National Party (KNP) | | | 2.7 | | | | | | | | | | | |
| Reformed Political League (GPV) | | 1.3 | 0.7 | 0.6 | 0.7 | 0.7 | 0.9 | 1.6 | 1.8 | 1.0 | 0.8 | 0.8 | 1.0 | 1.2 |
| Pacifist Socialist Party (PSP) | | | | | 1.8 | 3.0 | 2.9 | 1.4 | 1.5 | 0.9 | 2.1 | 2.3 | 1.2 | |
| Farmer's Party (BP) | | | | | 0.7 | 2.1 | 4.8 | 1.1 | 1.9 | 0.8 | | | | |
| Democrats '66 (D66) | | | | | | | 4.5 | 6.8 | 4.2 | 5.4 | 11.1 | 4.3 | 6.1 | 7.9 |
| Democratic Socialists '70 (DS'70) | | | | | | | | 5.3 | 7.1 | 0.7 | | | | |
| Dutch Middle Class Party (NMP) | | | | | | | | 1.5 | 0.4 | | | | | |
| Roman Catholic Party of the Netherlands (RKPN) | | | | | | | | 0.4 | 0.9 | 0.4 | | | | |
| Reformed Political Federation (RPF) | | | | | | | | | | | 1.2 | 1.5 | 0.9 | 1.0 |
| Evangelical People's Party (EVP) | | | | | | | | | | | 0.5 | 0.7 | 0.2 | |
| Centre Party/Centre Democrats | | | | | | | | | | | 0.1 | 0.8 | 0.4 | 0.9 |
| Green Left | | | | | | | | | | | | | | 4.1 |
| Other (all parties never having achieved parliamentary seat) | 1.0 | 1.6 | 1.4 | 0.8 | 0.6 | 1.6 | 2.6 | 2.1 | 0.6 | 1.5 | 1.8 | 1.4 | 1.3 | 1.2 |

Moreover, economic factors have begun to play a role in Dutch electoral behaviour. Given the nature of the structured model of party competition, it seems safe to assert that the state of the economy could have had only a minor impact upon voter choice. In a more open model, this is surely no longer the case. Within the battlefield area the degree of satisfaction with governmental economic policy has been shown to be strongly correlated with the vote. Those who were satisfied tended to vote retrospectively for the government coalition partners, particularly the party of the Prime Minister, whereas those who were dissatisfied voted for the opposition. Slogans such as 'Let Lubbers finish his job' in 1986 certainly played upon economic concerns in wooing votes for the CDA.

*Candidates*

In addition to issues, the limited evidence available seems to indicate that the party leaders are having an increasing impact upon voter choice. Of course, even when voters voted primarily according to their social group, they were concerned that the group had quality leaders who could inspire the confidence of the party faithful. However, such leadership served more as a reinforcement of a pre-existing choice than as a reason to choose a party. In recent years, with fewer voters' choices being determined in advance, the popularity of leaders may actually influence voters to make a choice for the party. This was evident in 1986 when the Christian Democrats chose the slogan just mentioned. The emphasis was on the popular prime minister rather than the party. Moreover, 'his job' referred to improvement of the economic position of the country, rather than any issue more directly associated with the ideology of the party.

Again, research showed that the attitude towards the leaders of the major parties could help to explain deviations from the expected voting position of those in the heartland and battlefield areas of the figure above. Since Lubbers was particularly popular in 1986, his party profited accordingly. In addition to Lubbers in 1986, there are other recent examples of the importance of party leaders in determining the vote. In 1977, Labour Prime Minister Den Uyl was quite popular; the party tried to capitalise on this with the slogan 'Elect the Prime Minister'. In 1982, the Liberals had a popular young man, Ed Nijpels, leading the ticket and fared quite well. In 1989 Hans van Mierlo helped revive the fortunes of D66. On the other hand, weak leadership can cost a party votes, as the Liberals discovered in 1989.

## Conclusion

To a considerable extent this chapter has been a consideration of change. Events in the 1960s have continued to have an impact upon the electoral and political system. In analysing electoral change between 1963 and 1977, one of the authors spoke of *Dutch Voters Adrift* (Andeweg, 1982). We might equally well speak of parties adrift. Both voters and parties were crossing a new sea, lacking the landmarks of half a century. Traditional identification with religious and social groups remains important for many voters, but is no longer a sufficient explanation of voter choice. Short-term issues as well as long-term ideological positions must now be taken into account. Governmental performance, particularly in the area of the economy can also influence voters, and popular candidates can win votes.

With more floating voters, the parties have been changing also. Campaign strategies and techniques have adapted to technological changes and have brought new ways of approaching the voters. New challenges remain on the horizon.

# 5

# The Cabinet

Dutch government is coalition government. The causes of coalition government in the Netherlands (socio-cultural minorities, multi-party system, PR) have been discussed in the three preceding chapters. In this chapter we turn to the important consequences of the coalition imperative for Dutch government. The first part of this chapter is devoted to the formation of governments. The process itself is described, as well as the critique and attempts to give Dutch voters more say over the composition of the government. We shall compare the outcomes of the process with the predictions based on rational-choice models of coalition building. The second part of the chapter looks into the decision-making by Cabinets once they are formed. The structure of the Cabinet is outlined, and the twin pulls of administration and politics on Cabinet decision-making are discussed.

## Building the Governing Coalition

'Dutch Without Government', 'Power Vacuum in The Hague': Dutch politics does not often attract the attention of the international press, but when it does, it is usually with headlines such as these in connection with the formation of a new government. Any hint of episodes of anarchy would be an exaggeration, but the suggestion that the interregnum between two Dutch governments is both important and different from the practices for the transfer of power in other countries is undoubtedly correct.

Important as they are, elections seldom have a determining impact on the formation of a government. At most the election outcome may deny a majority to a particular combination of parties, as in 1981, when the Christian Democrats and the Liberals would have preferred to govern together but won only 74 of the 150 seats in the Second Chamber of Parliament. This, however, is the exception rather than the rule, and a party that has 'won' in the election may lose the government formation. For the Social Democrats the relation between electoral gains and participation in government even seems to be inverse in the last two decades: whenever the Labour Party increased its share of parliamentary seats it lost its seats in the Cabinet (1977, 1982, 1986), and when it lost in the elections, it returned to government (1981, 1989). In the past, new governments were sometimes formed even without consulting the electorate. The most well known case occurred between 1963 and 1967. Following the 1963 elections a Cabinet of the three Christian Democratic parties (KVP, ARP, and CHU) and the VVD was formed. Two years later, this Cabinet fell and a new coalition of KVP, ARP, and Labour was formed. A year later, this Cabinet too was gone and a coalition of KVP and ARP filled in the time until new elections were held. Thus three coalitions of quite different political composition governed the country, only the first coalition being formed after elections. Since then, and largely because of this episode, it is generally accepted that a new government can be formed only after elections: that it is 'unhygienic to change partners without changing the sheets'. This new political morality has done little to alter the fact that, given the inconclusive outcomes of elections, the interregnum between the resignation of the old, and the swearing in of the new, Cabinet is one of the most important (but also one of the most controversial) moments in Dutch politics.

*Procedures of Cabinet Formation*

The provision that 'The King appoints and dismisses Ministers at his pleasure' was dropped from the Constitution in the 1983 revision. The position of the Dutch monarch in politics is much the same as that of the other constitutional monarchs in Europe. The ministers are responsible to Parliament for everything the Queen says or does, which forces her to say or do nothing without ministerial consent. If the Queen influences Cabinet decisions, it is through persuasion, rather than formal power. She may, in fact, be in a more influential position with regard to the formation of the Cabinet than some of her European colleagues. In countries where elections, with a little help from the electoral system, produce parties with a parliamentary majority (as in the UK), the role of the monarch is limited. In some countries without such parliamentary majorities, an elected official is charged with the responsibility for the formation of a government, as in Sweden. In the Netherlands the inconclusive outcome of the elections necessitates an impartial arbiter, and it is the Queen who takes the initiative as soon as the election results are known.

She does not form the new government herself but, after intensive consultations involving all parliamentary parties' leaders, she appoints a *formateur* or an *informateur* to preside over the negotiations between the prospective governing parties. It is through her choice of *(in)formateur*, and through the wording of his assignment, that the Queen exercises her influence. As soon as the appointment is made public, the appointee's political past is scrutinised, as were the entrails of a sacrificial beast by Roman augurs, or the beliefs of a candidate for the US Supreme Court, for any sign of coalition preference. Since 1945, 29 *formateurs* and 25 *informateurs* have come from the CDA or its constituent parties; there have been 9 *formateurs* and 7 *informateurs* from the Labour Party, and the Liberal Party has had only one *informateur*. The appointment of, for example, a Social Democrat or a Left-wing Christian Democrat is interpreted as a royal preference for a centre–Left coalition. If the *(in)formateur* is instructed to form 'a Cabinet that can be relied on to have the confidence of a majority in the States-General', minority coalitions are obviously excluded, which is not the case if the royal assignment speaks simply of the formation of 'a Cabinet'. Sometimes the Queen desires the formation of 'a cabinet that enjoys the broadest possible support in the States-General'. This is then interpreted as an instruction to form a Cabinet including CDA and PvdA, as these are usually the two largest parties. The Queen is sometimes criticised for her role in the formation of governments but, given their political importance, it is surprising that her decisions are not challenged more often.

The distinction between *formateurs* and *informateurs* is of little significance. Originally, only *formateurs* were appointed. However, since the Second World War, due to often complicated inter-party relationships, no *formateur* has succeeded in forming a Cabinet on the first attempt. The Queen often resorts, therefore, to appointing an *informateur* initially. As his title implies, his duty is to inform the Queen as to the viability of various options left open by the election outcome. The main attractiveness of the office of *informateur* lies in the fact that, whereas a *formateur* can fail, an *informateur* cannot; information can always be obtained, whereas a Cabinet cannot always be formed. Thus, the political risks involved in being an *informateur* are far less than those inherent in the position of *formateur*. In practice, however, *informateurs* no longer confine themselves to the gathering of information, and it is now customary for an *informateur* to leave only the recruitment of new ministers to a *formateur*, who is the Prime Minister designate.

Once appointed, an *(in)formateur* must seek answers to several questions, in roughly the following order: which parties are to form the new Cabinet? What will be the content of the new government's programme? How will ministerial portfolios be distributed over the governing parties? And, finally, who will be nominated as ministers? At any of these stages, the negotiations may be derailed. Often a new *(in)formateur* or even a team of *(in)formateurs* will be called upon to get the train back on the tracks. This happened, for example, in 1977, when talks between Labour, the CDA, and D66 broke down three times on the question of abortion, on a plan for a profit-sharing law, and on the distribution of ministerial posts. Each time the deadlock was broken by the appointment of a new *(in)formateur*, but finally, after 163 days of negotiations, no agreement could be reached on the appointment of the Christian Democrat Frans Andriessen as Minister of Economic Affairs. The whole procedure had to start anew, this time with the Christian Democrats and the Liberals.

The *(in)formateur's* first and most important task is to determine which parties will be invited to the negotiating table. His choice is restrained by the Queen's instructions, by the fact that some combinations of parties may not be able to muster the support of a majority in Parliament, and by the relations between the parties. In 1959 the Liberals publicly announced that they would not join any Cabinet including Social Democrats. The Labour Party soon reciprocated. Despite recent cautious overtures, this mutual exclusion still continues. In 1972 three parties – Labour, D66, and the Radicals – had formed a 'progressive' electoral alliance, pledging not to enter into a coalition with any other parties. After the elections it became clear that not only did this combination lack a majority, but so did the alternative combination of Christian Democrats and

Liberals. It was only after one of the longest and most complicated of Dutch Cabinet formations that a new government, consisting of 'progressives' and two Christian Democratic parties, could be sworn in. Very occasionally the answer to the *(in)formateur's* first question is clear and there is no room for manoeuvre at all. Prior to the 1986 elections the then governing parties, the CDA and the Liberal Party, announced that they would continue to govern together if their parliamentary majority were renewed. As they were not denied a majority the outcome of the formation was a foregone conclusion.

Once the combination of parties is settled, the negotiations can start in earnest. The leaders of the parliamentary parties (and not the party chairmen as in Belgium) represent the prospective governing parties in these talks. Usually, the new government's policy programme is the most important item on the agenda. In all countries governed by coalitions, there is no majority party election manifesto that becomes a government programme as soon as the new Cabinet is sworn in. If the Dutch way of forming a coalition government differs from that in Belgium, Italy, Germany, or the French Third and Fourth Republics, it is probably in the importance that is attached to the government agreement. Since the 1960s, this agreement has steadily become more important. Before the 1960s it consisted only of broad policy guidelines and more detailed compromises on a few controversial issues. Upon their appointment, the new Cabinet's ministers would then add to this agreement their own (or, more often, their department's) proposals. Today ministers can add or alter little. By means of the programme, the parties in the coalition try increasingly to bind both the ministers to the parties, and the parties to one another. It is a kind of political contract that holds the coalition together. Thus, political conflicts that bring down coalition governments in other countries may, to some extent, be prevented before the government takes office.

The programme has also increased in volume: the 1989 programme consists of 54 densely printed pages, not counting the many appendices. It contains detailed proposals for legislation, ranging from environmental protection to commercial television, and sets strict limits to the size of the budget deficit and the level of taxation. The programme contains only part of what the government is planning to do. It is a codification of mistrust. The preface to the 1989 programme states explicitly that there are many questions on which the parties agree, and that the programme contains only those questions on which they had conflicting views. As nearly all post-war coalitions included both Christian Democratic and secular parties, ethical issues are foremost among the controversies to be defused in the government programme. As we discussed in Chapter 2, a compromise can rarely be found on issues such as abortion or euthanasia. In such cases the programme often contains some procedural formula that is expected to depoliticise the conflict, at least for the duration of the government.

When the parties have agreed on a programme, the *(in)formateur* and the party leaders turn their attention to the distribution of seats in the Cabinet. This is normally a matter of proportionality. If satisfactory proportional distribution of ministerial posts cannot be achieved, inequalities may be compensated for at the level of junior ministers (called *staatssecretarissen*, or state secretaries). The Prime Minister customarily comes from the largest governing party. Although there are occasional disagreements about the number of portfolios to which each party is entitled, the matching of portfolios to party preferences is often even more difficult. Such preferences originate from the party's ideology or from the interests it represents. That the Liberal Party is disproportionately represented in the list of post-war ministers of Economic Affairs need not surprise us, and neither should the overrepresentation of Christian Democrats at the Department of Education, nor of Social Democrats at Social Affairs. However, it is less in line with expectations that the Social Democrats have been disproportionately often in charge of Finance and of Agriculture. Party preferences are sometimes ignored, as in the Lubbers III Cabinet, formed in 1989, in which the PvdA received Education and the CDA Social Affairs. At times party preferences are not honoured for political reasons: in Chapter 2 we saw how the Catholics were denied the portfolio of European Affairs in 1952 for fears of a Catholic Europe (see also Chapter 9).

Finally, once the portfolios have been apportioned, the government has to be staffed with ministers and junior ministers. Names are put forward by the party leaders, but they must be acceptable to the coalition partners. Ministers need not be recruited from Parliament but, if they are (as in the French Fifth Republic), once appointed as minister, they must give up their seats in Parliament. This feature of the Dutch Constitution has important consequences for the policy-making culture of the Cabinet, as we shall see later in this chapter. The incompatibility of ministerial office and membership of

Parliament is one of the few aspects of the government formation regulated by the written constitution.

Once all has been agreed upon, the *formateur* reports back to the Queen with his recommendations for a new government. The Queen then makes the formal appointments and the formation process is ended symbolically with a photo of the new ministers and the Queen. There is also no formal end to the Cabinet formation in the form of an investiture vote in Parliament. The procedures that we have described so far are extrapolated from government formations in recent years. The traditions and customs that determine the procedures are continually evolving and can be set aside completely whenever political expedience requires.

*Attempts at Reform*

The way in which governments are formed in the Netherlands has frequently provoked criticism. One complaint is that too much time is wasted in forming a government. In 1989 the formation of the third Lubbers government took 61 days. By Dutch standards, two months is actually considered rather quick, the post-war record being just 31 days (1948). At the slow end of the spectrum, there have been formations that took 108 days (1981), 122 days (1956), 163 days (1972) and even 208 days (1977)! Table 5.1 gives details of the duration of post-war Cabinets and their formations.

During the post-war period, on average almost a month per year is spent on government formations. This is sometimes seen as detrimental to effective government. During an interregnum the old Cabinet continues as a caretaker government and retains all its powers, but any controversial legislative proposals usually have to wait until the new government is sworn in. When outgoing ministers know that their party will not participate in the new government, they are sometimes reluctant to take necessary measures that may prove unpopular.

In general, however, the problem of a power vacuum should not be overstated. To a large extent, the long duration of the government formations is accounted for by the negotiations over a detailed government programme that is intended to prevent later conflicts. In a sense, a long interregnum is the price that is paid for Cabinet stability.

**TABLE 5.1**

**Duration of Cabinet formations and Cabinets, 1945–89**

| Date installed | Prime Minister | Duration of Cabinet formation in days | Duration of Cabinet in days |
|---|---|---|---|
| 24 June 1945 | Schermerhorn | 47 | 374* |
| 3 July 1946 | Beel I | 47 | 766 |
| 7 August 1948 | Drees I | 31 | 950† |
| 15 March 1951 | Drees II | 50 | 537 |
| 2 September 1952 | Drees III | 69 | 1502 |
| 13 October 1956 | Drees IV | 122 | 800† |
| 22 December 1958 | Beel II | 10 | 148* |
| 19 May 1959 | De Quay | 68 | 1527 |
| 24 July 1963 | Marijnen | 70 | 630† |
| 14 April 1965 | Cals | 46 | 587† |
| 22 November 1966 | Zijlstra | 38 | 134* |
| 5 April 1967 | De Jong | 49 | 1553 |
| 6 July 1971 | Biesheuvel I | 69 | 380† |
| 20 July 1972 | Biesheuvel II | 22 | 295* |
| 11 May 1973 | Den Uyl | 163 | 1683‡ |
| 19 December 1977 | Van Agt I | 208 | 1362 |
| 11 September 1981 | Van Agt II | 108 | 260† |
| 29 May 1982 | Van Agt III | 17 | 159* |
| 4 November 1982 | Lubbers I | 57 | 1348 |
| 14 July 1986 | Lubbers II | 52 | 1212† |
| 7 November 1989 | Lubbers III | 61 | — |

\* Interim Cabinet, intended for short duration.
†Life of Cabinet shortened by political conflict.
‡ Cabinet ended in political conflict, but this did not affect its duration.

The maximum interval between parliamentary elections is specified by the Constitution to be four years. Depending upon certain technical circumstances, it is actually possible for a Cabinet to be in office slightly more than four years. Yet few last even four years; between 1945 and 1989 there were 20 Cabinets, lasting an average of 810 days (or almost two years and three months). However, five of these Cabinets were caretaker governments, intended to be in office for only a short period prior to new general elections. If these Cabinets are excluded, the average Dutch Cabinet was in office for nearly 3 years. Moreover, some Cabinets saw their life span cut short for reasons other than political conflict: of all 20 post-war Cabinets until 1989, only seven perished prematurely for political reasons. Most Dutchmen would, therefore, probably agree with Gladdish, who noted that the relatively long interregnums in the Netherlands 'are scarcely a pathological feature, since the system depends upon the patient reconciliation of the ambitions of a number of minority parties; and they do not connote the kind of government instability associated with the French Fourth Republic' (Gladdish, 1972, p. 344). Compared with Italy or Belgium – two other countries always governed by coalitions – the Netherlands seems a haven of stability.

A much more serious criticism of the whole procedure is its lack of democratic legitimacy: voters propose, politicians dispose. Elections have little impact on which coalition is formed. This is the Achilles heel of the Dutch political system, and several reforms have been proposed in the course of the years to remedy the situation. All proposals have sought to increase the government's democratic legitimacy by moving the coalition negotiations from after to before the elections, but they have tried to achieve this end by different means. The proposed reforms can be divided roughly into two categories: those modelled on the British example, and those inspired more by the American system of government.

The 'British' reforms have concentrated on the party system, rather than on the institutions of government. In a celebrated essay in 1967, a young Social Democrat (now mayor of Amsterdam), Van Thijn, argued that in Dutch politics the displeasure of the voters cannot be channelled into 'turning the rascals out', as opposition votes are not concentrated on an alternative government party but are dispersed over many parties. In such a system, according to Van Thijn, an inherent tendency exists for the extremes to grow at the expense of the centre until the centre is crushed between extremist anti-system parties. To avoid such a Weimarian showdown, he advocated a remodelling of the party system along the lines of the British one (as it existed when he wrote), in which the pendulum of power could swing freely back and forth according to the electorate's preference. Since in the Netherlands more than two parties are relevant in Sartori's sense, these parties ought to form blocs or pre-election coalitions, so as to offer the voter a clear choice between two competing alternatives. It was hoped that, eventually, these blocs would transform into parties. Van Thijn's dreams of a dichotomous party system were inspired by the heavy losses that the centrist Christian Democratic parties began to suffer in those years. The feeling that the Christian Democrats

would gradually be reduced to electoral insignificance was reinforced
by growing discord within the KVP. Soon talks were under way
between the Social Democrats and smaller left-of-centre parties about
a single, broadly based Progressive People's Party. In the 1971
election campaign these 'progressive' parties presented a shadow
Cabinet, but they came nowhere near a parliamentary majority. In
1972 the progressive parties negotiated a joint manifesto before the
elections but, as we have already mentioned, in a protracted
government formation they were forced to accept Christian Democratic participation in 'their' Cabinet. The reform was then watered
down: if the Leftist preelection coalition did not achieve a parliamentary majority, it would govern only if it could have a majority of
the seats in Cabinet. Gradually even this 'majority strategy' proved
unworkable, and the reform of the party system is now forgotten. The
reform failed because the Christian Democrats did not disappear. On
the contrary: the Progressive People's Party never materialised, but
the Christian Democrats did manage to set aside old rivalries between
Catholics and Protestants to form a unified party. Ironically, it was
the new CDA that, having formed a pre-election coalition with the
Liberal Party in 1986, obtained a majority and thus excluded the
Social Democrats at all stages of the negotiations for a new
government.

The proposed 'American' reforms involved radical institutional
changes, and would have transformed the Netherlands almost into a
presidential system. The intellectual godfather of this type of reform,
Leyden Law professor Glastra Van Loon (1964), started from the
familiar assumption that PR may lead to an adequate reflection of
popular political opinion in Parliament, but not to a strong
democratic executive. Prior to 1918 the electoral system resembled
the current French system, in which a run-off election is held in each
district where no candidate obtains an absolute majority in the first
round. Under the Dutch system only the two highest placed
candidates participated in the run-off (see Chapter 4). As in
France, this system led to the formation of coalitions between the
first and second round, and from 1888 to 1913 a regular alternation of
government between two blocs of parties could be observed. PR
contains no such incentive to form pre-election coalitions. However,
PR has become so ingrained in Dutch political culture, and is so
central to consociational democracy, that the reintroduction of a
majoritarian electoral system was not seen as a feasible option by

Glastra Van Loon. Instead, he suggested giving the electorate the right to choose the Prime Minister: parties, or pre-election coalitions of parties, could nominate a candidate, and the office of Prime Minister would go to the party or coalition with the plurality of votes in the parliamentary election. This would considerably strengthen the position of the Prime Minister, but stop short of a presidential system. Glastra Van Loon's ideas formed the basis of more radical proposals put forward by D66, the party that originated from unhappiness with the way in which governments are formed in the Netherlands. The D66 manifesto called for a separate, direct election of the Prime Minister, and the abolition of ministerial responsibility. A Government Advisory Committee later recommended a moderate version of the D66 proposal, and it has been formally put before Parliament several times, but each time without success. Although the debate on democratic reform is resuscitated now and again, it seems to focus more and more on the possible introduction of referenda, or on an electoral system with a combination of nation-wide PR and electoral districts, as in Germany, rather than on a change in the procedures for building governing coalitions in the Netherlands. The link between election outcome and government formation is thus likely to remain a tenuous one.

*Coalition Theory and Dutch Cabinets*

If election results cannot predict the outcome of the formation process, can political science? Most theories view coalition formation as a game in which players act rationally. The assumption is that political parties want to maximise power by sharing it with as few other parties as possible. Hence 'minimal winning' coalitions will be formed that contain no parties that are not necessary for obtaining a parliamentary majority. Yet interestingly, before the 1970s, most Dutch coalitions contradicted such theories by being 'oversized' rather than minimal-winning (see Table 5.2).

This Dutch exception can be explained in several ways. A first explanation points to the fulcrum position of the Christian Democrats and, before this party was formed in 1977, of the largest of its predecessors, the KVP. This position enables it to play off the parties to its left and to its right against each other, and explains in part why it has always been represented in government since 1918. As De Swaan pointed out, still speaking of only the KVP: 'The most

**TABLE 5.2**
**Prime Ministers and composition of Cabinets**

| Date installed | Prime Minister | Composition* | Size of coalition majority[†] | Status[‡] |
|---|---|---|---|---|
| 24 June 1945 | Schermerhorn | PvdA/KVP/ARP/np | | |
| 3 July 1946 | Beel I | PvdA/*KVP*/np | 61:100 | o |
| 7 August 1948 | Drees I | PvdA/KVP/CHU/VVD/np | 89:100 | o |
| 15 March 1951 | Drees II | PvdA/KVP/CHU/VVD/np | 76:100 | o |
| 2 September 1952 | Drees III | PvdA/KVP/ARP/CHU/np | 81:100 | o |
| 13 October 1956 | Drees IV | PvdA/KVP/ARP/CHU | 85:100 | o |
| 22 December 1958 | Beel II | KVP/ARP/CHU | 77:150 | mw |
| 19 May 1959 | De Quay | KVP/ARP/CHU/VVD | 94:150 | o |
| 24 July 1963 | Marijnen | KVP/ARP/CHU/VVD | 92:150 | o |
| 14 April 1965 | Cals | PvdA/*KVP*/ARP | 106:150 | o |
| 22 November 1966 | Zijlstra | KVP/*ARP* | 63:150 | m |
| 5 April 1967 | De Jong | KVP/ARP/CHU/VVD | 86:150 | mw |
| 6 July 1971 | Biesheuvel I | KVP/*ARP*/CHU/VVD/DS70 | 82:150 | mw |
| 20 July 1972 | Biesheuvel II | KVP/*ARP*/CHU/VVD | 74:150 | m |
| 11 May 1973 | Den Uyl | PPR/*PvdA*/D66/KVP/ARP | 97:150 | o |
| 19 December 1977 | Van Agt I | CDA/VVD | 77:150 | mw |
| 11 September 1981 | Van Agt II | PvdA/D66/*CDA* | 109:150 | o |
| 29 May 1982 | Van Agt III | D66/*CDA* | 65:150 | m |
| 4 November 1982 | Lubbers I | CDA/VVD | 81:150 | mw |
| 14 July 1986 | Lubbers II | CDA/VVD | 81:150 | mw |
| 7 November 1989 | Lubbers III | PvdA/*CDA* | 103:150 | mw |

* Party of the PM in *italics*; np = non-partisan.
[†] Number of seats of governing parties in Second Chamber : total number of seats in Second Chamber. [‡] o = oversized; mw = minimum winning; m = minority.

effective way to exploit this position was for it . . . to carry the advantages of a pivotal position into the government coalition itself. By including both Social Democrats and centre-right parties, the Catholics could play both sides against the middle at every cabinet meeting' (De Swaan, 1982). Parties were thus added to the coalition even if they were not necessary for obtaining a parliamentary majority. This observation was an interesting improvement over existing rational coalition theory, because it takes into account that what is rational for one party need not be rational for another party, and that a centre party is in an excellent position to impose its definition of rationality on the other players.

The centre position of the CDA may also help to explain a puzzling aspect of the 1989 government formation. In that interregnum the

Christian Democrats announced as their first preference a coalition of the CDA and the Liberal Party *with* D66, and as their second preference a coalition of the CDA and Labour *without* D66. On a simple socio-economic Left–Right dimension D66 is positioned between Labour and CDA. Omitting the centre–Left D66 from a centre–Left coalition was seen by many as arbitrary, and was at odds with another widely accepted tenet of coalition theory: that coalitions should be 'closed' (i.e., should consist of ideologically adjacent parties). Dutch politics being a two-dimensional game (see Chapters 3 and 4), it might be argued that the Christian Democrats were wary of a secular majority in the Cabinet. The Labour Party plus D66 would have outnumbered the Christian Democrats, whereas the Liberals plus D66 would not. However, as votes in Cabinet are rare, it is unlikely that the CDA attached that much weight to numbers alone. It is more likely that the Christian Democrats realised that they would be the pivotal party in a coalition with D66 to its left and the Liberals to its right, but that D66 would take this position in a coalition of the CDA, D66 and Social Democrats. So the concept of a pivotal party may help us in explaining some of the oddities in Dutch government formation, but whether it can explain the oversized coalitions of the past is less evident. As Table 5.2 shows, since 1966 oversized coalitions have become the exception rather than the rule. De Swaan's explanation does not account for the disappearance of the theoretical deviation.

A second explanation does account for the emergence after 1966 of minimal-winning coalitions. In Lijphart's original theory, elite cooperation was a reaction to pillarisation (see Chapter 2). The more parties represented in the governing coalition, the better in terms of elite cooperation. 'Executive power sharing or grand coalition' is mentioned as one of the basic principles of consociational democracy. However, grand coalitions (in the sense that all major parties took part) have never been formed. Even the so-called 'broad coalitions' (Drees I, Drees II) left one of the principal parties, the ARP, in opposition. However, an oversized coalition certainly approximates Lijphart's ideal consociational Cabinet. Of all the characteristics of what Lijphart now calls consensus government, this is the only one that he finds to have changed: between 1946 and 1967 the country was governed for 13 per cent of the time by minimal-winning Cabinets; between 1967 and 1988 Lijphart finds this percentage to have risen to 71 per cent (Lijphart, 1989, p. 147).

It is surely not accidental that the disappearance of the oversized coalition has coincided with the decline in pillarisation. However, the definition of minimal winning and oversized is based on the number of parties and their seats in Parliament. Prior to 1977, the major Christian Democratic parties – KVP, ARP and CHU – often collaborated, but were three distinct parties. In 1977 they merged into a single party. If we were to treat them as a single party prior to the merger, the calculations would be quite different. If the three were counted as a single unit in all Cabinets in which all three were represented (as was usually the case), oversized coalitions would always have been the exception.

Whatever the explanation, the emergence of minimal winning coalitions has brought Dutch Cabinets more in line with coalition theory. Today, political science has more predictive power than in the past, but not much more. Most elections allow for several alternative minimal-winning coalitions. In 1989, for example, the theory of minimal-winning coalitions would not have been able to choose between a government of the CDA and the PvdA; of the CDA and the VVD; or of Labour, Liberals, and D66. The Dutch political scientist Daudt has attempted to arrive at a more precise prediction of the government's composition by making a distinction between parties advocating a radical change of society (which he calls parties of the Left), and parties preferring to keep things more or less as they are (which we shall call parties of the Right). Daudt argues that the KVP of the past, and the present CDA, is not a party of the centre, as is so often assumed, but a party of the Right. As such the CDA has a natural preference for a coalition with the Liberals. Only in cases of 'dire necessity' will the Christian Democrats enter into a coalition with the Social Democrats. Such a necessity can be numerical (when a coalition with the Liberals has no majority) or political (when Social Democratic participation in government makes it easier to get social acceptance of unpopular measures). Although Daudt argues that the Christian Democrats have an ideological preference for a government with the Liberals, such a coalition is also advantageous to the CDA because the Liberal Party tends to be much smaller, and therefore less demanding than the Labour Party (Daudt, 1982).

Daudt's theory was intended to explain the outcome of coalition formations until the 1970s, but, in the debate that followed his analysis, most authors have argued that the theory is historically incorrect. The Christian Democrats attracted voters who shared a common religion, but who had very different socio-economic positions and interests. The political strategy of the Christian Democrats was, therefore, a careful balancing act to satisfy all factions within the party. To have only the Liberal Party as a partner in government coalitions would sooner or later have led to dissatisfaction of the Left wing of the Christian Democrats. Today, however, Daudt's theory is nearer the truth as the CDA has clearly moved to the right since the 1970s. Because of split-offs to the Left (see Chapter 3), and because there is no longer a separate Catholic trade union, the Left wing is weaker now among Christian Democratic activists and MPs. The electorate of the CDA has also become more Right wing. According to opinion polls, more than half the Catholic voters (the largest contingent within the present CDA) preferred a coalition with the Social Democrats in the 1970s, and only about one-third wanted a coalition with the Liberals. In the 1980s this has changed completely. In 1982, 21 per cent of Christian Democratic voters were in favour of a coalition that would include the Labour Party, whereas 87 per cent preferred a government in which the Liberals would participate. Even a conflict in 1989, when the Liberals brought down the government, did little to change the sympathies of Christian-Democratic voters: 65 per cent were in favour of CDA + VVD ( + D66), and 27 per cent in favour of CDA + PvdA ( + D66).

The 'updated' version of Daudt's theory was put to the test in 1989. There was no necessity for the CDA to turn to the Social Democrats: the Christian Democrats and the Liberals had a majority, albeit a small one, and there were no major political questions on the agenda that made Social Democratic participation in government impera-tive. Nevertheless, despite all such theoretical predictions, a coalition of the CDA and the PvdA was formed. At this moment little is known about the motives of the CDA for making this theoretically 'irrational' choice. The official reason given by party spokesmen is that they considered the one-seat majority with the Liberals too small. Yet this can hardly be the real motive: in 1977 the Christian Democrats and the Liberals governed with only one seat more. Besides, a CDA–VVD coalition could count on picking up a few votes in Parliament from small parties of the Right, or even from D66, on most questions. The most likely explanation is that the choice was the result of a factional struggle within the CDA. The small remnant of the Left wing in the CDA used the slender majority, and the fact that the Liberals were 'guilty' of the 1989 government crisis, as arguments against a continuation of the coalition of the CDA and the VVD. The internal compromise was a first preference for a coalition with the Liberals, but only if D66 would agree to reinforce this coalition, and a second preference for a coalition with the Social Democrats, but only if D66 would not be part of the government. Because of this second condition, the Right wing probably gambled that D66 would join a centre-Right coalition, whereas the Left wing anticipated that this would not happen. Although this explanation is not yet more than an educated guess, it illustrates one of the weaknesses of most theories of coalition formation, which consider political parties to be homogeneous units and pay no attention to political struggles that go on behind the façade of the party label. Each of the theories discussed sheds light on one potential motive behind the government formation, but the composition of Dutch Cabinets is determined by as yet unpredictable combinations of different motives.

## Collective and Collegial Government

*The Position of the Prime Minister*

Since Dutch governments are invariably coalition Cabinets, this has important consequences for Cabinet decision-making. If Cabinets are placed on a scale from prime ministerial government to collegial government, Dutch Cabinets are clearly positioned towards the collegial end. In fact, the Netherlands ranks second only to Switzerland in terms of collegiality of leadership (Baylis, 1989). In a 1955 English-language article, Hans Daalder wrote about Dutch ministers serving *with*, not *under*, a Prime Minister. It took him over an hour to convince the journal's editor that this was not a foreigner's linguistic mistake, but a correct reading of Dutch Cabinet practices.

Compared with his British, French, or even his German colleagues, the Dutch Prime Minister has very few formal powers. He draws up the agenda and chairs all meetings of the Cabinet and its committees. He casts the deciding vote when there is a tie. But the Prime Minister does not appoint the ministers; names are agreed upon in the negotiations between the parties, and formal appointment is then made by the Queen. The Prime Minister cannot remove a minister or 'reshuffle' the Cabinet by assigning ministers to other portfolios. The

Prime Minister of the wartime government in exile twice dismissed a minister without even consulting the Cabinet. He was immediately criticised for such 'Persian constitutional morals', and after the war a parliamentary inquiry repudiated the claim that the Prime Minister should have the power of dismissal. The Prime Minister can ask the Queen to dissolve Parliament when there is a political crisis or at the end of a regular parliamentary term. It is doubtful, however, whether the Queen would honour such a request simply because the electoral prospects of the governing parties look favourable. Although the Prime Minister is entrusted with the task of coordinating Cabinet policy, he has no authority to settle conflicts between ministers unless they agree to his arbitration. He cannot give any directives to ministers.

The Prime Minister's staff is relatively small. He heads the Department of General Affairs, which employs about 350 civil servants, but most work in the Government Press Office, on the staff of the Scientific Council for Government Policy, or for one of the intelligence services. Only 10–12 act as advisers to the Prime Minister. All are career civil servants, and only occasionally does a Prime Minister bring in some political appointees. The Cabinet Secretariat is part of the Department of General Affairs, but has a semi-independent position. Except for the Cabinet Secretary, the Secretariat is formed by a handful of young civil servants seconded from other departments for a few years.

Despite the paucity of staff and formal powers, there is a feeling among many Dutch commentators that the position of the Prime Minister has been strengthened in more recent years, even though the use which is made of this position varies considerably with the personality of the Prime Minister and the political situation of the moment. The ever-increasing demand for coordination of government policy (see Chapter 7) may have strengthened the hand of the coordinator, but the impression of a stronger Prime Minister is largely fed by his increasing external role. Since Prime Minister De Jong's tenure (1967–71) the Prime Minister gives a weekly press conference and a television interview in which he explains and defends the Cabinet's decisions. Increasingly the Prime Minister represents the country at EC and other summit meetings. It is difficult to ascertain the extent to which the growing external role of the Prime Minister reflects a somewhat stronger position inside the Cabinet, but from a comparative perspective there can be no doubt that Daalder's observation that ministers serve *with* rather than *under* a Prime Minister is as valid today as it was in 1955 (Andeweg, 1991).

Collegial and collective government has long historical roots in the Netherlands. With the possible exception of the first two or three decades after 1813, the Dutch never experienced absolute monarchy. In Chapter 2 we mentioned Daalder's critique of Lijphart's 'self-denying prophecy', based on the tradition of elite bargaining and compromise dating back to the early days of the Republic of the Seven United Provinces. Consociational practices, whether they date back to 1579 or to 1917, are less conducive to a monocratic premiership than majoritarian democracy. After all, the Prime Minister, being one person, can belong to only one of the pillars.

The tradition of collegial and collective government is constantly reinforced by the coalition character of Dutch Cabinets. In a coalition Cabinet the jealousy of the other governing party (or parties) provides a powerful antidote to any monocratic ambitions fostered by the Prime Minister. Many of the institutional constraints mentioned above, such as his inability to staff or reshuffle his own Cabinet, or to take policy initiatives, stem from the circumstance that Cabinet members from other parties will only accept the Prime Minister's leadership as long as he is acting as leader of the coalition  and not as leader of his own party.

This balancing act between partisanship and impartiality is influenced by the composition of the coalition. In the four- or even five-party coalitions that were customary before 1977, a Prime Minister could make use of rivalry among governing parties other than his own to 'divide and conquer', particularly when his own party was the centre party in the coalition. This is no longer possible in the two-party coalitions that have since become current. In such a coalition the balance of power between the two governing parties has a significant effect on the Prime Minister's leadership.

The two most likely coalitions in the Netherlands are Christian Democrat/Liberal, and Christian Democrat/Social Democrat. The former is a coalition of a large and a small party, the latter of two parties of nearly equal size. In a coalition with a much smaller party, the Prime Minister is less constrained by the conflict between his role as party leader and his role as chairman. More ministers from his own party also means easier access for the Prime Minister to more departments. Prime Minister Lubbers has governed with the Liberal Party as well as with the Labour Party, so we can control this comparison for the Prime Minister's personality. In his two governments with the Liberals, Lubbers was seen as a rather dominant Prime Minister, but the numerical strength of the Social Democrats seems to have made him the first partner in a duumvirate with the Deputy Prime Minister (the leader of the PvdA). Conflicts among ministers are now often mediated by them together. When the Christian Democrats were in a coalition with the Liberals, Lubbers regularly intervened in the portfolio of the Minister of Finance, a fellow party member, sometimes even bypassing him by presenting his own budget proposals directly to Cabinet. In the Lubbers III Cabinet of CDA and PvdA, Finance Minister Kok is also the Deputy Prime Minister and leader of the Labour Party. There have been no more prime ministerial budget initiatives as any attempt by the Prime Minister to bypass this Minister of Finance would risk a full-blown Cabinet crisis.

All this would have changed if the proposal to introduce a directly elected Prime Minister had succeeded. As we saw, the primary aim of this proposal was not a strengthening of the Prime Minister, but such a consequence may well have been in the back of the minds of those who successfully opposed this reform.

Traditions and coalitions are not the only factors contributing to the culture of collegial and collective Cabinet government. The Dutch Cabinet is not merely a coalition of political parties, but also a board of heads of departments. All departmental ministers (but not junior ministers) are members of the Cabinet. Even the Minister without Portfolio for Development Cooperation *de facto* represents a part of a department. Departmental ministers enjoy a strong position. In Chapter 7 we shall discuss at length the degree to which Dutch policy-making can be characterised as neo-corporatist. One of the consequences of neo-corporatism is a high degree of autonomy for the various policy sectors. Each department has developed its own network of interest groups, quangos, advisory bodies, and specialised parliamentary committees. Ministers define their role primarily as being the head of a department. As a consequence, the Prime Minister is constrained not only by political envy of other governing parties, but also by the departmental jealousy of individual ministers. Even against the Prime Minister, ministers jealously guard their departmental turf, sometimes even in a literal sense. For example, the 1973–7 Den Uyl government was divided over the building of a particular dam as part of the Delta works to protect the Province of

Zeeland from flooding. Prime Minister Den Uyl then decided that he wanted to see the estuary where the dam was being planned, and he commissioned a customs cutter to take him there. By coincidence the Minister of Public Works heard about this, managed to get hold of a faster ship, and chased the Prime Minister out of his 'territorial waters'. In another case, during the summer of 1990, several proposals for administrative and political reform were (again) discussed, both in a parliamentary committee and in Cabinet. One suggestion, to give the Prime Minister more room for manoeuvre when representing the country at international summits, immediately prompted a threat of resignation by the Minister of Foreign Affairs, a fellow party member and close political associate of the Prime Minister.

A final factor worth mentioning in this respect is the Cabinet's small size. Not even the literature on group dynamics provides us with an exact cut-off point, but common sense dictates that true collective and collegial decision-making is inversely related to Cabinet size. The number of ministers rose from just 9 ministers in 1917 to 16 ministers (plus 17 junior ministers) in the 1973–7 government. By 1989 the number had been reduced again to 14 ministers (including the Prime Minister and one minister without portfolio). Junior ministers, now 10 in number, have no voting rights in Cabinet, and are invited to attend only when Cabinet discusses matters relevant to their portfolio. 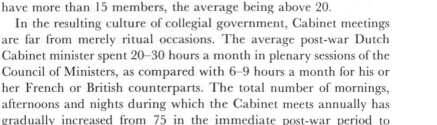 On average, about 15 ministers are present. Most countries' Cabinets have more than 15 members, the average being above 20.

In the resulting culture of collegial government, Cabinet meetings are far from merely ritual occasions. The average post-war Dutch Cabinet minister spent 20–30 hours a month in plenary sessions of the Council of Ministers, as compared with 6–9 hours a month for his or her French or British counterparts. The total number of mornings, afternoons and nights during which the Cabinet meets annually has gradually increased from 75 in the immediate post-war period to about 125 in the 1970s. In 1976 the Den Uyl Cabinet probably set a record by meeting on 163 mornings, afternoons, or evenings for a total of 478 hours. Since then the frequency of meetings has declined somewhat. In these meetings many matters are considered and an average of 26 decisions are taken. Moreover, these decisions are far from being simply rubber stamps. A careful reading of the minutes for one year, 1968, showed that 21 per cent of all decisions differed from the original proposal put to Cabinet.

*The Politicisation of the Cabinet*

Given the fact that all Cabinets are coalitions of political parties, it is surprising that the Dutch Cabinet remained a relatively apolitical, technocratic body until the 1960s at least. Before then, ministers regarded themselves primarily as departmental chieftains, and most conflicts in Cabinet were caused by divergent departmental interests. Several factors may account for the relative lack of politicisation of the Cabinet. First we must again mention consociational democracy. If stable government was threatened by subcultural strife, the Cabinet had to remain aloof from the daily political squabbles; it had to be depoliticised to be acceptable to all pillars. Sayings such as 'The closer to the Crown, the less partisan' about ministers, and 'The sounds from the Tourney Field only faintly reach the Salle de Trêves, where Cabinet usually meets' about Cabinet decision-making, testify to this depoliticisation. Ministers had little or no contact with the parliamentary party that had nominated them. When Zijlstra (later Prime Minister) was appointed Minister of Economics in 1952, as a political novice he sought the advice of his party's leader in Parliament. The latter declined to help 'because they had separate responsibilities'. To symbolise the apolitical nature of their office, in the Second Chamber of Parliament Dutch ministers are seated behind a separate table, facing the members of Parliament (see Exhibit 6.1).

A second factor contributing to depoliticisation was the relatively non-political nature of ministerial recruitment. Even before the incompatibility of ministerial office and a seat in Parliament was written into the Constitution, it was customary for an MP to resign his seat upon being raised to government rank. Moreover, ministers have often been recruited from outside Parliament. Of all ministers appointed between 1848 and 1967 only 35.2 per cent had parliamentary experience. The selection criteria were often more technocratic than political: a banker or economist at Finance, a lawyer at Justice, someone with trade union credentials at Social Affairs, a farmer or farmer's son at Agriculture. This 'rule' has not been adhered to without significant exceptions. In the post-war period purely non-political specialists have become rare (a few non-partisan diplomats at the Foreign Office, for example), although most government formations produce rumours that one or two ministers hastily had to become party members before taking the oath of office.

Although most ministers did have a prior political affiliation, they were not recruited mainly for their political experience but for their expertise in the policy area for which they were to assume responsibility. Even Prime Ministers have not always been the political heavy-weights one would expect in that position. Between the introduction of parliamentary democracy in 1848 and 1992, there were 42 Prime Ministers, 19 of whom had not been an MP, and 17 of whom had not previously been a Cabinet minister. With the exception of the Labour Party, the governing parties often preferred to keep their leader in Parliament. As late as 1973 Norbert Schmelzer, a former leader of the KVP, remarked: 'Being the parliamentary leader of the largest governing party is a much more influential, powerful, and creative function than being Prime Minister.'

A third factor contributing to the emphasis on a minister's departmental rather than political role is the absence of political advisers or a 'cabinet ministériel', as exists in France, Belgium, and Italy. As in the UK, ministers are briefed on Cabinet papers by their department, and these departmental briefings are based on rather narrow interpretations of the department's interest. If the civil servants involved do not think their department affected by a proposal, however politically controversial it may be, they have been known to advise their minister not to partake in the deliberations.

The consequence of such attitudes is that it has been, and to some extent still is, frowned upon when a minister joins a debate in which his department has no stake. 'One is not going to pester one another unnecessarily', one minister remarked. Recurrent violations of this tacit agreement of 'non-intervention' sometimes meet with a collective reprisal from the other ministers. For one of the most recent years for which the minutes of Cabinet are accessible, 1968, we have calculated that nearly four-fifths of all contributions to the debates in Cabinet could be traced to the speakers' departmental interests. Even if we correct the calculations for the fact that the Prime Minister's portfolio includes everything and that junior ministers are only allowed to participate when their portfolio is at stake, less than a quarter of all the contributions bore no relation to the ministers' department.

It should be emphasised that these figures are for 1968. In those years the politicisation of the Cabinet had just begun. Unfortunately, we have no access to the most recent Cabinet minutes, but we should expect 'non-intervention' to have declined and politically-inspired contributions to the debate in Cabinet to have increased in number. Several developments point to such a politicisation of the Cabinet. In the first place there has been a change in the recruitment of ministers. As we mentioned above, only 35.2 per cent of all ministers appointed between 1848 and 1967 had been MPs, but if we extend this period to 1983, the comparable figure rises to 42.3 per cent. In Table 5.3 we present a more detailed picture of the change in ministerial recruitment.

**TABLE 5.3**
**Technical expertise and political experience**
**in ministerial (first) appointments: 1848–1986**

| Period | Percentage technical expertise | Percentage political experience | Number of cases |
|--------|-------------------------------|--------------------------------|-----------------|
| 1848–88 | 71 | 36 | 118 |
| 1888–1918 | 79 | 50 | 72 |
| 1918–40 | 72 | 41 | 61 |
| 1940–46 | 59 | 14 | 29 |
| 1946–67 | 72 | 57 | 68 |
| 1967–86 | 65 | 73 | 75 |

*Source*: Bakema and Secker (1988).

As ministers may have both specialist qualifications and political credentials, the figures for any given period add up to more than 100 per cent. Political experience is defined broadly, and is not limited to membership of Parliament. It is interesting to note that only since 1967 is the percentage of political appointments higher than that of technical appointments. The year 1967 is usually associated with the beginning of the end of pillarisation. It may be that with the demise of pillarisation the need for 'government above politics' also declined.

There was a second development in the 1960s; since then the coalition agreement has gradually gained in importance as a political contract. Here the 1963 programme marks the beginning of the politicisation of the Cabinet. For that time, the agreement was uncommonly detailed, and the governing parties considered themselves bound to it. The programme was also referred to more often in Cabinet meetings. In the nearly four years of the De Quay Cabinet

(1959–63), the Cabinet minutes mention the government's pro-gramme only six times. During the less than two years of the Marijnen Cabinet (1963–5), the programme was mentioned at least 28 times in the Cabinet minutes. Since then, the government programme has not only increased in size and detail, but has been adhered to more and more strictly.

A third contribution to politicising the Cabinet is that an elaborate system of weekly political consultations has developed, in which party leaders meet with the party's ministers to prepare that week's Cabinet meeting. In the 1950s and 1960s, for example, the entire Cabinet met once a week informally for dinner. Only on the day of the Cabinet meeting itself did ministers from each governing party lunch separately. As a first sign of the 'politicisation' of the Cabinet, it became customary for the parliamentary leader of a governing party to attend his party's ministers' lunch. The lunch then became so important that decisions were seldom taken in the Cabinet's morning session. In 1973 the lunch was replaced by a dinner on the eve of the Cabinet meeting, during which a party's ministers, junior ministers, the party's leader in the Second Chamber of Parliament (and sometimes also the party's leader in the First Chamber and the party chairperson) discuss the next day's Cabinet agenda. Occasion-ally party discipline is enforced, and the decision taken by Cabinet differs from the one that would have emerged had all ministers followed their individual judgment.

The open surge barrier in the Scheldt estuary is probably the biggest monument to the politicisation of the Dutch Cabinet. After the 1953 flooding it was decided to close the estuary completely with dams that would reduce the risk of another inundation. In the early 1970s, as the time approached to build the final and largest dam at the mouth of the Easterscheldt, conservationists argued against the construction of a dam and in favour of a surge barrier that would be open to the tides in fair weather, but could be closed in case of a storm. The Den Uyl Cabinet (1973–7) had to choose between the less costly closed dam, advocated by the government's own specialists, and the much more expensive open surge barrier. The Cabinet was a coalition of coalitions: ten ministers from PvdA, PPR, and D66 formed a 'progressive' bloc, and six ministers from KVP and ARP formed a Christian Democratic bloc. If all ministers had followed their own judgment, all the Christian Democratic ministers and a minority of the progressive ministers would have constituted a

Cabinet majority in favour of simply closing the estuary. Within the progressive bloc, however, the majority in favour of the open surge barrier used the Thursday evening dinner to impose its will on the other progressive ministers. When, on the eve of the crucial Cabinet meeting, the Social Democratic Finance Minister gave in to party pressure, the ranks had closed and a whipped vote produced a ten to six majority in favour of the open surge barrier. Other, though less spectacular, examples of the politicisation of the Cabinet could be given. As we shall see in the next chapter, this development is closely linked to changes in the relationship between government and Parliament.

Despite the growing influence of the parties on the Cabinet, it is probably still fair to say, as former Prime Minister Drees did in 1965, that 'functional [i.e., departmental] conflicts tend to be more important than political conflicts'. Nevertheless, today's ministers wear two hats, and this does complicate decision-making from time to time. In 1989 the Lubbers II Cabinet fell because of a disagreement with the VVD over the financial aspects of an environmental protection plan. Most of the Liberal ministers in the Cabinet had treated this issue as a purely interdepartmental conflict in which they did not want to take sides, whilst their parliamentary party was treating it as a political conflict. They realised that they had put on the wrong hats only when it was too late. It has proven particularly difficult to improve coordination mechanisms inside the Cabinet because of the combined problems of departmental envy and political jealousy. In the 1965 government formation the party leaders agreed that the new Cabinet should have a 'presidium' or inner Cabinet, consisting of the Prime Minister and one minister from each of the other governing parties. This would facilitate political coordination, and was acceptable to all governing parties (as they would all be represented in this presidium). It was, however, not acceptable to all departments, as some departments would, but others would not, be represented. At the very first meeting of this Cabinet it was voted down because of departmental jealousy. Strengthening the Prime Minister to improve coordination between departments is less controversial among ministers because the Prime Minister has no departmental interests himself. Any suggestions in this direction, however, meet with political jealousy from the other governing parties.

The fact that the Dutch Cabinet is both a board of departmental ministers and a coalition of political parties also has its advantages. Ministers are moderated in their pursuit of narrow departmental interests by political cross-pressures. Parties are kept informed about departments headed by ministers from other parties because junior ministers from one party are sometimes appointed as 'watchdogs' at a department of another party's minister. Often they do not really operate as such, but rather provide a channel of communication between their department and the ministers from their party. Deadlocks may be broken by transforming a departmental issue into a political one, or vice versa. Trench warfare between the departments of Justice and of Internal Affairs for years prevented a planned reorganisation of the Dutch police force. Only after the governing parties agreed to a political solution in 1989 could the reorganisation be realised. Similarly, for decades abortion seemed an insoluble political conflict, until the Van Agt I Cabinet (1977–81) delegated the search for a compromise to the two departmental ministers involved (Justice and Health). Thus depoliticised, it proved easier to find a solution on which new legislation was eventually based.

In the past, the consensus-seeking that is so characteristic of consociational democracy took place in all sorts of institutions throughout society. The breakdown of pillarisation has not led to a demise of consensus-seeking, but it seems to have concentrated consensus-seeking in the Cabinet. The fact that the Cabinet has become a dual institution, in which both sectoral interests and political ideologies have to be reconciled, has increased its importance in the Dutch political system. It has also reinforced the tradition of collective and collegial government. In that sense, the Dutch Cabinet probably comes closer to the ideal of Cabinet government than governments in many other countries.

# 6

# Parliament

Once sworn in by the Queen, the Dutch Cabinet is dependent for its survival on the continued confidence of a majority in the States-General, the bicameral Parliament of the Netherlands. If the fact that Parliament can dismiss a government is to be taken as the defining factor for a parliamentary system, then the Netherlands must be placed in this category. Nevertheless, there are features of the Dutch Constitution which are more characteristic of presidential systems than parliamentary systems. In discussions among Dutch constitutional experts and parliamentary historians, the focus is on the question of whether the relationship between the Crown and the States-General is 'monistic' or 'dualistic'. 'Monism' refers to the absence of a clear distinction between Parliament and Cabinet, as one would expect in a parliamentary system, whereas 'dualism' is meant to describe the situation in which government and Parliament have distinctive roles and responsibilities, more akin to what one would find in a presidential system.

One important feature indicating this dualistic relationship was mentioned in the previous chapter: the position of government minister is incompatible with membership in Parliament. MPs who are recruited as ministers must resign their seats.

A second dualistic feature emphasises the independence of the Cabinet. The Queen appoints the Cabinet and, although it is dependent upon parliamentary support for its survival, no formal vote of investiture is necessary.

The architecture of the chambers of the two houses of Parliament symbolises this dualism (see Exhibit 6.1). Ministers are seated behind a separate table, facing the MPs (see Figure 6.1). The new building

135

**EXHIBIT 6.1**

**The interior design of the Second Chamber of Parliament**

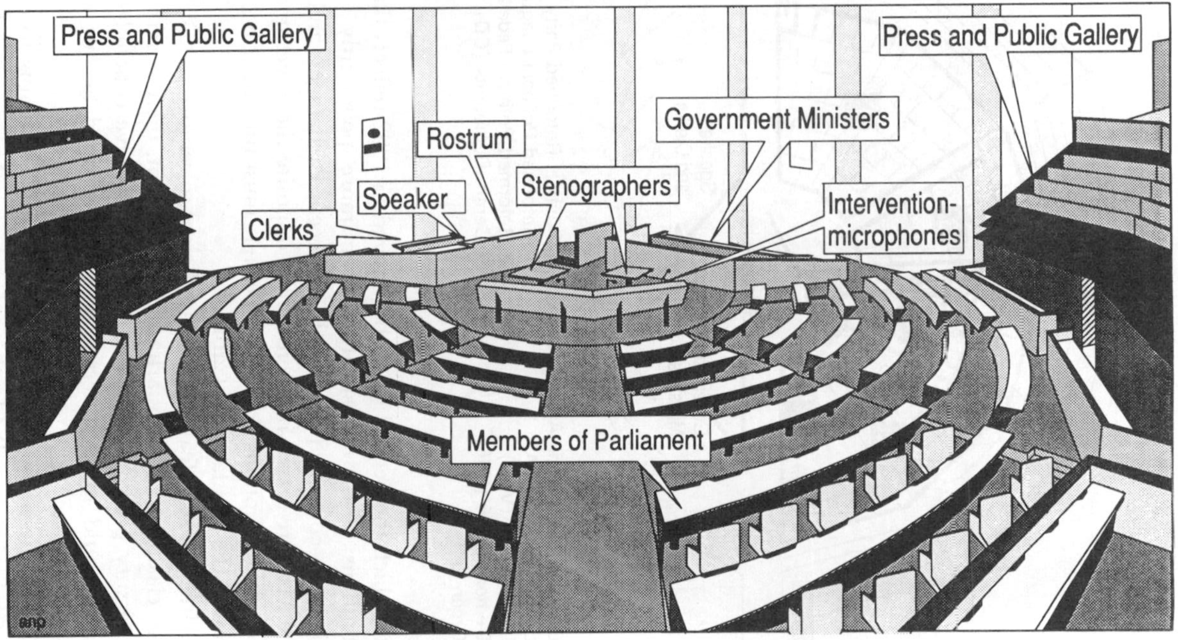

Press and Public Gallery

Intervention-microphones

Government Ministers

Stenographers

Rostrum

Speaker

Clerks

Members of Parliament

Press and Public Gallery

**FIGURE 6.1**
**Seating arrangements in the Second Chamber of Parliament**

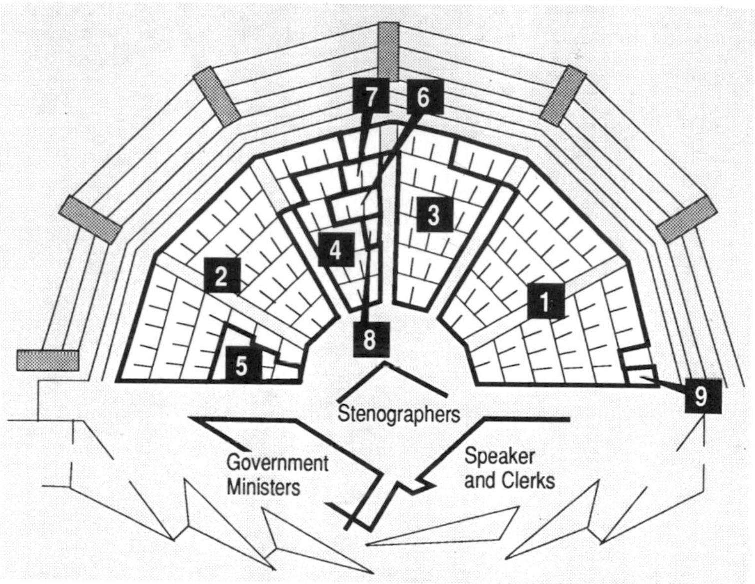

| | |
|---|---|
| 1 Christian Democratic Appeal (CDA) | 6 Political Reformed Party (SGP) |
| 2 Labour Party (PvdA) | 7 Reformed Political League (GPV) |
| 3 Liberal Party (VVD) | 8 Reformed Political Federation (RPF) |
| 4 Democrats '66 (D66) | 9 Centre Democrats (CD) |
| 5 Green Left | |

into which the Second Chamber moved in 1992 reflects the dualistic intentions of the Constitution even more poignantly. Debate is primarily construed as debate between Parliament and Cabinet. The MPs are seated in a semi-circle opposite the government's table and, if interruptions are made, speakers must turn their backs to their fellow MPs and face the Cabinet.

Although such features are insufficient to remove the Dutch system from classification as a parliamentary system, there is certainly some ambiguity present. Most Dutch observers have concluded that the system could in their terms best be described as one of 'limited dualism'.

The same ambiguity is evident in other attempts to classify the Dutch Parliament. Polsby, for example, has drawn a useful distinction between parliaments as transformative institutions, and parliaments as arenas. In transformative parliaments, the internal institutional structures and procedures affect the behaviour of the MPs and the outcome of the legislative process. Parliaments of the arena variety do not affect policy-making in this way, but offer a platform on which outside forces, primarily governments and political parties, may try to exert their influence. Polsby describes the US Congress – a parliament in a system of separation of powers – as a transformative institution, and the British House of Commons – a parliament in a parliamentary system – as an arena. Given the Dutch attempt to combine aspects of both parliamentary and presidential systems, it is not surprising that Polsby describes the Dutch Parliament as a moderately transformative institution (Polsby, 1975, pp. 292, 296).

In this chapter we shall discuss the position of the States-General *vis-à-vis* government in the light of these theoretical dichotomies. We shall argue that there has been a long-term development from Parliament as an institution to Parliament as an arena, but that this development is incomplete, so that the contemporary States-General has several appearances: institution, arena, and market. But first we shall briefly introduce the Dutch Parliament's organisation and procedures.

## Parliamentary Organisation and Procedures

Although the Dutch Parliament is still officially called the States-General, and proudly celebrated its 500th anniversary in 1964, it bears little resemblance to its feudal and Republican predecessors. The National Assembly during the French occupation (1795–1813) or the first Parliaments of the Kingdom of the Netherlands probably provide a more useful starting point for a discussion of the development of the Dutch Parliament. In searching for the roots of the modern Parliament it is symbolic that Parliament's most important House, confusingly named the Second Chamber, until very recently convened not in the hall where earlier the Republican States-General met, but in the ballroom converted for use by the National Assembly of the French period.

Originally a unicameral Parliament, the First Chamber, or Senate, was added in 1815, as a direct result of the short-lived merger of the Netherlands and Belgium (see Chapter 1). In contrast to the south there was less nobility in the north. Soil conditions in the once powerful provinces of Holland and Zeeland were not conducive to a landed gentry, and the absence of a monarch had prevented the creation of new peers for two centuries. Both factors did not apply to the Austrian Netherlands, where the nobility had fared better. The southern aristocracy was not content with merely being one of the estates represented in the States-General, as was the northern tradition. Thus a First Chamber was created, its members appointed for life by the King. Although Belgium became independent in 1830, the First Chamber remained a feature of the Dutch system.

The most important moment in the development of Parliament came in 1848 when, in reaction to the wave of revolts that had spread across Europe in that year, various reforms were introduced that set down the basic relationship between Crown, Cabinet, Parliament, and the people. Prior to 1848 the Second Chamber had consisted of delegations from the provinces; subsequently members were elected directly by the people. From that date ministers were to be held responsible to Parliament, rather than to the King alone. The ability of the King to appoint members of the First Chamber was replaced by election by the provincial legislatures. The powers of Parliament were expanded by giving the Second Chamber the right to amend bills rather than merely accept or reject them as previously, and control over an annual budget.

Some years would pass, however, before these fundamental reforms would become fully effective. The right of citizens to participate in direct parliamentary elections was severely restricted and only slowly extended until, as we saw in Chapter 4, suffrage became virtually universal in 1919. Parliament itself began to assert its new rights based on ministerial responsibility only gradually. Between 1866 and 1868 a number of conflicts occurred that settled some of the remaining ambiguities regarding the new powers: ministers were also held to account for the King's remaining prerogatives, and Parliament could not be dissolved more than once for the same reason.

Since 1848 the formal organisation and procedures of Parliament have changed little. There have been minor reforms, such as the enlargement of the Second Chamber from 100 to 150 members and of the First Chamber from 50 to 75 members in 1956, and the development of a committee system, but the only major reform has been in its method of election. As we noted in Chapter 4, with the introduction of universal suffrage all electoral districts were abolished and nationwide PR was introduced. Compared with parliaments elsewhere, the absence of any form of geographical representation in the States-General is one of its most striking characteristics, and has important consequences for parliamentary behaviour.

*The Structure of Parliament*

*The First Chamber.* Although the First Chamber (or Senate) was introduced during the short-lived union with Belgium, after the latter's independence the First Chamber remained. Since then the bicameral structure of the Dutch Parliament has been controversial, and proposals to eliminate it have frequently been made. Until now, however, such proposals have never met with success, in part because the First Chamber must assent to its own abolition.

The First Chamber is not directly elected by the voters, but by the members of the provincial legislatures. The members of all provincial legislatures form an electoral college by which the Senate is elected under a system of PR very similar to that used for the Second Chamber. The political parties present their lists of candidates to this college and strict party discipline is enforced during the elections. There is no electoral campaign and, except for honest mistakes or an occasional rebel, the outcome of the election is a foregone conclusion. The composition of the First Chamber thus indirectly reflects the size of the parties at the provincial elections. Despite their election by the provincial legislatures, members of the First Chamber in no way represent the various provinces.

Since a constitutional revision in 1983 the 'elections' for the First Chamber are no longer staggered; the entire Senate is elected at once. This election takes place therefore once every four years, soon after the newly elected Provincial Councils have first met. As the provincial elections do not coincide with the elections for the Second Chamber, the political composition of the two chambers can be different. In recent history, however, the governing parties have always held a majority in the First as well as in the Second Chamber.

Despite its appellation as 'First' and its unofficial title of 'Senate', the First Chamber is secondary in importance to the directly elected Second Chamber, which is the real political arena. In contrast to the full-time members of the Second Chamber, Senators are part-time politicians, usually meeting only one day a week. They have no personal staff, and are paid only a per diem in addition to expenses.

Although the First Chamber has the same powers of governmental oversight as the Second Chamber, it concentrates almost exclusively on legislation. However, lacking the right to initiate or amend bills, the First Chamber is primarily a chamber of revision. To its critics, the Senate can do no good. If it accepts the legislative proposals already approved by the Second Chamber, it is said to be redundant. If it rejects legislative proposals it is accused of encroaching on the primacy of the directly elected Second Chamber.

Since the First Chamber may make no amendments to a bill, there is no need for a procedure to iron out differences between the bills as they are adopted by the two Houses. Even if Senators discover technical errors in a bill, or have objection to only part of the proposal, their only choice is either to swallow their reservations, or to reject the bill in its entirety. For example, in 1976, a number of Liberal Senators were opposed to the period of pregnancy during which abortion would be allowed under new legislation initiated in and approved by the Second Chamber. Lacking the opportunity to propose amendments, they voted with opponents and the bill was rejected. Sometimes the First Chamber 'usurps' the power of amendment by threatening to reject a bill unless the minister promises to interpret the bill in a specific way, or even to introduce a new bill modifying some aspects of the bill under consideration. In recent years, this has led to renewed proposals to give the Second Chamber the power to override a Senate veto by a simple majority. It is doubtful, however, whether the First Chamber will consent to a weakening of its absolute veto into a suspensive veto.

*Parliamentary committees.*   Both Houses of Parliament have always known a committee system, with only minor differences between the two Houses. Here we look primarily at the committees in the more important Second Chamber. Between 1848 and 1953, with only minor modifications, a simple committee system was in effect. The Second Chamber was divided into five general committees, composed three times a year by drawing lots. Each committee examined all bills submitted. After consideration, each committee assigned a *rapporteur* to convey its findings to a central committee consisting of all committee chairmen and the Speaker.

After 1888 more specialised select committees gradually developed next to these five standing committees. Finally, in 1953 the old standing committees were abolished and the select committees took over the consideration of bills. There are probably two causes for this development: first, it was felt that the ever more detailed and technical proposals from the government required a level of specialisation from MPs that could not be guaranteed by randomly composed committees; and second, the more general political discussion of new bills had gradually moved from the standing committees to meetings of the newly developing parliamentary parties.

Today there are nearly 40 committees in the Second Chamber, more than 30 of which are permanent. The committee system reflects the structure of the bureaucracy, with most government departments being monitored by two or three parliamentary committees. In addition there are a few committees with more general tasks, such as the Committee on Petitions, or the Committee on Parliamentary Procedure. In general, committees have a function with regard to legislation as well as oversight of governmental activity. However, when a particular governmental action seems to require more extensive investigation, a special Committee of Parliamentary Inquiry is set up exclusively to investigate a particular policy.

Officially, the Speaker appoints the members of committees, but in practice he is left little choice. The partisan composition of committees is roughly proportional to the strength of the parties in the Chamber, although special consideration is given to the smaller parties. The smaller parties are often given latitude in the choice of committees on which they wish to serve. Once the party composition is known, the leader of each parliamentary party nominates his party's representatives. Proportional representation also dictates the distribution of committee chairpersons over the parties, and chairpersons may come from opposition as well as government parties. The leaders of the parliamentary parties meet informally to discuss which party will get which chairs. One of the considerations appears to be that the committee chairperson should be of a different party from the minister whose policies the committee is supposed to oversee.

*Parliamentary Procedures*

*Legislation.* The Constitution stipulates that legislation is a joint venture of Crown and States-General. With the exception of a few bills that can be introduced only by the government (most notably the budget), both ministers and Second Chamber MPs have the right to initiate legislation. Although there are no formal or informal limitations on the introduction of private members' bills, the number proposed is quite small and in practice the vast majority of bills originate in the Cabinet. During the readings in the Second Chamber members may introduce amendments that can be adopted by a simple majority. If a minister has introduced a bill, the government is allowed to alter (or even to withdraw) its proposal up until the final vote is taken in the Second Chamber. The bill is then referred to the First Chamber where, as we just noted, it can only be adopted or rejected.

Once adopted by both Houses, a bill must be signed by the Queen and countersigned by a minister before it is promulgated. In 1976 the Minister of Justice, a Christian Democrat, threatened to withhold his signature from any bill liberalising abortion. Although such a refusal is constitutional, political conflict or even crisis would undoubtedly ensue. So far, no such incident has occurred; in the case mentioned the rejection by the Senate of the proposed bill headed off an otherwise inevitable conflict.

Whether or not the Queen may refuse to sign a bill is less clear. In general, her political role is similar to that of other constitutional monarchs, with a possible exception for Cabinet formations (see Chapter 5). No situation comparable to the Belgian King Baudouin's refusal to sign an abortion bill in 1990 has ever occurred in the Netherlands. It is well known that the former Queen Juliana refused to agree to the execution of a number of German war criminals who had been sentenced to death. The government then prevented a constitutional crisis by commuting the sentences to life imprisonment. There are, however, no known cases of bills which, having been passed by both Houses, have met with a royal refusal. This is not necessarily because the Queen exercises no influence on legislation or has no opinions, but because she provides the government with ample prior warning concerning her views. In the early 1970s, for example, the Biesheuvel Cabinet suddenly and without apparent reason withdrew a bill regulating ministerial responsibility for members of the royal family. It is highly probable that the Queen had announced her intention not to sign the bill, and that the Cabinet preferred to have no legislation rather than an open constitutional conflict.

The procedure for changing the Constitution is only slightly more complicated than that for passing legislation. According to the constitutional procedure, after a constitutional amendment has been adopted by both Houses, Parliament is dissolved and new elections are held so as to give the electorate an opportunity to voice its opinion on the change. The newly elected Parliament must then adopt the amendment by a two-thirds majority. Theoretically, this gives the electorate a voice and potential veto. In practice, parliamentary dissolutions for reasons of constitutional revision are timed to coincide with regular parliamentary elections. Amendments are first adopted at the end of a parliamentary period just preceding regular elections. Discussions of constitutional amendments have never played a role in election campaigns, and it is likely that the electorate is completely unaware that it is passing judgment upon constitutional amendments as well as electing new representatives.

Dutch legislative procedures do not deviate widely from what is customary in most parliamentary systems. There is, however, one aspect that may be more idiosyncratic. In most countries bills die after a dissolution of Parliament. In the Netherlands, once introduced, bills never die. On average, about 250 bills are introduced each year and take 14 months before they are adopted by the Senate. However, there is no official time limit to the legislative process for a particular bill, the record being 26 years! Although the fact that bills can survive governments or Parliaments may seem a minor detail, its importance lies in the fact that the government is usually not under any time pressure with regard to its legislative programme, and therefore has no need to intervene in the agenda of Parliament. It is the Speaker and the Presidium of the House who set the agenda, without the kind of government interference that is customary in most parliamentary systems.

*Oversight.* Parliamentary oversight is based on Article 42 of the Constitution: 'The Government shall comprise the King and the Ministers. The Ministers, and not the King, shall be responsible for acts of government'. It is to Parliament that the ministers are thus responsible. Parliament can ask for information, which the government is not allowed to refuse, except for *'raison d'état'*. Written questions are the most widely used means to obtain information. Oral questions (or, more accurately, oral answers to written questions) also exist, but are used more for political purposes than the acquisition of factual information. The same applies to emergency debates, or interpellations, during which there is an opportunity for other MPs to join the debate once the minister has answered the question of one of their colleagues.

In terms of oversight, there is no formal distinction between the First and the Second Chamber, but in practice it is the Second Chamber where most of the relevant activities take place. Each House also has the power to collect its own information by calling for a Parliamentary Inquiry. An *ad hoc* Parliamentary Committee is then set up, with far-reaching powers: hearing witnesses under oath, and even imprisoning witnesses who refuse to testify. In the history of the Dutch Parliament only 13 such Parliamentary Inquiries have been held, probably because a majority of Parliament is needed for setting up an Inquiry. Attempts to give minorities of one-fifth or one-third of the members the right to a Parliamentary Inquiry have been vetoed by the First Chamber, even though that house has itself never held an Inquiry.

Parliament may adopt resolutions (or motions) at any time: for example, when it deems a minister's answer unsatisfactory. Any MP is allowed to introduce a motion, as long as it is seconded by at least four other MPs. Motions adopted are not binding on the government, and ministers do occasionally ignore them. During the Vietnam war, the Second Chamber several times adopted a motion requesting the Foreign Affairs Minister to protest to the American government, but the long-serving and wily Minister Luns always refused to do so.

It is generally accepted that a motion of no confidence, if adopted, cannot be ignored and must result in the resignation of the minister or of the Cabinet as a whole, or in the dissolution of Parliament. This rule is not to be found in the Constitution. Actually, nowhere does the Constitution mention that Cabinet needs the confidence of Parliament, and votes of confidence do not even exist. Perhaps for that reason, Parliament has in the past occasionally used other means to unseat a minister, such as rejection of his budget, or lowering his salary by one, very symbolic, guilder. Sometimes it is not even clear whether a motion is a censure motion or not. In 1966 the Cabinet stepped down after a motion criticising the government's financial policy was adopted, even though the MP who led the critics always maintained that it was not intended as a motion of no confidence. In 1981 the adoption of a motion led to a debate on whether it was a motion of no confidence or not. To end the confusion, the MP who had introduced the controversial motion introduced a second one, stating that the first motion was indeed intended to censure the government. The House then rejected this second motion. The ambiguity over censure motions has no real significance, but does symbolise the fact that the Dutch Parliamentary system has a touch of separation of powers.

## Executive–Legislative Relations

*From Institution to Arena*

These institutional characteristics of the Dutch Parliament, and the formal powers of 'the' Parliament *vis-à-vis* 'the' government were shaped before political parties were formed. As has been noted, Parliament has changed little since 1848, whereas the first political party, the ARP was founded only in 1879 (see Chapter 3). Before disciplined parties were formed, there was no coherent majority in the Second Chamber to sustain 'its' ministers for the duration of a Parliament. Instead, more or less *ad hoc* majorities had to be put together on each issue. In the absence of parties, the King continued to determine the composition of Cabinets to a considerable extent. This royal (and indirectly, through the monarch, even divine) legitimation in a sense 'elevated' the Cabinet above Parliament. The separation of powers was further emphasised because the very position of Parliament *vis-à-vis* the King and his ministers was one of the major political issues of the period between the shaping of Parliament and the forming of political parties.

When political parties developed around the turn of the century, they gradually wrested the power to form a government away from the monarch. When, for example, the Queen tried to reinstate the royal Cabinet formation in 1939, her ministers were censured at their first appearance in Parliament. However, for some time the parties in Parliament were content with their new role in the formation of Cabinets, and did not extend their influence to the government once formed.

In the previous chapter we mentioned the relatively apolitical recruitment criteria for ministers, the taboo on contacts between ministers and their fellow party members in Parliament, etc. There we also discussed possible causes of this curious self-restraint on the part of the parties in Parliament, such as the 'rules of the game' of consociational democracy. Here it is important to note that the notion of Parliament as an institution, as a collective body, confronting another institution, the government, survived the formation of disciplined political parties longer than in many other countries. However, as the basic unit of Parliament was no longer the individual member but the parliamentary party (or 'fraction', as it is referred to in Dutch), conflicts between ministers and their own parliamentary party were not uncommon. In the post-war period, at least two Cabinet crises resulted from such intra party conflict. In 1951 the Liberal Party in Parliament introduced a motion of no confidence aimed at the plans for the decolonisation of Dutch New Guinea of the Liberal Minister of Foreign Affairs. This led to the resignation of the entire Cabinet. In 1960 the Cabinet resigned when the ARP introduced a motion of no confidence in reaction to the plans of its own Minister of Housing. However, when individual ministers have been forced to resign because of criticism in Parliament, the victim's party normally has chosen to replace him rather than escalate the conflict into a full-blown Cabinet crisis. After all, the minister was often a political outsider, and the parliamentary party had not been consulted in advance about the issue that led to the unfortunate minister's downfall. The prestige of the party was thus not at stake.

In Chapter 5 we also described how the Cabinet was gradually politicised from the 1960s onwards. Ministers without previous parliamentary experience have become less common; weekly consultations between a governing party's ministers and its parliamentary leaders have been set up, and the coalition programme has gained in importance, binding not only the ministers but also the parliamentary parties making up the governmental majority. By 1979, 68 per cent of all MPs interviewed in a survey agreed with the statement that 'Government policy is formed in close consultation and cooperation with the parliamentary parties in the governmental majority.' Of all MPs 84 per cent agreed that 'More than in the past, the government is dependent on what the parliamentary parties in the governmental majority want.' Party discipline has increased significantly, although it is difficult to gauge actual party unanimity accurately as roll calls are rare and thus possible dissenters not registered. The Proceedings of the Second Chamber normally record the votes of parliamentary parties rather than of individual MPs. The Dutch political scientist, Wolters, has argued that this practice suggests a low level of intra party dissension, and cites estimates of party unanimity of 92–98 per cent during the 1967–71 Parliament (Wolters, 1984, pp. 182–5). Obviously, party discipline is strongest when agreements made between the parties during the Cabinet's formation or the weekly consultations are at stake. The government can, therefore, count on a loyal and firm majority; on average, less than one government bill per year is defeated in the Second Chamber.

As a result, the characteristic lines of conflict are now between parties, rather than between the institutions of Parliament and government, pitting ministers and MPs of one party against (ministers and) MPs of another party. Of these lines of conflict, the one between ministers plus MPs of the governing parties on the one hand, and opposition MPs on the other hand, is most visible, but also rather sterile in terms of policy outcome. By definition, the opposition is a minority, and therefore powerless except for the rare occasion when a wedge can be driven between the governing parties. Conflicts between the governing parties, both in government and Parliament, are much more interesting, as the outcome is less predictable and directly affects government policy.

This shift has reduced the importance of the elements of a separation of powers in the Dutch constitution. In the language of Dutch constitutional law, executive–legislative relations have become more 'monistic' and less 'dualistic'. This development has had important consequences. Beginning in 1965 we have seen a new type of Cabinet crisis, which did not occur previously, in which the Cabinet falls after a conflict along party lines *within* the Cabinet (e.g., 1965, 1972, 1977, 1981, 1982). Moreover, individual ministers are no longer censured by a parliamentary majority. In the past a parliamentary party often accepted, albeit grudgingly, the forced resignation of one of its appointees. Now that ministers tend to be prominent party members, and the parliamentary party is always consulted and involved in advance, to repudiate a party's minister is to repudiate that party itself. If a minister is forced to withdraw from the Cabinet, his party is likely to withdraw from the coalition, thereby bringing down the whole Cabinet. This forces the other coalition parties to choose between criticism of an individual minister and the survival of the Cabinet, with generally predictable results. The first case in which this mechanism prevented the censure of an individual minister occurred in 1977 when a Catholic Minister of Justice was accused of being responsible, through personal negligence, for the escape of an alleged (later convicted) war criminal. The spokesman for one of the other coalition parties, the Social Democrats, doubted the minister's capabilities for leading a department, but refused to support a motion of no confidence:

> We have judged this minister as Minister of Justice. He is more. He is the Deputy Prime Minister, he is a member of this Cabinet. As such he is a partner in compromises that we have made. That is what we have to consider. That is what is on the scales. If we weigh that, we can come to no other conclusion [than to refrain from censuring this minister].

Since 1977 there have been several similar cases. There is currently some debate among constitutional lawyers as to whether ministerial responsibility to Parliament is still effective now that Parliament seems unable, or unwilling, to apply the ultimate sanction of a vote of no confidence. Undoubtedly the separation of powers has decreased, and the Dutch system has moved towards a more typical parliamentary system. Today, Parliament is less an institution confronting other institutions and more an arena in which political parties try to influence government policy. This development is sometimes depicted as one of the factors contributing to a 'decline of Parliament'.

### The Paradox of Parliamentary Activism

Paradoxically, however, at the same time that Parliament operates less as an institution and is supposed to be in decline, Parliament has become noticeably more active. Although recent years show a development towards somewhat less hectic parliamentary years, the overall trend is clearly in the direction of heightened·activity. There has been only a slight increase in the annual number of plenary sessions, but the number of committee meetings has trebled since the early 1960s (see Table 6.1). The number of amendments to bills has risen from between one and two hundred to over a thousand per year. The number of amendments receiving majority approval has kept pace with the increase in amendments introduced. In addition to a small rise in the number of interpellations, there has been a spectacular rise in the number of written parliamentary questions, as well as motions introduced and adopted. There has been an increase in the number of private member bills from a total of merely 8 in the period between 1945 and 1965 to 93 between 1965 and 1985.

## TABLE 6.1

Use made of assorted parliamentary rights (average per year during four year periods, 1956–89)

| Period | Meetings | | Legislation | | | Oversight | | |
|---|---|---|---|---|---|---|---|---|
| | Plenary | Committee | Total number of bills introduced | Private member bills | Amendments introduced | Written questions | Interpellations | Motions introduced |
| 1956–60 | 74 | 273 | (258) | 0 | 101 | 228 | 6 | – |
| 1960–4 | 79 | 354 | (252) | 1 | 187 | 268* | 5 | 20* |
| 1964–8 | 58 | 368 | (282) | 1 | 150 | 621* | 3 | 63* |
| 1968–72 | 87 | 639 | (276) | 7 | 262 | 1389* | 15 | 171* |
| 1972–6 | 100 | 597 | (274) | 3 | 493 | 1498* | 12 | 249* |
| 1976–80 | 94 | 736 | (303) | 5 | 728 | 1532* | 15 | 639 |
| 1980–4 | 96 | 1124 | (322) | 4 | 1483 | 1305* | 15 | 831* |
| 1984–8 | 102 | 1286 | (266) | 7 | 1460 | 1011 | 15 | 597 |
| 1988–9 | 93 | 1062 | (305) | 7 | 1217 | 796 | 9 | 409 |

*Note:* The number of 'Bills introduced' encompasses bills introduced by the government and private members' bills.

*Sources:* asterisked figures from G. Visscher, 'De Staten Generaal' in H. Daalder and A. Nauta (eds) *Compendium voor Politiek en Samenleving in Nederland* (Houten: Bohn Stafleu Van Loghum, 1986); all other figures from Central Bureau of Statistics, *Statistisch Jaarboek* (The Hague, various years).

There has also been an interesting rediscovery of the Parliamentary Inquiry. Between 1848 and 1887 eight such Inquiries took place, but thereafter this powerful parliamentary weapon fell into abeyance for nearly a century with only one exception: an Inquiry that was held in 1947–8 to investigate the government's activities while in exile during the Second World War. Recently, in a ten-year interval, four new Parliamentary Inquiries were held: into government subsidies to the shipbuilding industry (1982–3); into housing subsidies (1986–7); into the failure to develop a new tamper-proof passport (1987–8); and into the implementation of social insurance programmes (1992–3). Moreover, the nature of the Inquiry has changed. Whereas the nineteenth century Inquiries dealt with social problems (contagious cattle diseases, working conditions in factories), recent Inquiries have tended to investigate government fiascos. Two Inquiries even led, directly or indirectly, to the resignations of one Cabinet minister and two junior ministers.

Several factors have probably contributed to this increased parliamentary activism. The development of the welfare state involves more government intervention, and hence more work for Parliament. MPs are better educated than they were in earlier times, and they are better paid, allowing them to function as full-time professional politicians. There is also more staff available, for each House as a whole, for the parliamentary parties, and for individual MPs. In 1960 the States-General had a budget of only 5 million guilders for its own activities; in 1986 this figure had risen to over 98 million guilders (a substantial increase even in the face of inflation). Some authors have pointed to the fact that the political climate has become more volatile, so that MPs have to be more active, constantly jockeying to improve their chances for renomination and reelection.

All this sounds plausible enough, but does not explain the paradox of a simultaneous decline of Parliament, due to 'monism', and increased parliamentary activity. There seem to be two rival explanations for this paradox. One argues that the decline of Parliament is more apparent than real and that, in fact, the opposite is the case; parliamentary activism has strengthened Parliament *vis-à-vis* the government. Because of more intensive parliamentary oversight, the ultimate sanction of censuring a Cabinet or a minister no longer needs application and, because of the increase in amendments and private members bills, it is no longer necessary to defeat the government on a bill. In short: barking dogs do not bite, because their bark is a sufficient deterrent. According to this explanation the separation of powers has not disappeared; Parliament as an institution is still alive and kicking.

It is difficult to disprove this theory; much of it hinges on the assumption that ministers, more nowadays than in the past, avoid antagonising Parliament. The 'law of anticipated reactions', however, is difficult to prove. There seems to be more evidence for a second explanation, which takes the opposite view: the dogs are barking more because they are no longer allowed to bite. It is interesting to note that more than half of all censure motions introduced since 1848 were introduced after 1971, after which date neither Cabinets nor even individual ministers have been brought down by a vote of no confidence. This second explanation is also supported by the fact that, although parties become more active when they move from a governmental to an opposition role, and less active when they move from opposition to governing coalition, parliamentary activism cannot be accounted for entirely by the opposition. MPs in the governmental majority have also become more active: for them barking is the only activity allowed. It has even been argued that increased parliamentary activism has contributed to the 'decline of Parliament', as it has led to an 'inflation' of parliamentary powers. In the past the mere introduction of a motion was an important event attracting considerable attention in the daily press; today even motions that are adopted often go unnoticed by the media. Note that in this explanation of parliamentary activism Parliament as an institution has given way to Parliament as an arena.

*Parliament as a Marketplace*

The Dutch Parliament has a third appearance. In addition to the constitutional institution and the political arena, Parliament may take the form of a marketplace in which social interests are traded. Because of the electoral system, regional interests have little impact on parliamentary behaviour but socio-economic interests are well represented, and their representation does not necessarily coincide with party membership. In the parliamentary marketplace, departmental ministers and specialised MPs of all parties join forces to defend their common sectoral interests against the tradesmen with other interests. The Minister of Agriculture, together with all the parties' spokesmen on agriculture in Parliament defending the farmers' interests, is often cited in this respect. This coalition was known as the 'Green Front' long before 'green' took on another meaning, and by no means stands alone. Parliament as a marketplace takes its place in the neo-corporatist policy networks that will be described in the next chapter.

The occurrence of Parliament as a marketplace is more difficult to date than its development as an arena. Clues to its timing may be found in a few related developments. In the first place, until recently political parties, and especially Christian Democratic parties, tried to appeal to a socio-economic cross-section of the electorate by putting candidates on their list who came from various interest groups: so-called 'quality seats'. This practice became possible only after the introduction of PR and the list system of candidate nomination in 1917. By its very nature this encouraged MPs to operate as 'stallholders' for the interest group involved. The 'quality seats' are a symptom of the general emphasis placed on specialisation and specialists in Dutch political decision-making, which is also evident in the parliamentary marketplace.

Another important factor was the replacement of the non-specialised by specialised Parliamentary Committees in 1953. These specialised Committees consist primarily of MPs who are experts in the policy area concerned, sometimes because of prior activities in one of the relevant interest groups. As we have seen in Table 6.1, the number of committee meetings has increased substantially. These specialised committees are the market stalls, where the specialised tradesmen from governmental majority and opposition jointly discuss the market strategy for their common interest.

These dates, 1917 and 1953, indicate that Parliament as a marketplace seems to have coexisted with both Parliament as an institution and Parliament as an arena.

*The Coexistence of Institution, Arena, and Marketplace*

Despite its historical decline, Parliament as an institution has not vanished altogether. Actually, from a normative point of view, the institutional perspective still seems to dominate the interactions between ministers and MPs. There appears to be a remarkable gap between 'is' and 'ought' in this respect, as can be seen from Table 6.2.

**TABLE 6.2**

**MPs opinions on executive–legislative relations (1990)**

| | Who should determine the broad outlines of governmental policies? | Who actually does |
|---|---|---|
| Parliament | 28.5 | 8.1 |
| Government and Parliament | 18.2 | 4.4 |
| Government | 32.1 | 19.1 |
| Government plus parliamentary parties in the coalition | 18.2 | 55.1 |
| Government plus 'social partners' | 0.7 | 1.5 |
| Others | 2.3 | 11.8 |
| Total | 100.0 | 100.0 |
| *N* | 137 | 136 |

| | Who should judge the eventual policy outcomes? | Who actually does |
|---|---|---|
| The opposition in Parliament | 0.7 | 4.4 |
| The parliamentary parties in the coalition | – | 35.8 |
| Parliament as a whole | 94.9 | 49.6 |
| Others | 4.4 | 10.2 |
| Total | 100.0 | 100.0 |
| *N* | 138 | 137 |

*Source*: 1990 Parliamentary Study (only the answers of members of the Second Chamber are presented in this table).

Although 55 per cent of the MPs interviewed in 1990 agreed that policy is largely determined by the government plus the parliamentary parties belonging to the governing majority (as one would expect in a Parliament operating as an arena), only 18 per cent of them are of the opinion that policy ought to be determined in this fashion. There is near unanimous agreement that government should be controlled by Parliament as an institution, but the percentage drops from 95 to 50 per cent when the question deals with the practice of legislative oversight. This pattern can be observed within all parliamentary parties, although the parties with most experience in government – CDA, PvdA, and VVD – appear to be less critical of Parliament as an arena.

Parliament as an institution is not confined to the normative level only. That it coexists with Parliament as an arena or a marketplace at the empirical level can be learned from the fact that the institution is still capable of claiming victims in contemporary politics. In 1987 a Liberal minister and a Christian Democratic junior minister resigned after being criticised in the report of an all-party Parliamentary Inquiry Commission; in 1989 the Cabinet resigned after a conflict between Liberal MPs and Liberal ministers; and in 1990 a Christian Democratic Minister of Agriculture resigned when MPs of the coalition partner Labour Party threatened to support a censure motion, and his own parliamentary party refused to defend him. At the same time, however, other ministers in similar situations have successfully escaped this fate by preventing Parliament from transforming itself from arena into institution. Of the MPs interviewed in 1990, 53 per cent agreed with the statement that 'Parliamentary criticism of an individual minister too rarely leads to the minister's dismissal.' A minister's career is not cut short merely by the size of his failure, but probably also by the fact that he has become politically expendable in his own party.

The fact that separation of powers seems to have survived Primarily in Parliamentary Inquiries indicates that the kind of issue most likely to be dealt with by Parliament as an institution is a scandal or a policy fiasco. Parliament might also take this form when its position as a constitutional institution is at stake (as when the government tried, some years ago, to cut the budget of the States-General), when novice ministers do not abide by 'the rules of this House', or when ministers are reluctant to give an MP the information he or she asks for. If the form Parliament takes depends on the type of issue on the agenda, Parliament can be expected to take the form of a marketplace in the specialised parliamentary committees, when dealing with routine or technocratic matters, and generally anything involving sectoral interests which is not politically controversial. This idea that Parliament can 'shift gears' between institution, arena, and marketplace was put to MPs in the 1990 survey of parliamentary attitudes (see Table 6.3).

As can be seen from Table 6.3, 58 per cent of Second Chamber MPs agree that in general the best description of the relationship between government and Parliament is in terms of a political arena (ministers plus parliamentary parties of the governing coalition versus the opposition). That 27 per cent still describe the relationship as one

**TABLE 6.3**

**MPs' perceptions of executive–legislative relations (1990)**

|  | Best description of the relationship between Government and Parliament | | |
|---|---|---|---|
|  | In general | In budget procedures | During affairs and Inquiries |
| Cabinet v. Parliament (Parliament as institution) | 27.3 | 20.6 | 73.1 |
| Cabinet plus parliamentary parties in coalition v. opposition (Parliament as arena) | 57.6 | 49.3 | 24.6 |
| Sector specialists (MPs plus ministers) v. other sector specialists or generalists (Parliament as marketplace) | 15.2 | 30.1 | 2.3 |
| Total | 100.1 | 100.0 | 100.0 |
| $N$ | 132 | 136 | 130 |

*Source*: 1990 Parliamentary Study (only the answers of members of the Second Chamber are presented in this table).

between the institutions of Cabinet and Parliament is a sign of the continued importance of the doctrine of separation of powers in the Dutch Parliament. As expected, Parliament is seen primarily as an institution in the case of Inquiries.

Interestingly, only 15 per cent mention the marketplace. Some authors have linked the role of sectoral specialists in Parliament primarily to public finance. They complain, for example, about a 'parliamentary disease', driving public expenditure upwards: after the financial spokesmen of most parties have called for overall spending reductions, the spokesmen for each of the departmental budgets agree, but not for their particular sector (Daalder and Hubée-Boonzaaijer, 1976). One might therefore expect the market-place to be mentioned more often with respect to the annual budget proceedings in Parliament. Indeed, 30 per cent of the MPs interviewed agreed that the marketplace best describes executive–legislative relations during budget proceedings, but nearly half of the MPs feel that even then Parliament as an arena prevails. This can be explained by the fact that the marketplace is often integrated into the arena. In both the 1979 and the 1990 Parliamentary Study about 80 per cent of MPs interviewed fully agreed with the statement 'As a rule, the parliamentary party allows one considerable freedom of manoeuvre in parliamentary committees', while less than 5 per cent disagreed. At the same time, in the 1972 and 1979 studies there was widespread agreement with the statement 'As a rule, one votes according to the advice of the specialist': in 1972, 80 per cent fully agreed and 2 per cent disagreed; in 1979, 91 per cent fully agreed and only one MP disagreed. This statement was not used in the 1990 study, but it provides similar indications in the answers to a question about the centre of gravity within the parliamentary party's decision-making process: 66 per cent of the respondents mentioned the specialist or the parliamentary party's internal committee of specialists on a given issue, whereas only 26 per cent perceived the parliamentary party's plenary session, and a mere 9 per cent its leadership, as the most important factor. In other words, in parliamentary committees party discipline is relaxed, allowing MPs to operate as stallholders on a marker rather than as gladiators in an arena. As the parliamentary party usually takes its cues from its specialist(s), the marketplace then transforms into the arena. Of course, such complementarity of Parliament as an arena and Parliament as a marketplace is only possible as long as the issue involved is not central to the coalition agreement, or to the party's ideology or manifesto.

## Parliament and the People

The starting point of this chapter was the ambiguity of attempts to classify the Dutch parliamentary system as either 'dualist' or 'monist'; as a 'transformative institution', or a political 'arena'. We have shown that this ambiguity reflects the reality of Dutch parliamentary practice. It is the result of an incomplete development from Parliament as a more or less non-partisan constitutional institution to a political arena. The situation is further complicated by the existence of a third form of Parliament: the marketplace. There is still considerable normative nostalgia for Parliament as an institution. The resuscitation of Parliamentary Inquiries in the 1980s has kindled hopes for a revival of the institution. It may be argued that Parliament as a marketplace is less interesting in an era when a retreat of the state is fashionable, and budget cutbacks inevitable: the market stalls are empty. As a political arena, it may be argued further, Parliament is predictable and boring. Only as an institution may Parliament continue as the source of political legitimacy it was intended to be (Van den Berg, Elzinga and Vis, 1992, pp. 183–207).

Despite regular suggestions that people have turned their backs on parliamentary politics, in terms of the legitimation function for the democratic system, Parliament retains its fundamental role. Parliamentary debates are covered extensively by the media, including a nightly news programme showing excerpts from the day's debate when Parliament is in session. Although certainly not all MPs are familiar household names, national surveys have shown that more than 90 per cent of the populace can recognise photos and name the party of the parliamentary leaders of the major parties. When Parliament opened its doors to show its new building to the public in 1992, hundreds of thousands of visitors exceeded all expectations. Surveys held at the time showed that a vast majority of Dutch citizens still see Parliament as a cornerstone of the Dutch political system.

# 7

# The Policy-Making Process: Territorial Centralisation and Functional Decentralisation

The Dutch state was once known as the Republic of the Seven United Provinces. Today, it has occasionally jokingly been referred to as 'the Republic of the Thirteen Disunited Departments'. This chapter discusses the degree of (de)centralisation of the policy-making process, geographically as well as functionally. First, we review the role of provincial and municipal governments to see whether the Dutch political system is indeed at least as centralised as France, as it is often claimed to be. We then turn to functional decentralisation, and to the main factors that are supposed to contribute to the 'sectorisation' that characterises Dutch policy-making: neo-corporatist arrangements and the absence of a unified civil service. An evaluation of the (im)balance of decentralisation and coordination of governmental policy concludes this chapter.

## The Territorial Dimension

*Provincial Government*

The decentralisation that was characteristic of the confederal Republic was abolished during the Napoleonic occupation (1795–

158

1813) never to be reintroduced (Andeweg, 1989, pp. 42–3). It is ironic that the once sovereign provinces now form the most impotent of the three layers of government (national, provincial, and municipal). The 12 provinces have their own directly elected provincial legislatures and provincial governments but, with the exception of a few policy fields (such as physical planning and environmental protection), their independent impact on policy-making is limited. As an intermediary between local and national authorities, provincial government deals with other governments rather than with individual citizens. For the citizen, the province is important primarily as a board of appeal against decisions by municipal officials. Outside the northern and southern provinces few people identify with their province; only in the northern province of Friesland, with its own recognised language, do we find a Frisian Nationalist Party, but it is too small to overcome the low threshold for representation in the national Parliament. Traditionally there have been differences in political culture, with the Social Democrats stronger in the north-west and the Catholics stronger in the south-east, but these are decreasing rapidly.

In recent years the turn-out in provincial elections has fallen below that in municipal elections and even came close to that in elections for the European Parliament (see Figure 4.1). The first calls for the abolition of the provinces were heard. The provinces are simultaneously criticised for being too large and too small. Municipal governments have long felt the need for cooperation and the coordination of their activities with neighbouring municipalities in regions that are smaller than the current provinces. The big cities of Amsterdam, Rotterdam, The Hague, and Utrecht often view the provinces as unwelcome representatives of the small municipalities that surround them, and hinder their expansion. Since the Second World War, the creation of some form of regional (i.e. subprovincial) government has almost constantly been on the political agenda (Toonen, 1992). So far, however, fears of the complications ensuing from the creation of a fourth layer of government in what is, after all, a small country, have prevented any reform. An already existing regional authority, Rijnmond (Rotterdam and the area surrounding its seaway), was even abolished for this reason. Currently, the country is subdivided into 62 'cooperation districts' of neighbouring municipalities, but these districts have no democratic legitimation or formal powers.

Although the provinces may be too large to function efficiently as regional governments within the Netherlands, from a European perspective they are too small. Some of the Dutch provinces have established their own offices in Brussels to lobby for their interests, but they find it difficult to get official recognition. The territorial unit that the EC Commission is using as a basis for its active policy of regional development, the 'Euregio', is much larger than even the largest of the Dutch provinces. Currently, the Netherlands is one of the few EC member states without Euregios. It has been proposed to treat the whole country as a single Euregio, but it is more likely that the current provinces will be combined into three or four Euregios. Some of the provinces are already increasing cooperation with two or three of their neighbours in anticipation of such a development. If this occurs, and if some form of regional government finally materialises as well, one may wonder about the prospects of the current provinces.

*Municipal Government*

Local governments are clearly of more importance. There are now just over 700 municipalities in the country, a number that is slowly decreasing as a result of the central government's policy of combining municipalities of less than 10 000 inhabitants into larger units. The structure of local government is spelled out by an Act of Parliament dating back to 1848, which provides a uniform framework for all municipalities, regardless of their size. A municipal council is directly elected for a four-year term. Depending on the size of the population, this council consists of 7–45 members, and elects 2–6 aldermen. Together with the appointed mayor, the aldermen form the executive branch of the local government.

The structure of municipal governments is almost identical to that of provincial governments, but both differ in important ways from the way the national government is organised. The electoral system at the local level is quite similar to the one used for national elections (and described in Chapter 4), and the local executives are also coalitions of several parties. However, whereas ministers cannot be MPs, the aldermen are elected exclusively from among the council members, and they must retain their council seats. It might be expected that this would lead to a relatively more politicised local executive, but the opposite appears to be true. Most local executive coalitions are so-called 'mirror coalitions' (i.e., they reflect the composition of the council at large). Smaller parties may not always be represented in such a mirror coalition, but all major parties are, usually in proportion to their strength on the council. In municipalities with a mirror coalition, a distinction between governing coalition and opposition can hardly be made. In larger cities in particular, the local executive coalitions are less inclusive and more politicised, but on average three-quarters of all local executive boards are composed of mirror coalitions (Tops, 1990).

The role of the mayor probably enhances the depoliticisation of local government. Dutch mayors are still appointed by the central government from among applicants outside the municipality concerned. All prospective mayors are party members, and in making appointments there is an attempt to reflect the national proportions of the major parties, while taking local political circumstances into account to an extent. Occasionally, national politicians are parachuted into a mayoralty in one of the larger municipalities, but in general they are recruited more for their managerial skills or expertise in local government (e.g., as an alderman in some other town) than for their political experience (Andeweg and Derksen, 1978). For most occupants of the office, being mayor is a career, in which appointment to a larger municipality is regarded as a promotion which brings more prestige as well as a salary increase. The mayor is chairman of both the council and the municipal executive board, in addition to which he has a few responsibilities in his own right, such as the maintenance of public order. His appointment is for a six-year renewable term and, unlike the aldermen, he cannot be removed by the council. Despite the power of the central government over their appointments and careers, mayors do not act as agents of 'The Hague' and they are not subject to instructions from above; neither are they part of a bureaucratic hierarchy. Their role in local politics varies widely, however. In smaller communities, the mayor often dominates the council and the executive board, being the only full-time professional administrator, as well as someone who can serve as an articulate ambassador for the town at the provincial and national level. In the more politicised larger cities especially, full-time aldermen have stripped the mayor of all but his constitutionally prescribed functions. As Left-wing parties are strong in the cities, it should come as no surprise that they would prefer the mayor to be elected, either directly by the voters or by the council, arguing that an appointed mayor is an anachronism in a mature democracy. Being

better represented in the smaller communities, it is equally predictable that the Liberals, and especially the Christian Democrats,
favour the current practice, suggesting that an appointed mayor
brings continuity, impartiality, and professionalism to local government. In true Dutch fashion, this debate has been going on for
decades, while a pragmatic compromise has evolved in which mayors
continue to be appointed, but in which local leaders are increasingly
consulted in the nomination procedure.

Constitutionally, two concepts define the functions of local
government: 'autonomy' and 'co-government'. Autonomy refers to
the policy domain in which the municipal government has independent authority, whereas co-government implies its task in implementing national legislation. Paradoxically, it is in the field of co-
government rather than in the field of autonomy, that we find at
least some degree of decentralisation in Dutch politics. Municipal
autonomy is only very loosely defined; local governments are
responsible for municipal affairs. As the territorial dimension of
government is organised hierarchically, however, what is or is not a
municipal affair is eventually determined by the activities of the
central government: when national authorities decide to take on an
issue, it is by definition no longer a municipal affair. Thus, in 1990,
the Minister of Internal Affairs annulled a decision by several
municipal governments not to grant contracts to companies doing
business with South Africa, arguing that such a policy amounted to
foreign policy, which clearly is not a municipal affair. Moreover, even
in regulating what is left over for them, the municipal authorities
need the approval of the provincial governments for their annual
budget and most of their plans. The provinces, in turn, are also
subject to supervision by the national government.

The field of co-government is somewhat more promising if one
looks for signs of decentralisation. Co-government clearly outweighs
autonomy in local government policy-making. In 1980 it was
estimated that every working day the municipalities received more
than 20 instructions from central government departments, mostly
dealing with education and housing. Sometimes the implementation
of such regulations is mechanical, but often the central government
lays down the general outlines of a policy, permitting local authorities
to fill in the details. Through such 'details', municipal governments
are sometimes able to deviate substantially from the central

government's intentions (Toonen, 1987) despite supervision, new and more detailed central regulations, etc.

On the other hand, the municipalities are tied to the central government by 'golden ropes', i.e., by their financial dependence on centrally controlled funds. Dutch local governments raise only 9 per cent of their total revenues themselves (which is low in comparison to other West European countries), primarily through a real estate tax. About 25 per cent of municipal income is based on revenue sharing. The central government pays into a municipal fund, from which the money is distributed to the municipalities on the basis of a complex formula, taking into account such factors as the number of houses and inhabitants as well as the total length of the canals in town. There are no specific conditions attached to revenue-sharing, which brings the total proportion of municipal income that can be freely allocated by the local council (albeit subject to overall provincial approval) to about one-third. Two-thirds of municipal revenues therefore consist of subsidies and grants from the central government for specific purposes, further curtailing local autonomy. This percentage has not declined substantially over the years, although all Cabinets promise decentralisation. If budgetary items are transferred from specific grants to revenue sharing, it is often to allow the central government to cut back on its budget while hiving off the responsibility for poorer services onto local authorities.

There is no escaping the conclusion that, relative to most other West European countries, the Dutch policy-making process is highly centralised in territorial terms. The only real limit to centralisation is the familiar problem of the span of control: the inability of the central government to make full use of all its controlling mechanisms, even in such a small country. Centralisation also contributes to the relatively depoliticised atmosphere which is characteristic of local politics: most of the ideological issues that divide the population are taken out of the realm of local politics by the central government, the governing coalitions take in nearly all parties; the mayors are appointed and play a managerial rather than a political role; and the bulk of local government consists of implementing central guidelines. It is perhaps telling, that in Dutch, local politics is usually referred to as local *administration*, and that it is considered an appropriate object of study for students of public administration, rather than for political scientists.

## Functional Decentralisation

However, policy-making in the Netherlands is decentralised, as the remark with which we started this chapter implies. This decentralisation is no longer to provincial and local authorities but to largely autonomous 'policy sectors', each composed of interest groups, advisory boards, (sections of) a government department, and specialised committees in Parliament. This functional decentralisation is the result of many factors such as the cultural predilection for specialised expertise, and the political need for depoliticisation discussed in Chapter 2. The two most important factors, however, are the existence of neo-corporatist institutions and arrangements, and the absence of a single unified civil service. It is to these two factors that the remainder of this chapter is devoted.

### The Incorporation of Interest Groups

After consociationalism, neo-corporatism is probably the best-known characterisation of the Dutch political system. For our discussion of the role of interest groups in the policy-making process we shall avoid entering the fruitless debate on the exact definition of neo-corporatism to which such a large portion of the literature is devoted. As a common denominator we may safely use the concept to describe an empirical relationship between interest groups and the government that is based on an exchange (influence for support), and on cooperation rather than competition. Thus pressure groups no longer observe their definitional limits of organisations attempting to influence governmental policy-making *from the outside*, without taking part in the decision-making or accepting responsibility for the resulting policies; instead pressure groups are incorporated into the process and defend the outcomes to their members. The theoretical boundaries between the roles played by political parties and by pressure groups are blurred. For such a neo-corporatist model of policy-making to work, there are (at least) three pre-conditions: interest groups have to be strong and well-integrated; venues have to exist where the exchange between government and interest groups can take place; and, most importantly, all parties involved have to be willing to abide by the rules of bargaining and compromise, rather than conflict and competition.

*Interest Groups.* It is difficult to ascertain whether, in general, Dutch interest groups are strong and well integrated. If we define strength in terms of inclusiveness, i.e., of the proportion of actual members among the population that an interest group claims to represent, there seems to be at least as much variation as in other countries. A few professions operate as a closed shop: e.g., lawyers and medical doctors. High density is also achieved by interest groups representing organisations rather than individuals: the Dutch Association of Municipalities (VNG), for instance, organises nearly 100 per cent of all potential members. It is estimated that of all companies with ten or more employees, 90 per cent are affiliated to one of the large employers' organisations. The percentages are lower for associations of individuals: although 80 per cent of the farmers are organised, only 35–40 per cent of the retailers and small businessmen belong to their associations. As elsewhere, the inclusiveness of consumer organisations is very low.

For comparative purposes, the membership density rate of the trade unions is of particular interest (see Visser, 1990). Until the 1970s, 40 per cent of all workers were members of a trade union; the absolute number of members has since increased, but the density rate had dropped to 24 per cent by 1990. Even if we take into account that only the printing industry is a closed shop, these percentages are low, especially when compared to those of other so-called neo-corporatist states, such as the Nordic countries (nearly 90 percent), and Austria or Belgium (about 60 percent). In many countries the density rate has increased in recent years, so that today even the relatively weak Swiss trade unions organise a larger proportion of the work force than their Dutch counterparts. The relative lack of inclusiveness is evident in most sectors of the economy, most of all in trade and finance (9 per cent in 1985) or among women (13 per cent in 1985), and least in the public sector, although it declined even there from 60 per cent in 1970 to 46 per cent in 1985. If the trade union figures are representative of Dutch interest groups in general, the degree of inclusiveness does not seem to be very impressive. At first sight, the same can be said of the cohesiveness or integration of interest groups.

Although the peak organisations are usually stronger than the various affiliated branches, there are not many interests that are organised by just one single pressure group. Pillarisation often resulted in separate Catholic, Protestant, and 'general' (sometimes split into Socialist and Liberal) organisations for any particular interest. Depillarisation has reduced the number of separate organisations for the same interest, but many remnants of that era still persist. There are now two large trade union federations: the Federation of Dutch Trade Unions (FNV), a 1976 merger of the Socialist and Catholic trade union movements with nearly a million members in 1990, and a much smaller Protestant Christian National Trade Union (CNV) with a 1990 membership of 300 000. Both peak organisations represent a cross-section of both manual and non-manual workers, with the CNV attracting relatively more white-collar workers. In addition to the FNV and the CNV there are several small independent unions but, with the exception of a few white-collar organisations (combined in the MHP with a total of 125 000 members), they are not very important.

In an economy dominated by a few large multinational companies, one might expect these companies to try to influence the government directly, rather than through interest groups, and such direct lobbying undoubtedly does take place. Yet a sophisticated study of the actual influence of business firms on the Dutch government concluded 'that in our investigation we did not find any indications for a comparatively great influence of the branches belonging to multinational concerns' (Braam, 1973, p. 339). Influence was more related to membership of, and position in, interest organisations. The employers' peak associations are as divided as the trade unions are. For the larger companies there are the Association of Dutch Companies (VNO), a combination of two secular employers' organisations founded in 1968, and the Dutch Association of Christian Employers (NCW), a merger of a Catholic and a Protestant organisation, formed in 1970. The organisations of farmers and small enterprises are also still divided by old cleavages.

Such divisions have done little to weaken the pressure groups. Through their integration into a pillar they once enjoyed close relations with a political party, giving them an additional channel of influence. Other than the ideological diversity among French or Italian interest groups, pillarisation did not lead to much competition among the pressure groups. It was therefore better to speak of parallel rather than rival organisations. Each organisation had its own constituency, without much hope of converting members from its counterparts in other pillars. Depillarisation appears not to have led to increased competition among interest groups, at least not to the same degree as among political parties. In general, they work together to protect the interest for which they stand. Within the trade union movement, for example, Christian unions were sometimes created from above in order to take the wind out of the socialists' sail, but such rivalry no longer plays a role. The CNV tends to be more moderate than the FNV, but it is rare for the CNV to accept an offer from the employers that is rejected by the FNV, or for the FNV to go on strike without at least the CNV's tacit approval. Between parallel organisations representing the same interest many informal, sometimes even institutionalised, mechanisms for communication and coordination exist, leaving little room for a government so inclined to 'divide and conquer'. One of the preconditions for neo-corporatism, solid interest groups – therefore seems to be met, despite less than impressive membership figures.

*PBO and advisory councils.* There can be no doubt that the second precondition, the existence of venues for consultation and bargaining between government and interest groups, is amply met. There is a bewildering variety of advisory boards, tripartite councils, and parastatal organisations. Dutch neo-corporatism is often illustrated by referring to a post-war project for the public law organisation of economic activity (PBO), with the Socio-Economic Council (SER) as its best-known and most important organisation. The intention of the PBO was that the government would transfer some of its responsibilities to independent regulatory commissions, in which representatives of employers and workers, together with government appointees, would regulate their particular sector of the economy. A network should have developed of vertical organisations, encompassing all companies that contribute to a particular product (such as the dairy product board), as well as horizontal organisations, comprising all companies in a particular branch of industry (such as the agriculture board). For outsiders, it is sometimes difficult to appreciate that the government bears no responsibility for the regulations issued by such boards. This was the case, for instance, when hothouse farmers from other EC countries protested to the Dutch Minister of Agriculture that he was giving their Dutch colleagues an unfair advantage by charging them less for natural gas. The minister had a hard time convincing the demonstrators that the price of gas had been negotiated between a natural gas distribution board and a greenhouse farming board, without his involvement. Such examples serve as evidence of Dutch neo-corporatism. However, the picture they paint is exaggerated. In reality, the PBO has been a major failure, with the food and agriculture sector and the SER as exceptions. In the rest of the Dutch economy, and especially in the manufacturing industry, fewer product- or branch-boards materialised than had been expected. There are now 43 PBO boards and 20 subcommittees in existence.

The SER remains a central institution in any discussion of Dutch policy-making. It is often described as a tripartite organisation, which is both true and not true. It is tripartite in the sense that it consists of three components of equal size (15 seats each), but usually 'tripartite' implies that the government is also represented, together with employers' organisations and trade unions. This is not the case with the SER, where the third element consists of 'Crown members' appointed by the central government, but acting independently. The Crown members include the Governor of the Dutch Bank, the Director of the Central Planning Bureau, and university professors of economics. As experts they may have a moderating effect on the debate between clashing interest groups, but they cannot take the government's place when the exchange of influence for support, so central to neo-corporatist policy-making, takes place. When it comes to bargaining between government and socio-economic interests, the SER (that showcase of neo-corporatism) plays no role. Paradoxically, it is a formally bipartite institution, the Foundation of Labour, set up by employers' organisations and trade unions, that in practice functions as a meeting ground for government and interest groups. If the SER plays a significant role in policy-making it is because the government is obliged to ask the Council's advice on a wide range of socio-economic and related legislation.

As an advisory board, the SER is something of a *primus inter pares*. According to the government's own estimate after an effort to clean up the jungle of boards and councils, there are now 249 official permanent external advisory councils remaining, including the 63 PBO boards mentioned above. Of all the members of these 249 councils, 75 per cent were recruited from organised interests. It is the government that decides which interest groups are to be invited to participate in the advisory councils and PBO boards. By certifying some organisations as 'representative', and by barring other organisations, the government intervenes directly in the world of the pressure groups. The most notorious example dates back to the early post-war years, when the government shut out the largely Communist trade union, EVC, of which 20 per cent of all organised workers were then members (more than the CNV). Partly because of internal disagreements, but partly also because it was denied the legitimacy and access which the government accorded to the other unions, the EVC weakened and was eventually disbanded in 1964. Membership of the advisory councils is thus itself part of the neo-corporatist exchange between government and pressure groups.

Some advisory councils also have regulatory powers (such as the PBO boards), or even judicial powers, but their primary task is to advise the government on a specific policy area. Formally such advice is not binding, but in practice it often cannot be ignored. First of all, the government is committed by having requested the advice in the first place and by having steered the discussions in the council through the exact wording of such a request. In some advisory councils the government is formally represented but, even when it is not, civil servants are often present during the council's proceedings. Second, the government is sometimes dependent on the councils for information. Often the interest group representatives on the council are better placed to estimate the social impact of a particular policy than government officials. Most advisory councils have their own expert staffs. For example, there are five major advisory councils on public health; combined they employ more experts on their secretariats than the government's Directorate of Public Health. When a government task-force to rationalise the advisory system realised this, it quickly shelved its plans to combine these five councils into one: it would have created a powerful counter-bureaucracy with a near-monopoly of expertise in this particular area. Third, when the representatives of often divergent interests agree on a particular recommendation to the government, a minister has to be very sure of himself to deviate from such unanimous advice. He will risk a strong reaction not only from the interest groups that endorsed the recommendation, but also from the political parties with which these interest groups may still have 'pillarised' connections. A 1977 study by the Scientific Council for Government Policy, itself one of the advisory councils, put the percentage of unanimous recommendations emanating from all the government's advisory councils at over 90 percent. Since then, increasing polarisation between employers' organisations and trade unions has probably reduced this percentage for the socio-economic sector (the SER rarely agrees on anything any more), but in other areas it may not have changed much.

It is through the advisory councils and PBO boards that the interest groups are incorporated into the institutional framework of Dutch policy-making. There is no gainsaying the significance of this institutional framework, but it should be emphasised that it is only the visible part of a network of largely informal contacts and consultations. A former Minister of Economics described in an interview how he and the Minister of Social Affairs would invite the trade union leaders and employers' representatives to his Amsterdam apartment, where they would bargain all Sunday afternoon in the living room, and have the results officially confirmed in the SER or some other council the next day. Protestant and Catholic politicians and interest group representatives meet regularly in what is called the 'Christian Social Convention'. It is in such informal meetings that many of the exchanges take place, or are prepared.

*The sources of neo-corporatism.*   So we have the means (cohesive interest groups) and the opportunity (both institutionalised and informal consultations) for neo-corporatism. We now turn to the motive: why do interest groups and government officials behave in this way? There are (at least) three different explanations for the incidence of neo-corporatism in the Netherlands.

A first explanation views neo-corporatism as the outcome of corporatist ideologies. It is pointed out that corporatism is an important feature of Christian, and particularly of Catholic, political philosophy. The Catholic principle of subsidiarity requires the government to devolve decision-making to the lowest possible level. Furthermore, Dutch Calvinists developed the idea of 'sovereign spheres' in society, created by God and subordinate only to God, in which the government should not interfere. Although the Catholic principle is more hierarchical than the Calvinist idea, they both call for a transfer of government responsibilities to corporatist institutions. The Dutch Social Democrats and Liberals were not averse to such a transfer. The Social Democrats had already adopted the idea of 'functional decentralisation' into their programme of planning (rather than nationalisation) in the 1920s and 1930s, and Dutch liberalism, being more organic than individualistic in its ideological origins, did not object much as long as corporatist institutions could emerge voluntarily. After 1945 there was some predictable argument about the exact role of the state and the voluntary nature of corporatism, but a consensus soon developed and at first a junior minister (subsequently a cabinet minister) was appointed to develop the PBO. The role of corporatist philosophy should not be overstated, however. As we pointed out before, if Dutch policy-making is neo-corporatist, it is not because of the PBO which had only very limited success. If the PBO has political ancestors, they are German rather than Dutch: it was the German occupation which initiated the creation of corporatist institutions. After the war they were not disbanded, but modified (fewer powers for the chairman of a board, better representation of trade unions). Earlier Dutch corporatist ideas merely provided a fertile ground for the Nazi initiative.

The other two explanations both start from the idea that the Netherlands is a small state. The small state argument is a dangerous one. It has also been used, for example, to account for consociational democracy by arguing that small states have only small problems, and can therefore afford the luxury of consociationalism! In his book, *Small States in World Markets*, Katzenstein (1985) offers a less simplistic argument. He points out that small states have small domestic markets, making them dependent on the international market. In an open economy (see Chapters 1 and 8) the government is relatively powerless to steer the economy and the option of protectionism would be suicidal. According to Katzenstein such open economies can only adapt to world market changes. Such adaptations are in the interest of all parties involved (government, employers, and trade unions), which facilitates their cooperation. Neo-corporatism is, therefore, functional in a small state with an open economy.

The third explanation is more cultural in nature. As former Prime Minister Zijlstra stated in an attempt to explain the continued existence of the SER:

> As long as they are talking, they are not shooting. That is not because Holland is Holland, but because Holland is a small country. It is such a terribly small country. You forget this when you are living abroad, but we are just like a village. You meet each other at the village pump each evening, and you talk. (Klamer, 1990, p. 52)

The interviewer, a Dutch economist teaching in Washington, DC, goes on to generalise this argument by emphasising the 'family-feeling' of the Dutch in comparison with US culture. While such a 'family-feeling' can be detected in Dutch culture, it is doubtful whether this results from idyllic gatherings around the village pump, given the fact that over 15 million people live in this 'small state' (see Chapter 1). In Chapter 2 we noted that corporatism and consociationalism are interrelated. This is certainly true in cultural terms. Also in Chapter 2 we discussed the Dutch cultural predilection for consensus and compromise. Even if one agrees with Daalder that at the elite level this culture goes back to the days of the confederal Republic, it is less obvious what its roots at the mass level are. The average citizen may not be familiar with the concept of 'neo-corporatism', but will be able to recognise the phenomenon as 'the harmony model'; he or she is more likely to refer to employers' organisations and trade unions as 'the social partners' than as 'pressure groups'; and the word 'compromise' has no negative connotation. This culture of consensus may very well be a product of the long-term influence of religion on Dutch society. Both Catholicism and Dutch Protestantism view society as a natural organism, all parts of which are functional and complementary rather than incompatible. Conciliation is regarded as morally superior to conflict. This brings us back to the first explanation, although the religious influence is probably less through precise philosophical blue-prints and more through diffuse popular culture.

*'Still the century of corporatism?'.* Neo-corporatism and consociationalism also have in common that both are supposed to have withered away as soon as they were discovered by political scientists. In both cases this decline is supposed to have set in around the late 1960s or early 1970s. 'From Corporatism to Statism' or 'The Neo-Liberal Backlash' are titles that testify to this perception. Such a view is based on a number of developments that cannot be denied. First, there is an increased polarisation of divergent interests, most visibly of employers' associations and trade unions. This polarisation is due partly to the success of neo-corporatism. After the Second World War the trade unions accepted wage restraint in return for full employment. Full employment was more or less a fact in the early 1960s when the registered labour reserves were less than 1 per cent of the total work force (see Chapter 8). In order to attract workers employers started to pay 'black' wages in addition to the official wage level determined in the tripartite bargaining process. This put the trade unions in an awkward position and, faced with a decline in membership, they opted for a more radical course of action. There were huge wage

increases in 1963 (13 per cent), 1964 (15 per cent), and 1965 (10 per cent). The centrally-guided policy of wage restraint was abandoned. In the mid-1970s some FNV trade unions even withdrew from a number of PBO boards. Later, with rising unemployment and an economic recession, trade unions were in too weak a position to extract major concessions from the employers.

A second development is the more prominent and less reactive role played by the government. Depillarisation has loosened the ties between pressure groups and political parties somewhat, allowing the parties, and a government formed by the parties, more room for manoeuvre. The decline of economic growth presented the social partners with a zero-sum game: the neo-corporatist bargain could no longer be facilitated by according each partner a bigger slice of the national cake. In the ensuing stalemate the government was forced to seize the initiative (see Chapter 8).

To declare the era of neo-corporatism over on the basis of these developments is, however, the result of too narrow a definition of neo-corporatism and of contrasting a stereotyped picture of Dutch neo-corporatism in the past with an exaggeration of the changes. It seems an unnecessary limitation of neo-corporatism to require the relations within the tripartite system to be symmetrical, and not all authors in the international literature on neo-corporatism make this proviso. The relations within the system may vary with economic and political circumstances. The economic recession and the long reign of a Christian Democrat/Liberal coalition reduced the power of the trade unions, and strengthened the employers' organisations and the government. Economic and political fortunes change, however, and may alter the relations within the neo-corporatist triangle. Such changes within the system do not necessarily amount to abolition.

In addition, the changes are often exaggerated. The past was more statist, and the present is more corporatist than is often assumed. Even in the past not all Dutch policy-making fitted the neo-corporatist mould. It is interesting to look at the distribution of advisory councils over government departments. The Department of Welfare, Health and Culture is surrounded by 49 advisory councils; the Department of Agriculture has 14 councils, to which we should add a large number of the 63 PBO boards. Other departments that are well endowed in this respect are Internal Affairs, Education, Transport and the departments of Economic and Social Affairs. On the other hand, the departments of Finance, Defence, Foreign Affairs, and Housing have only 4–5 advisory councils each. If we take the number of advisory councils as an, admittedly imperfect, indicator, it would seem that the incorporation of interest groups in policy-making is less extensive in policy areas presided over by regulatory rather than spending departments, departments that date back to before the development of the welfare state.

Even where neo-corporatist arrangements prevailed, the relations between the government on the one hand and the interest groups on the other were not always symmetrical in the past. Statist intervention and neo-corporatist consultation often went hand in hand. The phalanx of advisory councils in the area of education policy, for example, developed only in the late 1950s, when the Department of Education modified its traditional role of passive guardian of the financial rights of the religious schools in order to take on a more active role. Several Dutch authors have argued that the role of the government in the 1945–63 period has been underestimated (Woldendorp, 1985), and that it even dominated some PBO boards (Fernhout, 1980).

In the descriptions of the changes in policy-making, too much attention has been focused on the institutions of neo-corporatism, and particularly on the SER. As Wassenberg points out:

> Radicalization and symbolic polarization are delegated to the micro-level of interest implementation and to the macro-level of interest articulation where it is written large and heroic. On the meso-level of the politics of accommodation, where interest group leaders together with sector-bureaucrats are 'constantly forced to undo with one hand what they do with the other', accommodation becomes habit forming. (Wassenberg, 1982, p. 92)

For interest group leaders the unquestionably more active role of the government is a blessing in disguise:

> Frequent government intervention alters the expectations of social partners: there is no need to make concessions and reach agreements if the government is likely to intervene and impose a settlement anyway. Instead it is possible to stand fast and maintain positions which help to sustain the support of followers. Blame for imposed solutions, which may or may not be acceptable, can then be assigned to the intervening third party – in this case the government – rather than on leaders who have failed to represent

followers as effectively as they might have. As a result, the distance between social partners on matters such as incomes policy is not necessarily as great as it would appear to be on the surface. In other words, neo-corporate relationships prevail. However, the form and the extent of cooperation vary considerably, depending on the circumstances . . . It is sufficient to note that government decisions, coupled with the tacit consent of trade unions and employers may be at least as effective as policies worked out and administered through tripartite structures such as the Social and Economic Council. (Wolinetz, 1983, p. 12)

Even if we look at the visible, institutionalised part of the policy-making process, obituaries of neo-corporatism seem premature. Of all currently existing advisory councils 41 per cent were created after 1973, when this mode of policy-making was supposed to be disappearing. There has been only one Cabinet, the 1982–6 Lubbers I coalition of Christian Democrats and Liberals, which has deliberately tried to ignore organised interests, but in 1986 the new coalition agreement explicitly stated that 'The social partners will be given more say over and will be closely involved, also financially, in important parts of socio-economic policy-making.' The 1989 coalition agreement promised that 'Policies and procedures should create the conditions for broad social cooperation, in the first place through definite agreements with the social partners, social organisations, and local authorities.' This is not mere rhetoric: immediately upon its formation in 1989 the Lubbers III coalition of Christian Democrats and Social Democrats negotiated a 'policy framework for social cooperation' with the employers and the unions, and in 1990 the system of employment exchanges was changed to create regional job centres run by tripartite institutions.

If this analysis is correct, the incorporation of interest groups into the decision-making process, although perhaps less ostentatious, and with a more active role of the government, is still characteristic of Dutch policy-making in many fields. One of the consequences of neo-corporatism is that it strengthens the functional decentralisation and subsequent sectorisation of policy-making. Pressure groups fight for one interest only, thereby focusing on a particular policy area without much attention for the whole range of government activities. This is their proper function, and we should be surprised if it were otherwise. It is estimated that 80 per cent of all advisory councils are established for very specific policies (the Advisory Commission on Working and Resting Hours for Crew-Members of Dutch Airplanes on Regular Routes is an admittedly somewhat extreme example); 15 per cent of the councils advise on a policy area (e.g. the Banking Council, or the Advisory Council on Peace and Security); only 5 per cent of the councils are regarded as 'intersectoral', but many of the councils in this category are still primarily consulted by only one department (e.g. the Central Council for Environmental Protection) (Van Delden, 1989). The sectorisation of policy-making is further strengthened by the structure of the Dutch bureaucracy.

*The Fragmentation of the Bureaucracy*

The most striking characteristic of the Dutch civil service is that as such it does not exist; each department is largely autonomous. The only things all departmental employees have in common are a psychological test as an entrance requirement, and the conditions of service. The Minister of Internal Affairs is the formal head of the governmental apparatus, but his role is confined to matters such as conducting the negotiations with the civil service unions over pay and working hours. A General Personnel Service exists to administer the psychological test and to serve as an internal job centre, but the departments are not obliged to recruit new staff through this office. Most departments do their own hiring, except perhaps for secretaries and tea ladies (see Table 7.1).

In the absence of a general entrance examination as in Great Britain or France, each department sets its own standards, generally requiring training or expertise in a specific policy area. The main sources of new civil servants are the universities and, to a lesser extent, organised interests. There are sometimes clear links between particular universities and particular departments: thus, the Department of Agriculture employs many graduates from the Agricultural University at Wageningen, Transport and Waterworks attracts many engineers from the Technical University at Delft, Economic Affairs houses a large number of economists trained at Erasmus University in Rotterdam, and the Justice Department has recruited many graduates from Leyden University's Law School. Although positions at the top level within a department are usually filled from the department's own ranks, horizontal entry is not uncommon. It is estimated that about one quarter of all top level appointments are

**TABLE 7.1**

**Personnel and budgets of government departments, 1992**

| Department | Number of personnel | Budget (in millions of guilders) |
|---|---|---|
| General Affairs | 334 | 51.9 |
| Foreign Affairs* | 3 683 | 7 769.7 |
| Justice† | 35 939 | 4 184.6 |
| Internal Affairs | 2 192 | 4 513.7 |
| Education | 3 479 | 33 104.6 |
| Finance‡ | 31 332 | 4 012.0 |
| Defence | 23 628 | 14 087.0 |
| Housing and Environment | 7 593 | 15 540.3 |
| Transport and Public Works | 14 685 | 9 338.9 |
| Economic Affairs | 5 455 | 3 570.3 |
| Agriculture | 10 686 | 3 002.2 |
| Social Affairs | 2 669 | 38 248.2 |
| Welfare, Health, and Culture | 6 967 | 12 199.6 |

\* Includes development aid.
† Includes police.
‡ Includes the tax office.
*Source: Miljoenennota 1992* (1992).

outsiders, coming from other departments, or (much more likely) from outside the central government bureaucracy (Rosenthal and Roborgh, 1992, Table 8). Sometimes departments recruit directly from organised interests (and vice versa). A few years ago, for example, the Minister of Internal Affairs appointed as his Director General for Government Personnel the leader of the FNV trade union. Earlier in his career he had been chairman of the FNV civil service union, negotiating with the very official he was now succeeding! Such a reversal of roles may be rather exceptional, but it epitomises the permeability of the bureaucracy to outside interests. Once appointed to a particular department, however, a civil servant tends to spend his or her entire career within the confines of that department, often even within a single Directorate. There is no policy or practice of rotating officials from one department to another. Any attempt to increase the mobility of the civil servants is frustrated by their high degree of specialisation.

This emphasis on technocratic specialisation is not offset by political appointments. Political considerations do play some role in the appointments of civil servants, especially at the highest levels, not only with an eye to ensuring that advisers are loyal to a particular minister, but also as part of the proportional distribution over all major parties, so central to consociational democracy. This proportionality has always been a rough one (Rosenthal and Roborgh, 1992, Table 7), with some departments being dominated by one party (e.g., Foreign Affairs by the VVD, and Agriculture by the CDA). In recent years there have been signs that governing parties have given preferential treatment to their own candidates, but it is still a far cry from a spoils system. As we mentioned in Chapter 5, political advisers are rare and French-style *cabinets ministériels* even non-existent in Dutch departments.

The recruitment of departmental specialists has important consequences. Experienced observers can detect distinct departmental cultures, even in dress, ranging from corduroy or jeans at Welfare, Health and Culture to blue blazers at Internal Affairs, or pin-striped suits in the Foreign Office. Cultural differences also exist with regard to the relations between civil servants and their political masters. One study found a relatively low incidence of classic Weberian role orientations in the newer welfare state departments, such as Welfare, Health and Culture, Education, and Social Affairs, whereas such role orientations prevailed in older departments such as Internal Affairs, Justice and Agriculture (Eldersveld, Kooiman and Van der Tak, 1981, p. 85).

Moving from one department to another can therefore be like moving into quite a different world. It takes some time to get to know the acronyms by which Directorates, Sections and Bureaus within a department are known. The structure of departments also varies: some are top-heavy with officials in the higher grades (General Affairs, Internal Affairs, Foreign Affairs, Education, Economic Affairs), while other departments put more emphasis on the medium and lower grades (Finance, Justice, Welfare, Health and Culture). Some Departments are extremely hierarchical (e.g., Internal Affairs) and others have a rather horizontal organisation (e.g., Welfare, Health and Culture). To add to this confusion, a particular position may have quite different functions: e.g., the Permanent Secretary in the Department of Economic Affairs is the minister's top adviser on macro-economic policy, whereas his colleague at Finance is the top manager of the departmental apparatus.

The fragmentation of the Dutch bureaucracy in terms of departmental recruitment, culture, and structure has several causes.

It is obvious that the neo-corporatist networks surrounding each department tend to reinforce departmental autonomy. It is telling that civil servants often refer to the pressure groups with which they have to deal as 'our clients': the farmers are the Department of Agriculture's clients, the local authorities the Department of Internal Affairs' clients, the workers the clients of the Department of Social Affairs, and so on. It is argued that the ties between departments and organised interests have grown stronger in recent decades: as depillarisation deprived some interest groups from automatic access to a political party, direct contacts between such groups and departments have increased (Wassenberg, 1982, pp. 103–4).

More indirectly, consociational democracy has also contributed to departmental fragmentation. The rule of 'depoliticisation' (see Chapter 2) gives policy-making in the Netherlands a distinctly technocratic flavour: in order not to offend any one of the minorities, decisions are often based on technical rather than on ideological motives (see Chapter 10). This is why civil servants must be highly specialised in a particular policy area, rather than in more general managerial skills. We have seen in Chapter 5 that the emphasis on technocratic expertise even extends to ministerial nominations. When specialised ministers were directly recruited from organised interests – or, as also happened, from the department itself – the contribution to departmental autonomy was strongest.

We should point out, however, that departmental fragmentation predates both consociational democracy and neo-corporatism. Departmental autonomy has its roots in a historical coincidence: the Dutch bureaucracy developed *after* the introduction of individual ministerial responsibility and *before* the strengthening of collective responsibility. During the Republic, the absence of an absolute monarch prevented the development of a strong and centralised bureaucracy. The Republic was a state composed of local offices rather than of central officials (Daalder, 1966, pp. 190–2). It was only during the Napoleonic occupation, and under King William I's subsequent reign, that a hesitant and modest beginning was made in building a bureaucratic apparatus. Ministerial responsibility was accepted relatively early in the Netherlands (1848), but in the absence of political parties and coherent governmental majorities it was the individual minister who oversaw the building of the bureaucracy. Once suffrage was widened, and parties developed that joined in governing coalitions, the notion of collective responsibility gained importance. By that time, however, departmental autonomy had become firmly entrenched. Moreover, the new departments that developed, mostly as splits from the Department of Internal Affairs, were set up to oversee a particular sector of the new welfare state. Other than the traditional regulatory departments, these new departments were much more in need of specialised knowledge.

Whatever the causes of departmental fragmentation, its consequences are significant. Differences in recruitment, culture and structure cannot but leave their mark on the resulting policies. Lawyers refer to 'Thirteen Legal Families' to indicate that each department has its own predilection for using specific instruments: older departments maintain a preference for legislation, while other departments rely more on regulation, permit systems, or subsidies. It has been argued that this variety reflects profound differences of opinion about the government's proper role in society, with some departments clearly being more interventionist by nature than others. Another effect of departmental fragmentation is its contribution to the functional decentralisation and sectorisation of Dutch policy making.

*The Quest for Control*

Sectorised policy-making does not stop with the incorporation of organised interests and the fragmentation of the bureaucracy. In Chapter 5 we noted that, despite the increased politicisation of the Cabinet, ministers still tend to see themselves primarily as heads of a department. The custom not to intervene in Cabinet discussions when one's own department has no stake in the policy being deliberated prevents Cabinet from being the 'Government against Subgovernments' that Rose assumes Cabinets in parliamentary systems to be (Rose, 1980). When a minister then defends his policies in Parliament, sectorisation continues. In Chapter 6 we saw how sectoral interests play a role even there. In the past organised interests were represented directly through the 'quality seats', and today their membership of one of the specialised committees introduced in the 1950s forces MPs to concentrate on a particular policy area. It has been asserted that interest groups have enclosed government policies in a pincer movement: through their incorporation into the policy-making process they are closely involved in preparing a policy, and through their representatives or contacts in parliamentary committees they control the outcome.

This would be an exaggeration of the interest groups' real influence, but it is fair to say that policy-making in the Netherlands consists of an 'Iron Ring' composed of 'closed policy circuits' (Van den Berg and Molleman, 1975), or 'Iron Triangles'(De Vries, 1990), one for each policy area, in which organised interests, the relevant department, and the relevant parliamentary committee determine policies for that area in a nearly autonomous fashion.

*Weaknesses and exceptions.* For a general description of Dutch policy-making, the Iron Ring, the Iron Triangles, sectorisation, and functional decentralisation are all pertinent terms. Yet we should be careful not to make this description into a straw man. The very fragmentation of policy-making limits the fit of any single model to the process. We have already drawn attention to the variation in the degree of incorporation of organised interests. This should be kept in mind when we discuss economic policy – often the product of neo-corporatist bargaining – in Chapter 8, and foreign policy – made largely without interference from organised interests – in Chapter 9. We should also point out that there are countervailing powers to the autonomy of the sectors. The Prime Minister, the Minister of Finance, and their departments, as well as parliamentary party leaders, all see their role as 'generalists' and coordinators of government policy. The coalition agreement is an important policy instrument in the hands of these generalists, even though interest groups try to influence its contents and specialised MPs are sometimes involved in drafting sections. The most important antidote to sectorisation is political conflict. As we have seen in Chapters 5 and 6, ministers and MPs are forced to forsake their role as head of department or sectoral representative whenever an issue is, or becomes, politically controversial. The growing politicisation of the Cabinet and the increasing party discipline in Parliament undoubtedly occur at the expense of sectoral autonomy.

So far, we have not touched upon the consequences of European unification for Dutch policy-making. This is not because it had no impact, as we shall see in Chapter 10, but rather because it is not clear what its effect on functional decentralisation has been. On many policy issues, the government now has to negotiate both with its 'social partners' at home and with the other member states of the EC in Brussels. This gives the government a certain amount of leeway, and an opportunity to put the blame for measures to which the interest groups object on the Community. Realising this, interest groups try to exert their influence in Brussels as well as in The Hague, but it often proves difficult to form a common front with their counterparts in other member states, and the system of advisory boards is not well developed on the European level. A European Socio-Economic Council, for example, exists but hardly plays a role. On the other hand, the sectors may sometimes reinforce their autonomy as the result of European unification. Within the EC, policy-making is often as fragmented as it is in the Netherlands (see Exhibit 7.1), and it is almost impossible for Dutch generalists to fight sectoral policies when such policies have the seal of supranational approval.

Both scenarios – a weakening and a strengthening of functional decentralisation – can be observed. Agricultural policy-making provides an interesting example. In the past the EC seems to have strengthened the 'green front', as this policy sector was known in the Netherlands. A former minister of Agriculture explained to one of the authors how he enthusiastically pushed for a European agricultural policy: 'In the Dutch Council of Ministers I met the ministers from other departments, and I had to defend the farmers' interests against other interests, but in the EC Council of Ministers I met only other ministers of agriculture, and we all agreed on the importance of agriculture.' A recent study of Dutch fisheries policy-making has shown, however, how the well-integrated 'Iron Triangle' in that sector came under tremendous pressure because of the fishing quota agreed upon in Brussels (De Vries, 1990). As a result of EC policies to reduce the grain surplus, the policy network on arable farming disintegrated, leading to sometimes violent demonstrations by farmers. Today the autonomy of this policy sector seems weakened, rather than strengthened by, European unification.

*Advantages and disadvantages.*   Despite all the exceptions and caveats discussed above, functional decentralisation is still sufficiently important to engender an ongoing debate on its advantages and disadvantages. On one aspect of functional decentralisation, the incorporation of organised interests, the disagreement in both the Dutch and the international literature is particularly pronounced. Neo-corporatism is at the same time denounced as the cause of all

**EXHIBIT 7.1**

**Coordinating Dutch EC policies**

Nowhere is the fragmentation of Dutch political decision-making more acute, and controversial, than in its confrontation with the more unified political systems of other West European countries in the process of EC decision-making. For a long time departments coordinated their negotiating position in Brussels not with other Dutch departments but with their 'clients'. In some policy fields, especially agriculture, it became standard practice to give temporary civil service status to representatives from interest groups or PBO boards in order to be able to include them in the official Dutch delegation (Robinson, 1961). Attempts to improve domestic coordination of EC policies failed for at least 15 years because of unchecked rivalry between the Department of Economic Affairs and the Foreign Office, which had created competing directorates for the preparation of the Dutch position within the EC. When, in 1964, negotiations started over Nigeria's association with the EC, two Dutch delegations arrived, both claiming to represent the Netherlands. As Griffiths sums up:

> Valuable ministerial time has been wasted in resolving blistering interdepartmental rows over both policy-content and departmental competence. Furthermore, in order to accommodate various departmental interests, the size of Dutch delegations at international negotiations has often proved large, unwieldy and cumbersome. Finally, and most importantly, the continuous squabbling has seriously weakened attempts to impart some unity to the overall direction of European policy. (Griffiths, 1980, p. 286)

Eventually, in 1971, a system for coordinating Dutch EC policies was put into place, ending the rivalry between Economic Affairs and Foreign Affairs in favour of the latter. A committee of civil servants from all departments (CoCo), meeting weekly, is chaired by the Junior Minister of Foreign Affairs. He is the only junior minister who is always present at Cabinet meetings, and he is also a member of the Cabinet Committee for European Affairs (REZ), which meets the most frequently of all Cabinet committees. In terms of procedures, this looks satisfactory. On a scale from 1 (no coordination) to 9 (government as unitary rational actor), Metcalfe rates the Dutch system of European policy coordination at 6, which is lower than Denmark and the UK, but at the same level as France, and higher than Germany (Metcalfe, 1988). However, the formal procedures have done little to stop the empirical fragmentation. Departments pursue their own European policies or, at best, they do their own coordination. 'As a result, EC policy coordination in the Netherlands can best be regarded as a patchwork of more or less distinctive patterns of coordination lines across the various substantive fields of policy' (Van den Bos, 1991, p. 85).

This fragmentation is generally felt to have weakened the impact of the Dutch position in Community decision-making. Proposals to give more power to the Prime Minister with regard to Dutch EC policy, or even to equip him with a European unit composed of high-level civil servants from all departments, are examples of reforms that are advocated in this respect. There is, however, little evidence that fragmentation actually is detrimental to Dutch interests. It might also be argued that the Dutch fragmentation is ideally suited to EC decision-making. After all, 'Brussels' is at least as fragmented, with the Council of Ministers meeting in different policy-related compositions, with the Commission's powerful Directorates, and especially with the nearly 200 specialised 'working groups' providing the level where most of the negotiating takes place. The Dutch delegations, with their highly specialised civil servants (sometimes seconded by interest-group representatives) may well be more effective than delegations with better coordination, but less expertise.

current economic difficulties, and also hailed as the only solution to these problems. It is argued that the welfare state has been undermined because of the incessant demands made on the government by interest groups, and that the government is unable to act decisively to remedy the situation because of being overloaded by demands, or because it lacks the necessary room of manoeuvre (pluralist stagnation). Thus, in 1990, an OECD report on educational policy blamed the dense network of advisory councils for the tardy adaptation of Dutch education to new developments. Others, however, point out that the more neo-corporatist industrial democracies do not seem to be less successful in economic terms than their less neo-corporatist neighbours. It is hypothesised that if a government attempts to take on an economic crisis alone, its policies will fail for lack of support and legitimacy. The term *maatschappelijk draagvlak* (literally 'societal weight-bearing surface') has become a household phrase to describe the supposed need for government policies to be supported by organised interests. It is feared that a government that cuts itself off from interest groups and advisory councils will become 'autistic', lacking the learning capacity to take the appropriate measures. Even the overload argument is turned around, by arguing that functional decentralisation helps to prevent the central government from being overloaded.

There is less disagreement on two other aspects of functional decentralisation: its lack of democratic legitimacy, and the lack of policy coordination. As early as 1922, anxiety about the transfer of political responsibilities to boards and councils without political accountability led to a successful amendment to the Constitution, initiated by the Socialist leader Troelstra, stipulating that advisory councils can be established only by law. It has long remained a dead letter, but it was recently rediscovered as part of attempts to restore the 'primacy of politics' in policy-making. Others, dismissing such attempts as futile, have sought to give each autonomous policy-making sector its own legitimacy by splitting up Parliament into several 'functional Parliaments'. Still others are more inclined to legalise functional decentralisation by creating independent agencies to take over some responsibilities of government departments. From time to time it has even been suggested that the First Chamber of Parliament be transformed into a corporatist chamber.

The lack of policy coordination is a more recent concern. It is pointed out that there is ample opportunity for interest articulation in

Dutch policy-making, while interest aggregation is underdeveloped. In apparent reference to one of the many synonyms for neo-corporatist bargaining, 'concertation', Gladdish has likened Dutch policy-making to an 'orchestra with no conductor' (Gladdish, 1991, p. 144). In true Dutch tradition several commissions have been set up to study the problem and to recommend remedies. In 1971 a Government Advisory Commission on Interdepartmental Coordination recommended reforms such as a strengthening of the departmental leadership *vis-à-vis* the various divisions and bureaus, the creation of a Scientific Council for Government Policy, and giving some ministers the task of coordinating particular policy areas involving more than one department. In 1975 a study by the new Scientific Council led to the establishment of a Cabinet Committee on Interdepartmental Coordination, which recommended, among other things, cautiously allowing Cabinet Ministers to appoint political advisers. In 1981 an Advisory Commission on Administrative Reorganisation submitted proposals to combine the departments into five major policy areas with one ministerial 'overlord' each for the coordination within that policy area, to rotate civil servants among the departments and to abrogate sectoral advisory councils, etc. A Cabinet Committee to implement some of these recommendations was set up, but its reports or activities have not been made public except for the decision to appoint a Government Commissioner for Administrative Reform. This Government Commissioner published a series of reports suggesting, among other things, giving ministers a staff to help them prepare their position on Cabinet items that are proposed by other departments, and to update the coalition agreement regularly. In 1990 a Committee of the leaders of all major parliamentary parties once again recommended the creation of a unified civil service, and even suggested changing the electoral system to the German system where electors can vote both for a party list and for a constituency candidate. It was argued that such district MPs would be more likely to be generalists.

The results of all these plans have been meagre. Very few proposals have been accepted, let alone implemented. Interestingly, the proposals that fared best were those entailing the creation of new structures and institutions such as coordinating ministers, the Scientific Council for Government Policy, and special bureaus for the permanent secretaries of the departments. Proposals to abolish departments, and to reduce the number of ministers or the number of civil servants participating in Cabinet Committees have rarely met with success (Andeweg, 1989). The number of advisory councils has been brought down, but largely by scrapping 'dormant' or otherwise defunct councils. No real reform or reorganisation of the policy-making system has taken place. In the 1980s attention was shifted from reorganising government to reducing government. In 1982 the 'retreat of the State' became official government policy in the form of a number of 'major operations': decentralisation, deregulation, debureaucratisation, privatisation, and policy reappraisal (see Chapter 8). So far, these 'major operations' have not met any of their objectives, and they have certainly not affected functional decentralisation as the dominant pattern of policy-making in the Netherlands. The search for better coordination, 'the quest for control' (Van Gunsteren, 1976; Wassenberg, 1982), is still on.

# 8

# Socio-Economic Policy

## The Return of the 'Dutch Disease'

On Tuesday, 18 September 1991, Queen Beatrix began her reading
of the government's annual budget message on a sombre note:

> 1992 will not be an easy year, either internationally or nationally.
> Our economy will receive a backlash similar to that which has
> taken place in other countries. After a number of good years, the
> threat of increased unemployment is hereby faced.
>
> Therefore, retention and growth of employment must be given
> first priority. This is in order to absorb the backlash now and to
> profit maximally from international economic recovery thereafter.

Outside the Parliament buildings and around the country, large
groups had gathered. They were already well aware of the stern
measures that the Queen would soon announce, and were ready to
begin their protest. Work was stopped in the Rotterdam harbour;
buses and trams stopped running; teachers and professors stopped
their classes to watch the televised address and discuss the problems
with their students.

The measures proposed were hardly new. Employment must take
precedence over higher incomes. Welfare benefits would be cut by 3
per cent. Taxes would rise for upper income groups. Government
debt and the associated interest payments were still rising, thus
spending must be brought down.

Much of the protest in the streets could be attributed to the
disappointment that this was not all a thing of the past. When the
Labour Party returned to government in 1989, one had the feeling

that the dreaded 'Dutch disease' had finally been cured. With Social Democrats in government, a new period of 'social renewal' in the towns and cities could begin. Now it appeared as if the disease had only become latent and the symptoms were again becoming manifest. This time no one really wanted to take the medicine.

In Chapter 1 we gave a brief outline of the structure of the Dutch economy, its strengths, and its weaknesses. Among its strong points are the location of the country on the Rhine/Meuse estuary, its infrastructure of railways, roads and waterways, one of the highest levels of worker productivity in Western Europe, and one of the lowest annual averages of days lost through labour disputes. If in this chapter we concentrate not on such strengths but on some of the weaknesses and problems of the Dutch economy, it is because they have provoked reactions by the government in terms of policies.

In discussing economic policy, it should be underlined once again that the Dutch economy relies heavily on imports and exports. This openness renders the Dutch economy vulnerable to fluctuations in international market conditions, and severely limits the impact of government action on the state of the economy. As with governments in more autarkic economies, the Dutch government also has policies to stimulate industrial development, regulate domestic trade, etc., but the emphasis clearly must rest on cushioning the negative social effects of adverse international economic developments. Instead of just 'economic policy', it is, therefore, common to speak of the government's '*socio*-economic' policy in the Netherlands (a practice followed in this chapter's title). The results of decades of this socio-economic policy constitute one of the most elaborate welfare-state arrangements in Western Europe. In this chapter we focus on three aspects of the Dutch welfare state and government attempts to deal with them: unemployment; the size of the public sector; and the budget deficit. They have been chosen because they deal with broad regulation of the economy and the conditions under which the economy must function and, most of all, because they have been the most politically controversial of all aspects dealing with the economy.

It should be noted, however, that it is not possible to place strict boundaries between these three issues. Action taken concerning one almost inevitably influences the others. This is one of the reasons that they engender so much political controversy. We shall attempt to keep them separate, but the reader will realise that this is not completely possible and that to do so is in itself somewhat artificial.

# Unemployment

*The Size of the Labour Force*

Following the Second World War, full employment became one of the primary goals of governmental economic policy and is now laid down in Article 19 of the Constitution. With the miracle of economic recovery in the 1950s and 1960s, this goal was essentially achieved. Unemployment levels were generally no higher than the 1 or 2 per cent levels that are caused because people are in the process of changing jobs. The demands of economic growth were in fact so great that labourers from Mediterranean countries, primarily Morocco and Turkey, were recruited as 'guest workers', often to perform the most menial tasks.

However, to say that there was full employment does not present the complete picture. Even if we exclude children under the age of 15 and retired persons of 65 and over, by no means were all citizens of the Netherlands employed. Employment (and unemployment) figures are based upon those who are actually seeking work. Who does so is dependent upon various factors; thus the percentage of the population that actually holds a job may vary greatly according to the local situation and traditions of a particular country. The percentage of the Dutch population employed between the ages of 15 and 64 is 15–20 per cent lower than the percentage for the UK, and several similar countries (see Table 8.1). This relatively low level is not the result of unemployment, since figures from 1965 were only 2 per cent higher and in 1975 they were 1.4 per cent lower.

**TABLE 8.1**

**Percentage of the population aged 15–64 holding employment (1987)**

| Country | % |
| --- | --- |
| Netherlands | 58.4 |
| Belgium | 63.4 |
| Spain | 57.7 |
| USA | 75.6 |
| Federal Republic of Germany | 65.9 |
| Japan | 72.5 |
| UK | 74.8 |
| Sweden | 81.8 |
| Denmark | 82.8 |

*Source:* Wissenschaftszentrum Berlin, as reported in Alberda (1990), p. 92.

One of the major factors accounting for such discrepancies is the participation of women in the labour force. This percentage has been quite low in the Netherlands. Alberda has described this tradition as follows:

> The low degree of participation by women has been typical in the Netherlands throughout the 20th century. During the first half of the century, in particular, this was seen as a symptom of relative wealth. In fact, this was also the view at the beginning of the period following the Second World War. The emphasis placed on the bread-winners principle in our system of social insurance was based upon the widely held belief that a married woman should stay home and care for the house and the children. Child payments and public housing proceeded from this same view. The low degree of participation by women and the high birth rate in the Netherlands belonged together. The rapid expansion of the labour force in the seventies and eighties is also related to this phenomenon. When the Netherlands was attacked by recession, the views on the position of women had changed thoroughly. Actual participation of married women was still very low and the recession and unemployment prohibited further growth. (Alberda, 1990, p. 97)

To this one might add that, because of the German occupation, women were not brought out of the kitchens into the factory to support wartime production as in the USA and UK. Until 1960, no more than 20 per cent of women had ever worked at any one time. The figures for the Netherlands for participation of women were among the lowest in Europe. However, changes are taking place. In Table 8.2 a breakdown is given of the employment of men and women in the Netherlands, the USA, and Sweden. In order to illustrate the changes that are taking place, the figures have been further broken down into age groups.

The extent of change is illustrated by the figures showing that almost half of all Dutch women between the ages of 15 and 54 are now employed, as compared with only 10 per cent of women over 55. However, although female employment is on the rise in the Netherlands, the figures (even in the younger groups) still fall well below those for the USA and Sweden.

These figures also show that the low participation of women does not account completely for the low participation rate in the Netherlands. Only in the 25–54 age group does employment for

**TABLE 8.2**

**Participation of potential labour force by age and sex in the Netherlands, the USA and Sweden (1980 and 1987)**

| Country/age | Men | | Women | |
|---|---|---|---|---|
| | **1980** | **1987** | **1980** | **1987** |
| Netherlands | | | | |
| age 15–24 | 50 | 49 | 48 | 48 |
| age 25–54 | 94 | 91 | 37 | 46 |
| age 55–64 | 64 | 41 | 14 | 10 |
| USA | | | | |
| age 15–24 | 75 | 73 | 62 | 65 |
| age 25–54 | 93 | 93 | 64 | 72 |
| age 55–64 | 71 | 67 | 41 | 42 |
| Sweden | | | | |
| age 15–24 | 72 | 66 | 70 | 67 |
| age 25–54 | 95 | 95 | 83 | 90 |
| age 55–64 | 79 | 75 | 55 | 64 |

*Source:* SZW (Ministry of Sociale Zalken en Werkgelegenheid) (1989:81), OECD figures, as reported in Sociaal en Cultureel Planbureau 1990.

Dutch men closely approach that for American or Swedish men. Employment among Dutch young men aged 15–24 is only marginally higher than that for Dutch young women. Among Dutch men over 55, the percentages are considerably higher than those for women, but also considerably lower than those for American and Swedish men. Moreover, in only a seven-year period, the participation among this group dropped by 23 per cent. To understand these figures better we must turn to the problem of unemployment.

*Rising Unemployment*

At the end of the 1960s only about 70 000 persons, amounting to less than 2 per cent of the labour force, were unemployed, in the sense of actually seeking a job. Since some people are always between jobs, this was considered virtually full employment. At the beginning of the 1970s, the number of unemployed began to rise slightly. Political leaders spoke of the unacceptability of more than 100 000 unemployed. Nevertheless, by 1971 this figure had been surpassed and rates continued to creep up slowly to approximately 300 000 at the end of the decade. As the 1980s began, the rise in the unemployment rate began to increase dramatically. Between 1980 and 1981 the number added to the unemployment rolls exceeded the entire figure for 1973. A similar number was then again added in 1981 and 1982. At the peak in 1983 and 1984 the number unemployed had exceeded 800 000 and amounted to approximately 17 per cent of the labour force. These figures were often much higher for younger persons and ethnic workers.

International figures, which show lower levels due to different definitions of unemployment, nevertheless revealed that the Dutch figures were quite high in comparison with similar countries. In 1983 and 1984, the Dutch unemployment figures were roughly comparable to figures for Great Britain and Canada and were exceeded only by Belgium, Ireland, Turkey, and Spain among OECD countries.

*Combating Unemployment*

By the end of the 1970s, unemployment had become a major political problem. In national election studies carried out in 1977, 1981, and 1982, more than half of all respondents voluntarily named unemployment first as the most important problem in the nation. Even more mentioned it as a second or third important problem. Combating unemployment thus became a high priority for the government and its 'social partners', the employers, and the trade unions.

One cause of high unemployment was thought to be the high wage levels in the Netherlands, making Dutch goods more costly and export more difficult. Higher prices and inflation in the early 1970s had pushed wage costs up, but these had not declined during the recession. Thus one attack on unemployment focused upon lowering wage costs and making Dutch products more competitive in price. A natural reaction of companies was to attempt to cut costs by not hiring new employees or not replacing employees who retired or left for other reasons. Attempts were made to make it more attractive for companies to hire, by providing subsidies if they employed persons who were among the long-term unemployed. In 1981 and again in 1983 the minimum wage for workers under 23 was lowered in attempts to combat higher levels of unemployment among the young.

In a move reminiscent of the 1950s, when the trade unions cooperated with the government and the employers to keep wages low and make recovery possible, a dramatic settlement was reached in 1982. The trade unions agreed to a reduction of wages. In return the length of the working week was shortened. For civil servants, for example, this meant that the working week became 38 rather than 40 hours per week. In most cases this was accumulated to provide workers with 12 extra work-free days per year. From the point of view of the unions, the intention was that this free time be filled up by new positions, thus combating unemployment directly. This is not exactly how it worked out, however, since most employers did not attempt to fill up all such free time, but used the measure as a personnel-slimming and cost-cutting device.

Another area in which government, employers, and unions cooperated was the introduction of more flexible types of employment. Part-time employment was encouraged. By 1990 approximately 1.25 million persons, amounting to approximately a quarter of all employees, held part-time rather than full-time jobs. Part-time employment became particularly important for women. OECD figures for 1988 reported that 72 per cent of all women employees in the Netherlands held part-time jobs, the highest figure for OECD countries (*OECD in Figures*, 1990). By increasing the possibility for part-time employment, it became possible to increase the participation of women in the work force at a time of economic difficulty.

While on the one hand attempts were made to make it attractive for companies to hire younger workers, measures were taken to remove older workers from the labour force through early retirement. Rather than a general lowering of the retirement age, provisions were made whereby early retirees could receive almost their full net wages until they reached their formal retirement age. Through flexible determination of the age at which such measures were made available, both the government and private employers were able to influence the size of the labour force. For example, most governmental employees became eligible at 62 (later 61), but teachers could take advantage of the provisions at the earlier age of 59. In some companies, employees became eligible as young as age 57½. Early retirement became attractive to many older workers, especially if unemployment seemed a possible alternative, and by 1988 approximately 102 000 persons were participating in such programmes (Sociaal en Cultureel Planbureau, 1990, p. 74). It is these programmes which help to account for the substantial drop between 1980 and 1987 in male employment among the 55–65 age group (see Table 8.2).

Although not all provisions and programmes were equally successful, relief was found. Between 1983 and 1988 the Netherlands had one of the better records in creating new jobs; about the same as the UK and somewhat lower than the USA, but better, for example, than Germany, France, or Japan. After 1984 the number of unemployed dropped steadily to about 600 000 at the end of the decade. Yet Dutch figures for long-term unemployment remained high in comparison with other West European nations. Two things are noteworthy concerning the governmental budget message as read by the Queen. The first is direct: after the declines in unemployment, there was concern about new rises. The second is less obvious: it is the conclusion that the government, and presumably public opinion, now accept far higher levels of unemployment as normal than was once the case. Although a reduction from more than 800 000 to less than 600 000 unemployed is important, to speak of 'a number of good years' reveals a considerable change of thought when compared to statements around 1970 that 100 000 unemployed was unacceptable.

## The Size of the Public Sector

The Netherlands has one of the largest public sectors in the world. Most comparative figures show that its size is similar to that of Sweden and Denmark, but considerably larger than that in Great Britain or the USA. The large size is the result of the creation of extensive provisions to protect the citizenry against economic difficulties: i.e., the creation of an extensive welfare state. Many of these programmes turned out to be considerably more expensive than had originally been projected. Costs became so high that the size of the public sector became a political issue in the 1980s. An important goal of governmental policy was to reduce this size. In this section we briefly examine the growth of the problem and some of the attempts to reduce the size of the public sector.

*The Growth of the Welfare State*

Basic welfare assistance is paid for out of general governmental funds, and is not what is generally meant when one refers to the welfare state. Welfare state protection beyond the minimal level is guaranteed by means of a number of insurance programmes. There are two types of programme: so-called 'people's insurance' (*volksverzekeringen*) which provides coverage and benefits for all permanent inhabitants of the country, and 'employee insurance' (*werknemersverzekeringen*) which covers all persons who are employed. The premiums for these insurance programmes are paid either by the employees or the employers or both, but may be supplemented by governmental general revenue.

The first people's insurance programme was the old age pension scheme introduced in 1956. This was followed by a widows and orphans law (1959), child payments (1962; child payments for employees had been introduced in 1939 and amended in 1963) and major medical insurance (1967). Finally, a general programme for the handicapped was added in 1976.

The insurance programmes for the employed began with unemployment compensation insurance in 1949. Compulsory medical insurance was introduced in 1964. A law providing disability compensation was passed in 1967, and in the same year a new law replaced pre-war legislation and provided compensation for normal sickness leave. Some of the benefits from these programmes were quite generous by international standards. For example, unemployment benefits and disability payments were set at 80 per cent of the last earned wage. As will be discussed below, since disability benefits continued at this level (and were indexed to cover inflation) until the age of retirement, disability became, in some cases, an attractive alternative to unemployment.

Table 8.3 gives an overview of the amounts paid by employees and employers for social insurance programmes. The values in the table are percentages of the employee's income. In some cases, premium is not paid on all earned income, but stops after a maximum payment has been made.

Premiums for people's insurance programmes are all paid for by the employees. However, premiums for employee programmes are shared by the employee and the employer. There is no particular rationale behind the distribution of costs between the two; this distribution is the outcome of past negotiations between the trade unions, the employers and the government. This also explains the final row of the table, which indicates that an amount of 11 per cent has been transferred from the employee to the employer without a specific designation of what is involved. Whether or not a premium is officially paid by the employer or the employee, it represents a

**TABLE 8.3**

**Premiums for social insurance programmes**
**(as percentage of income in 1991)**

|  | Employee contribution | Employer contribution |
|---|---|---|
| General insurance programmes |  |  |
| Old age | 14.05 | 0 |
| Widows and orphans | 1.10 | 0 |
| General disability | 1.80 | 0 |
| Major medical | 5.80 | 0 |
| Employee insurance programmes |  |  |
| Sickness leave | 1.20 | 7.15 |
| Disability | 5.50 | 0 |
| Unemployment | 0.95 | 1.35 |
| Medical | 2.85 | 4.95 |
| Other | 1.00 | 2.40 |
| Transfer payments |  |  |
| (i.e., from employee to employer) | −11.00 | 11.00 |

*Source*:  *NRC Handelsblad*, 17 September 1991, Appendix 'Rijksbegroting', p. 4.

portion of the total wage cost that does not go into the pocket of the wage-earner. If we were to add all these amounts, we would see that just over 50 per cent of actual wages have been added to wage costs in terms of insurance premiums. However, this figure applies only to lower incomes, since in some cases the amount of the premium has been set at a maximum. If a person earns above a certain level, the premium is paid only over a set amount. In addition, required medical insurance participation applies only to those with lower incomes. Of course, for higher incomes private insurance coverage must be paid but, again, this will not be tied to the level of income. Given all these extra costs, in order to provide a worker with a particular level of income (before taxes), on average an additional 45 per cent must be added to direct wage costs. The insurance premiums drive labour costs up and thus help make Dutch products less competitive internationally.

   Besides providing coverage against economic difficulties, the Dutch welfare state has attempted to ensure that all citizens would share in the increased wealth of the nation and that a 'just' distribution of the national income would be realised. One of the most controversial measures taken in this regard was the linking of minimum wage levels and of levels of the benefits from most of the above mentioned insurance programmes to the rise in wages of those employed in the private sector. This idea is in a sense a logical extension of the automatic price compensation clauses that were introduced into labour contracts in the 1970s. If employees received additional wages, at least in part because of rises in prices, then those receiving benefits were similarly in need of an increase. Thus the principle of 'coupling' was introduced, whereby rises in benefits were 'coupled' to rises in wages. This principle was also extended to the salaries of governmental employees.

The result of 'coupling' was that, when new contracts were negotiated between the employers and the unions in the private sector, government costs went up automatically. More revenue was needed to provide for increases for civil servants, and the insurance programmes were forced to make higher payments to their bene-ficiaries. This often necessitated an increase in the rates of the insurance premiums and in taxes, which in turn produced greater wage costs. As a result, an automatic wage spiral was introduced which pushed up wage costs, and the size of the public sector increased accordingly.

In 1953 social insurance premiums amounted to only about 5 per cent of the net national income. During the ensuing decade, this figure had more than doubled to almost 11 per cent. As a result of new programmes introduced in the 1960s and early 1970s, the amount for insurance premiums continued to rise throughout the 1970s. Figure 8.1 shows the development of insurance premiums from 1970 until 1992. Beginning at 15 per cent in 1970, the percentage of net national income rose to 24 per cent at its peak in 1983, before dropping to just under 20 per cent in the early 1990s.

Tax revenues in this period have remained surprisingly steady. In fact, even if one goes back to an earlier date, these figures do not change as substantially as the figures for the social insurance premiums. After the Second World War, total tax revenues as a percentage of net national income amounted to about 30 per cent. Due to tariff reductions, this fell to 23 per cent in 1955 (De Wolff and Driehuis, 1980, p. 28). After this low point, however, as the government began to take on new responsibilities, taxes were gradually increased. The official government figures in Figure 8.1 are slightly lower than those reported by De Wolff and Driehuis, who

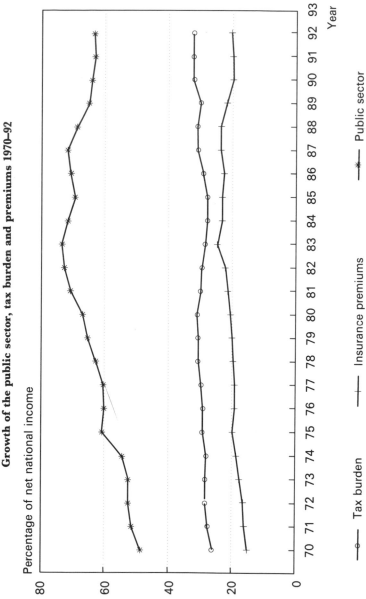

**FIGURE 8.1**

**Growth of the public sector, tax burden and premiums 1970–92**

give a level of 26 per cent for 1970. The figures rose only slightly until 1990 when tax revenues went up and insurance premium contributions went down.

The rise in tax levels and social insurance premiums contributed to the increase in the size of the public sector. However, careful examination of the three graph lines in Figure 8.1 shows that the public sector increased more rapidly than the increase in the sum of the other two figures. Total public expenditure, as revealed in the public sector figure, thus was increasing more rapidly than government income via taxation and insurance premiums. Much of the increase was due to the unexpectedly high levels of expenditures for the social insurance programmes (see below and Exhibit 8.2). The difference between governmental tax and premium revenues and governmental expenditures must be made up for through non-tax revenues or borrowing. The increasing gap, which is particularly evident from Figure 8.1 in the years between 1979 and 1984, led to concern for the size of the government budgetary deficit. This problem will be discussed below as the third major economic problem of this chapter.

*Reducing the Public Sector*

*The retreat of the state.* The rapid growth in the size of the public sector at the beginning of 1980s led to a general feeling that action was necessary to call a halt to further increases. When a coalition of Christian Democrats and Liberals took office in 1982, Prime Minister Lubbers announced that it was to be a 'no nonsense' government, committed to a reduction of the role of the state in socio-economic affairs. To this end, several 'major operations' were announced, including reappraisal of specific programmes, decentralisation, deregulation, privatisation, and debureaucratisation. The results of these programmes, however, are probably nearer to rhetoric than reality (after the title of a Dutch book on the 'major operations': see De Kam and De Haan, 1991).

The reappraisals of existing programmes constitute the most successful of the operations. Annually, committees consisting of civil servants from various departments and led by the Treasury, vetted programmes for both their effectiveness and efficiency, under an agreement by which ministers were not allowed to interfere. Despite their success, the result of all reassessments between 1982 and 1986 combined is estimated to amount to only 7 billion (i.e., 7 thousand million) guilders. The dismal record of territorial decentralisation in the Netherlands has already been discussed in Chapter 7. Despite its promise of deregulation, the Lubbers I Cabinet produced one of the most extensive legislative programmes in the post-war era. In an attempt to scale down the size of the central government's apparatus, it was announced that each year the number of government personnel was to be reduced by 2 per cent. This was an ambitious goal, especially because about half of the government's formation was exempted (tax officers, the police and armed forces, and teachers). It proved to be unattainable: in 1982 the central government had 163 397 people on its pay-roll; in 1986 this number had been reduced to 161 200.

The Dutch privatisation story is of particular interest because, other than the programmes just mentioned, privatisation is aimed directly at the government's economic role, and because it has been one of the most conspicuous features of contemporary economic policy in most West European countries, Britain and France in particular. In the Netherlands, privatisation was advocated for reasons of administrative efficiency and budgetary reduction; it was not motivated by an ideological crusade for free-market capitalism. This meant that parties of the Left could also support privatisation, and only the Green Left opposed it. The Dutch Social Democrats had already dropped nationalisation from the party manifesto in the 1930s, and provided no opposition to privatisation in the 1980s. Opposition from the civil service trade unions was largely bought off by 'social charters' accompanying each privatisation, guaranteeing newly privatised employees pension rights and even job security for a limited time period.

These measures are important in the Netherlands because privatisation has been largely defined as the legal transfer of government employees from the public to the private sector, regardless of questions of ownership and control. The most important of these privatisations have been those of PTT (Post, Telegraph, and Telephone) and the Post Bank. PTT was transformed in 1989 from a state enterprise into a company wholly owned by the state. The Post Bank was created in 1986 as a joint stock company of which the government was the sole share-holder. Through these (and other smaller) privatisations, 113 965 employees were stripped of their civil service status between 1982 and 1992, but only 900 of them were transferred to a privately owned company.

Some of the transformations of a state enterprise or government agency into a state-owned company have been intermediate stages in preparation for denationalisation proper. Although divestment of shares is not considered privatisation by the Dutch government, it has taken place. Sometimes, however, the Act of Parliament authorising the sale also stipulates that the state should retain a certain percentage of shares (50 per cent in the case of PTT). The most important of the divestments involve KLM Royal Dutch Airlines (from 78 per cent in 1984 gradually to 38 per cent in 1992), the chemical giant DSM (formerly the State Coal Mines; from 100 per cent to one-third in 1989), and the Post Bank, which merged with a commercial bank and an insurance company (after selling part of its shares in 1989 the government was left with a 23 per cent holding in the new company). These and smaller divestments brought the government a total of about $ 2.75 billion in the decade between 1982 and 1992.

One of the explanations for the meagre results of privatisation may be that most of the companies owned by the government produce additional revenues. Of the 45 companies in which the national government had an interest in 1990, only eight (most importantly KLM) were operating at a loss. The previous sentence also holds the key to a second, and much more important, explanation: the large size of the Dutch public sector is not due to considerable direct ownership of enterprises by the government. When the privatisation programme began, there were only four state enterprises (PTT, IJmuiden Fishing Port Authority, the Mint, and the Government Printing Office), and the government held all the shares in only 13 companies (the most important of which were DSM and Dutch Rail). Many comparative studies have shared the conclusion that, 'There are fewer public enterprises in the Netherlands than in the other countries [of the EC] and their share of the national economy is relatively small' (Parris, Pestieau and Saynor, 1987, p. 186).

The main reason for this comparatively small nationalised sector is probably that in most countries nationalised industries tend to operate largely on the domestic market. In some of these countries privatisation is in part necessitated by the breaking open of these domestic markets through EC regulations. The Dutch economy had always been open, preventing nationalisation in the past. In addition, the fact that the Dutch Social Democrats dropped nationalisation in favour of planning in the 1930s undoubtedly has contributed to the absence of a significant nationalised industry.

All this is not to say that the Dutch government has not intervened in economic activities in the past, and that it has not withdrawn from these activities to some extent. In the past, various companies and even entire industries have received governmental subsidies, which at times brought with them considerable governmental control. Government subventions are also the life-blood of numerous foundations for the arts and broadcasting, and for such activities as local swimming pools. In the 1980s the government's policy with regard to such subsidies changed radically. We should, therefore, add 'desubsidisation' to privatisation in order to get a correct picture of the withdrawal of the government from the Dutch economy. Exhibit 8.1 illustrates both the Dutch government's past mode of economic intervention and its recent change of policy by outlining the history of the government's involvement in the shipbuilding industry.

However, even privatisation and desubsidisation combined can have only a limited impact on the size of the Dutch public sector. As we mentioned above, the mushrooming of the Dutch public sector is not related to an increase in the government's economic interventions, but rather to a rapid growth of income transfers related to the social insurance programmes. Any attempt to scale down the public sector must therefore involve an attack on that, the heart of the welfare state.

*The attack on income transfers.*   The rapid growth in the size of the public sector at the beginning of the 1980s led to a general feeling that action was necessary to call a halt to further increases. Since then, many proposals have been made and, despite considerable controversy, some have been implemented.

Perhaps the most controversial measures taken have involved the 'reform' of the social welfare system. These reforms were aimed both at reducing the number of persons receiving benefits under such programmes and reducing the benefits provided. One measure taken was to abandon the principle of 'coupling'. In the early 1980s benefits were 'uncoupled', thus lowering costs since price increases no longer resulted in higher benefit payments. The principle of 'coupling' is particularly important to Social Democrats, who see it as a step towards a fair and just distribution of the national wealth. When they

## EXHIBIT 8.1

### The RSV story

The story starts in 1965/6 when a tripartite commission investigated the problems of the (private sector) Dutch shipbuilding industry and recommended rationalisation and modernisation as the only routes to recovery. The government assumed that such an operation required a concentration of the shipbuilding industry, which was then in the hands of seven independent companies. As a first step, the government established an interest-subsidy system on condition that individual beneficiaries would agree to cooperate with each other. This set in motion a gradual amalgamation of most of the shipyards. One company, led by a maverick and expansionist entrepreneur, Verolme, was later shown to be the most healthy and viable of the seven. Verolme tried to go it alone, but when he needed a government guarantee on a commercial loan to build a new dock, the government forced him into a merger with one of the ailing shipyards. This worsened Verolme's financial position, and soon he needed a government loan to tide him over. The government then forced him to merge his company with the others into a new conglomerate, RSV, and to step down himself.

The resulting new company was in fact a shotgun marriage, an artificial creation of the government. It remained a loose combination of shipyards in different parts of the country, and never became a viable entity. The government repeatedly had to step in to rescue the company with loans and guarantees. With some 30 000 employees, to seriously consider letting 'RSV go bankrupt was thinking the unthinkable'. The government observer in the company was the senior civil servant in charge of the Department of Economic Affairs' industrial policy. He became a double agent: it was never clear whether he represented the government in the company, or the company in the government. As the government was drawn in deeper and deeper, 'The Minister and his officials began to meddle in what were basically corporate decisions: the acceptance of orders (at any price), cost calculations, capacity plans and investments. The borderline between government and corporate responsibility became blurred.' The company eventually collapsed in 1983. The importance of this episode can be gauged from the fact that the government had spent 2.2 billion Dutch guilders (±£0.67 billion) on this company alone.

A Parliamentary Inquiry into the débâcle brought to light the degree of government interference in what was a private sector company. As a result the amount of government money spent on firms in difficulty declined sharply (from half a billion guilders in 1982 to around 14 million guilders in 1984). According to another report such subsidies dropped from 3 per cent of the net national income in 1982 to 1 per cent of net national income in 1987. Whatever the correct figures may be, government loans and guarantees to private sector companies have declined dramatically. It is safe to assume that this decline is accompanied by a decrease in government interference in the operation of these companies. The RSV story illustrates how the Dutch government could intervene in the economy and retreat again without nationalisation or privatisation.

*Sources:* 'Verslag van de Enquetecommissie Rijn-Schelde-Verolme (RSV)', Second Chamber of Parliament 1984–1985, 17817, n.16. The quotes are from the English language summary (see also Andeweg, 1988b).

joined the new coalition after the 1989 elections, they demanded that it be reinstated. However, with the poor economic outlook, as described in the Queen's speech, one of the unpopular proposals was to uncouple benefits again.

'Uncoupling' has also been applied to other areas. Salaries of governmental employees were uncoupled from levels in the private sector. Even this, however, was not sufficient and a general salary cut of 3 per cent was put through. Moreover, benefits of some programmes were also lowered. Benefits for sickness, disability and short-term unemployment had previously been set at 80 per cent of the last wage earned; these levels were cut to 70 per cent .

Existing programmes for short- and long-term unemployment were integrated into a new comprehensive programme. In doing so, the structure of benefits was changed, with the general effect that, for workers with shorter work histories, the duration of benefits was shortened. In the area of disability, additional measures have been considered. Exhibit 8.2 discusses in some detail the rapid growth in the number of persons receiving disability payments and attempts to limit these numbers. In 1991–2, this was one of the most divisive issues in the country, and at times has threatened to bring down the government coalition.

---

**EXHIBIT 8.2**

**The disability problem**

A major political issue, which is related both to the problem of unemployment and to the size of the public sector, has been the number of persons receiving disability benefits. In the 1960s the Netherlands was somewhat behind in its legislation concerning the disabled. The law that was passed in 1967 was intended to redress this position and be an example for the rest of Europe. It provided generous benefits for those who became unable to work due to a disability.

At the time the legislation was enacted, it was predicted that the number of persons receiving such benefits would eventually rise to between 150000 and 200000 persons. Yet, within four years, the predicted maximum of 200000 had been exceeded, and the number continued to grow. New legislation in 1976 expanded coverage to include the self-employed and those who had become handicapped early in life. This produced a jump in numbers to about 500000, but the end was still not in sight. By 1988 the number of persons receiving benefits had exceeded 800000 and it became conceivable that the 1000000 figure might be reached.

There seem to be two explanations for the fact that the numbers so greatly exceeded the predictions. One is that the accepted definition of disability has been altered with changing times. When the legislation was enacted, disability generally referred to physical disabilities incurred through on-the-job accidents. Gradually, both within the general population and among those charged with the administration of the programme, stress-related sicknesses and disabilities began to be included. In 1970, stress-related sicknesses and disability accounted for 13 per cent of new cases, and ranked below movement disabilities (25 per cent), and heart and circulatory diseases (21 per cent). By 1988, heart related diseases had fallen to only 9 per cent of the total number of new cases, but psychic disorders had risen to 31 per cent of all new cases, exceeded only by movement disabilities (33 per cent). In 1988, more than one-quarter of those receiving benefits were officially disabled because of stress-related or psychological problems. Some observers felt that the actual figure was even considerably higher.

A second explanation for the unexpected numbers is that disability became, under some circumstances, an attractive alternative to unemployment. When the legislation was enacted, disability payments were intended as a temporary benefit until the employee could find new employment in which the handicap was not a detriment. However, it quickly became apparent that most persons would never receive new employment and that they would remain recipients of disability benefits until they reached the age of retirement. Disability payments were set at 80 per cent (70 per cent after 1987) of the previous level of income and remained so, indexed to wage rises, until retirement. Unemployment benefits, on the other hand, also began at this level but dropped off after between six months and two years. In an economic situation in which reemployment seemed questionable, disability became not so unattractive, at least financially. Observers spoke of 'hidden unemployment'.

In order to soften the social pain of unemployment, employers who were forced to make job cutbacks often attempted to get as many workers as possible, often older workers, classified as disabled. This also helps to account for the decline in the percentage of labour participation among older age groups.

Comparative figures show that in 1984 expenditures for disability, work-related accidents and professional sicknesses in the Netherlands equalled 5.9 per cent of the GDP. This was the highest level within the EC, more than doubling that of France and the UK, and approached only by Italy and Luxembourg. This high level represents a considerable drain on public resources, while the high number of disabled and relatively high rates of days lost to sickness also lower productivity. In an effort to reduce the size of the public sector and to improve the position of Dutch industry, proposals were made in the 1992 budget message. One of the most controversial was that benefits would not be continuous until the age of retirement. Instead, it was proposed that the length of benefits after one year be made contingent upon the number of years that a person had worked. Labour Party members, in particular the Finance Minister, Wim Kok, were unprepared for the reaction within their party to these proposals. The trade unions were strongly opposed and organised demonstrations. The Labour Party executive was in disarray. Kok put his own position on the line to a special party congress in order to avoid the party withdrawing from the coalition. Eventually, the SER advised negatively on the proposals.

The controversy over disability programmes has not yet ended. In the summer of 1992 a new proposal produced controversy. The government junior minister responsible proposed that the control and administration of the insurance programme be separated. Currently both are in the hands of the industrial associations, '*bedrijfsverenigingen*', which are controlled by the employers and trade unions. Critics have felt that the unions and employers both had an interest in not controlling the growth in numbers too strictly. A more independent control might better accomplish a reduction in the numbers receiving benefits. In an attempt to understand what has gone wrong and whether there is a question of mismanagement, the Second Chamber of Parliament has decided to take the strong measure of holding a Parliamentary Inquiry.

The result of such reforms of the social security system has been a substantial decrease in benefit levels over the past ten years. For benefit recipients at the minimum levels, the decrease has amounted to about 10 per cent of real disposable income. However, since in some programmes the number of recipients has continued to increase, the total reduction has been limited. Expenditures for social insurance programmes has been stabilised at about 28 per cent of net national income (Goudswaard, 1990).

## The Budget Deficit

Paying for the welfare state is an expensive business. As has already been indicated, most programmes ended up costing more money than had been anticipated. Moreover, most programmes were initiated at a time of economic growth and full employment; as recession and unemployment became more serious, the numbers of persons needing assistance increased accordingly. Table 8.4 shows that throughout the 1980s expenditures for disability, early retirement, welfare and unemployment programmes grew at a rapid rate. During this period inflation was relatively low, so that most of the increases are real increases. Of course, these are not the only costs for the government by far. In addition there are expenditures for the other insurance programmes, as well as for usual government outlays such as for education, defence, housing, roads, development aid, culture, recreation, and health. And, as we shall see, almost one quarter of governmental expenditure is now related to the repayment of the national debt. All this money must come from somewhere.

**TABLE 8.4**

**Expenditures for disability, early retirement, welfare and unemployment (in millions of guilders), 1980–8**

| Year | Disability | Early retirement | Welfare | Unemployment |
|------|-----------|------------------|---------|--------------|
| 1980 | 13 704    |                  | 5 764   | 3 458        |
| 1985 | 16 809    | 814              | 10 739  | 6 090        |
| 1986 | 16 862    | 969              | 10 967  | 5 222        |
| 1987 | 17 228    | 1 073            | 11 233  | 4 381        |
| 1988 | 17 546    | 1 346            | 11 510  | 4 119        |

*Source:*    Metze (1990), p. 100.

Whereas the insurance programmes are financed primarily by premiums, the normal outlays of government are financed largely through taxation. For 1992, it was expected that somewhat more than one-third of the revenues for the national government would come from salary and income taxes, and somewhat less than one-quarter from VAT. However, as we have already seen in Figure 8.1, taxation and insurance premiums do not combine to produce sufficient revenue to finance all governmental expenditures. In the 1992 budget message, expenditures were estimated at 204.5 billion guilders. Taxes, duties, etc., were estimated to produce only 146 billion guilders. In addition, 28.7 billion was expected in profits, sales and other non-tax receipts. This left a gap of 29.8 billion guilders to be filled by other means.

The political controversies that have surrounded the gap in the budget have centred around two elements. First, discussion of the Dutch economy and the governmental budget is not complete without treatment of the role of natural gas. Second, since, natural gas revenues cannot cover the entire gap however they are used, the amount that the government must borrow to cover expenditures is a major concern. These two elements are discussed in the following sections.

*Natural Gas and the 'Dutch Disease'*

Natural gas was discovered near the village of Slochteren in the north of the country at the end of the 1950s. However, it was not until 1967 that accurate estimates were made concerning the size of the natural gas reserves. It is now assumed that the Netherlands has the fifth-largest reserves in the world.

When gas was discovered, the prevailing view on the future of energy resources was quite different from that of today. Oil prices were low and were expected to remain so; nuclear energy was expected to be an economical source of power in the future. Thus Dutch policy was concentrated on exploitation of the new finds as quickly as possible. Gas mains were laid throughout the country and heating and cooking facilities were quickly converted. This conversion led to higher consumption as houses had central heating installed, and gas was also used in industrial boilers for generation of steam and in electric power plants. Gas also provided raw materials for the chemical industry (see Lubbers and Lemckert, 1980).

The decision to supply gas at a low price was generally beneficial to the economy. As estimates of the size of reserves rose, the decision was made to stimulate the export of gas. This was in line with expectations that gas would become less popular or necessary in the future. In an effort to penetrate the market, a low price was charged. Some of the export contracts linked the price of gas to that of oil, although this was not looked upon particularly favourably at the time. Such views would change quickly!

The oil crisis of 1973 was to alter matters radically. The dramatic rise in the price of oil meant that the monetary value of gas also rose. Moreover, gas had environmental advantages that were becoming more apparent. Prices were brought more into line with market value as new contracts were negotiated and old ones renegotiated. Since the great bulk of the revenues generated by gas go directly into the government treasury, the government received a major financial bonanza. The balance of payments showed large positive figures and the Dutch guilder became one of the world's strongest currencies.

Yet natural gas may have been a mixed blessing: a 'poisoned apple', as one author put it. The poison produced a sickness known as the 'Dutch Disease'. 'The Dutch disease refers to a sickness whose syndrome is the use of temporary income, in the Dutch case obtained from the unexpected gas revenues, in order to finance permanent expenditures. The symptoms are increased governmental expenditures and a hard currency' (Metze, 1990, p. 25).

The strong currency placed Dutch entrepreneurs at a competitive disadvantage. At a time when the world economy was trying to absorb the effects of the oil crisis, Dutch products were more expensive because of the gas-induced high value of the guilder. While the reduced growth of world trade cost the Netherlands about 2 per cent of the growth in its GNP, gas production began to contribute an additional portion of the annual governmental budget. Around the beginning of the 1980s gas production amounted to about 7 per cent of the GNP and 15 per cent of the national governmental revenues.

These revenues were not invested in long-term ventures to produce new jobs, but were employed to shore up existing industry and to plug the gaps in the budget as the costs of the welfare state rose (see Figure 8.1). The 'easy money' led to expenditure patterns that, unless altered, would continue long after the gas reserves were exhausted. Thus many of the measures taken in order to reduce expenditures were necessary in order to reduce dependence upon gas revenues. This dependence has indeed been decreased, as the budget message for 1992 anticipated that gas revenues for 1992 would amount to only 4.7 per cent of total predicted revenues.

## *The Financing Deficit Reduced*

As revenues, even including gas receipts, have seldom matched expenditures, the government has been forced to borrow money not only for long-term investments but also for current outlays. In only a decade, the national debt rose from somewhat under 150 000 million guilders in 1982 to 339 000 million guilders in 1991. These figures amount to 43.8 per cent and 71.0 per cent of the national income respectively, and were expected to rise to 72.2 per cent in 1992. In the same period interest payments on debt have risen from about 2 per cent to almost 6 per cent of the GNP, a figure considerably higher than the average of the five larger EC countries.

The high level of governmental borrowing has been a major political concern in the Netherlands over the past ten years. The term 'financing deficit' (*financieringstekort*) has been a common term in political debate and is easily recognised by large segments of the population. This term refers not to the actual deficit in the current budget, but to the difference between revenues and expenditures, less the amount paid on long-term loans. The assumption is that as such loans are paid off, the amounts become available for new loans. When a gap is still existent between income and outlay, it can be plugged either by additional loans or by monetary measures, such as simply printing new money. Most Dutch economists view a financing deficit of between 4 and 5 per cent of Net National Income as tolerable. Until 1979 the financing deficit figure never exceeded 4.4 per cent , but thereafter it began to rise dramatically, reaching a peak of 10.7 per cent in 1982.

By this time it had become clear that the financing deficit had reached intolerable levels. Such borrowing by the government takes funds away from other areas of investment and burdens future budgets with higher interest payments. Discussion of the desirable level, or an agreed upon maximum level, of the financing deficit became a major focus in negotiations surrounding the formation of new Cabinets. It is not surprising that the Liberal Party pushed strongly for reducing the deficit, but by the end of the 1980s all parties were in agreement that reduction was necessary. When the Social Democrats joined the Christian Democrats in the 1989 coalition, they agreed to push the level down to 4.75 per cent in 1991 and 4.25 per cent in 1992. The Social Democratic leader and Minister of Finance, Wim Kok, has been trying hard to shed his party's free-spending image by holding the line. Even in the light of unexpected economic difficulties, he supported measures to keep this deficit at the level agreed upon.

## Conclusion

After the Second World War, the Dutch economy was in ruins. With austere governmental policies, harmonious cooperation between employers and trade unions, and efficient use of Marshall Plan aid, recovery came quicker than had initially been predicted. By the 1960s wages were increased and a period of unprecedented economic growth and a rise in the standard of living ensued. Building upon the foundations of the 1950s, a system of social welfare programmes was constructed to protect as much as possible against personal economic setbacks.

In the 1970s and into the 1980s economic growth slowed, in part because of the shock of the 1973 oil embargo. Unemployment shot up more rapidly than had ever been imagined. The number of people receiving benefits from unemployment and other social welfare programmes grew faster than had been predicted. By the beginning of the 1980s, the Netherlands was again faced with substantial economic problems.

Beginning with the 'no-nonsense' 1982–6 Cabinet, unpleasant measures have again been taken. Few countries have actually succeeded in cutting governmental expenditures, salaries of government employees, welfare benefits, and subsidies for all sorts of favourite activities in the way the Dutch government has. Obviously not all measures were popular and there has often been an attitude of 'Why me?' and 'You first', but there has also been a general acceptance of the gravity of the situation. This is symbolised by the 1982 agreement in which the trade unions agreed to wage measures. There has been no conflict between the working and non-working, no tax revolts, and no great crisis of government.

When he wrote his now classic analysis of *Pluralism and Democracy in the Netherlands*, Lijphart formulated Rule One of 'The Rules of the Game' of Dutch politics:

> The first and foremost rule of the Dutch political game is that politics should not be regarded as a game at all . . . it is a business. This attitude is in accord with Holland's long tradition as a merchant nation and with the crucial political role the merchant middle classes have played in Dutch history. This attitude toward politics has a pervasive and highly beneficial influence on democratic stability. (Lijphart, 1975, p. 123)

Although this rule was originally formulated decades ago, and before the problems discussed in this chapter emerged, it still seems to hold today. As the government and the public face the problems outlined in the pessimistic Queen's message quoted at the beginning of this chapter, it is to be hoped, but also expected, that a businesslike solution will again be found.

# 9

# Foreign Policy

## The Constants of Dutch Foreign Policy

*Peace, Profits and Principles* is the catchy alliterative title of a book on Dutch foreign policy by Joris Voorhoeve (1979), one-time parliamentary leader of the VVD (1986–90). Under these three headings he sought to analyse the major traditions of this foreign policy, which he defined as 'maritime commercialism' 'neutralist abstentionism' and 'internationalist idealism'. Others have objected to the concept of traditions in this respect, even arguing that the Dutch have insufficient historic sense for traditions. Such authors prefer to speak of tendencies, themes, or constants, and some of them have amended or enlarged Voorhoeve's list. On closer inspection, however, the themes mentioned by other authors remain closely related to the clusters of attitudes mentioned by Voorhoeve (Heldring, 1978; Rozemond, 1987; Scheffer, 1988). There is also little disagreement concerning the origins of such tendencies or traditions.

Both the size and geographical location of the country have left their imprint on the country's external relations. The Dutch domestic market being quite small but ideally located to serve as a gateway to the European hinterland, the Netherlands came to rely on maritime trade. This has brought an Atlantic perspective to its foreign policy, sometimes bordering on anti-continentalism. Already in the seventeenth century, Pieter de la Court, a Leyden merchant and political scientist, advocated creating a wide swathe of water to the east of the province of Holland, to separate it from the European continent. As late as the 1950s the Dutch Foreign Office proclaimed: 'The

212

Netherlands cannot exist without Europe, but it is a continental European nation neither in its history, nor in its character.' Despite altercations with the British first, and despite irritation over American pressure to decolonise later, the Netherlands has continued to rely on these two extra-continental powers. This reliance is due partly to the importance of maritime trade, but also to the desire to have a countervailing power to the dominant state on the continent, be it German or French.

The significance of trade for the Dutch economy has also led to another of Voorhoeve's traditions, 'neutralist abstentionism', a set of preferences described by others as 'economic pacifism'; it is a reluctance to accept changes in the status quo, or downright conservatism. The Dutch colonial empire could not be defended adequately, and was therefore best protected by a neutralist policy. The flow of commerce was best served by an opportunistic abstention from European power politics. Any disturbance of the balance of power could be detrimental to trade, and was therefore deplored. The Netherlands has been described as a 'satisfied nation', quite happy with things as they are in the world. After 1945 the failure of neutralism as a security strategy was recognised by Dutch politicians and the public alike, and the joining of the Atlantic Alliance has been interpreted as an unequivocal abandonment of the neutralist tradition. Other observers, however, maintain that NATO membership constitutes less of a break with tradition than it may seem at first sight. Now that the international status quo was no longer guaranteed by a Pax Britannica, the Dutch supported a Pax Americana. Both the old and the new situation in which the Dutch found themselves allowed them an *afzijdigheid in afhankelijkheid* (aloofness in dependence: Scheffer, 1988): 'membership in a Western bloc, dominated by one superpower has permitted a continuation of traditional Dutch neutrality within a new framework and has relieved them of the need to develop an ambitious foreign policy of their own' (Bodenheimer, 1978, p. 251). It was the perception of a renewed emphasis on neutralism in the 1970s that led Walter Laqueur to his diagnosis of 'Hollanditis' as a second 'Dutch disease' (Laqueur, 1981).

The third constant in Dutch foreign policy, 'internationalist idealism' in the words of Voorhoeve, is often attributed to the Calvinist church minister in every Dutchman, rather than to the merchant in him. Especially when this idealism transforms the Dutch government into a Dutch uncle, wagging an admonishing finger at other nations, the relation with Calvinist moralism is too obvious to miss. The same can be said of another manifestation of internationalist idealism, the emphasis on international law. Article 90 of the Constitution even charges the government with the promotion of 'the development of the international rule of law'. Such legalism is not entirely alien to Calvinist culture. Often, however, minister and merchant went hand in hand. Dutch attempts to codify international relations are sometimes perceived as symptoms of Dutch conservatism, of its clinging to the status quo. Moreover, ever since Grotius, the content of international law has rarely failed to serve the Dutch interest in free trade and open sea passages. The Dutch interest in neutralist abstention from power politics is easily disguised as moralism.

In this chapter we shall take a closer look at these three clusters of supposedly constant foreign policy preferences by examining the Dutch role in three international organisations. It is through its active involvement in a large number of international organisations that the Netherlands tries to rise above the status of a small country: in terms of territory the country ranks 117th in the world, in terms of population 40th, in terms of GNP 14th, but in terms of membership in international organisations it ranks second in the world (Voorhoeve, 1979, p. 19; Voorhoeve, 1991, p. 55) The three most important ones are also most suited to a discussion of the three constants in the foreign policy of the country: NATO ('peace'), the EC ('profits') and the UN ('principles').

## From Staunch Ally back to Neutral State?

The Dutch decision to join the Atlantic Alliance was opposed only by the Communist party, and has never been seriously questioned. The original support for NATO should be understood against the backdrop of, on the one hand, gratitude for the American effort to liberate the Netherlands in 1945 and for Marshall Plan aid for rebuilding the ruined Dutch economy, tempered only marginally by anger over American pressure to end the successful military actions against Indonesian insurgents and, on the other hand, of growing anxiety over Soviet imperialism, fuelled particularly by the Communist take-over in Czechoslovakia in 1948. Perhaps the Dutch embraced NATO membership because it allowed them to continue as a naval power by compensating for the loss of the colonies (Pijpers, 1991, pp. 64–5).

Despite later criticisms of the participation in NATO by the then dictatorial regimes of Portugal and Greece, despite opposition to American involvement in Indo-China and Latin America, and even despite misgivings over NATO's nuclear strategy, public support for NATO membership has never wavered. The percentage in favour of leaving the Alliance has never exceeded 20 per cent (Everts, 1983, p. 30), and no major party has ever advocated withdrawal from NATO, not even a 'French', partial, one. Especially during the first decades of the Alliance, the Netherlands acted as a particularly staunch ally and a loyal supporter of US leadership in the Alliance.

The Dutch share in NATO's defence expenditures has always been relatively high compared with that of other smaller member states such as Belgium, Turkey, Greece, Denmark, or Norway (Voorhoeve 1979, pp. 130–1). The Dutch were among the 15 countries that joined the USA in the Korean War (a UN mission *de iure*, a US mission *de facto*). In 1957 the Netherlands wasted no time in becoming the first European ally to accept American nuclear missiles on its territory. While other member states demanded a say in the engagement of such weaponry ('dual key'), the Dutch would have been happy to leave this responsibility entirely to the US government. Another quarrel with the Americans about Dutch colonialism, this time about the Dutch–Indonesian conflict over Papua New Guinea in 1961–2, did little to weaken the Dutch enthusiasm for the Atlantic Alliance. The long-serving Foreign Secretary, Joseph Luns (1956–71) stead-fastly refused to convey the protests of the Dutch Parliament over American intervention in Vietnam to Washington. As we shall discuss in the following section, the Dutch government always objected to plans for European rather than Atlantic defence arrangements, and served almost as an American proxy in the EC. One author even struggled to find a distinction between the Dutch role of faithful ally and that of a vassal or satellite state: the submission of the Dutch to American leadership, he suggests, was not imposed, but voluntary (Van Staden, 1978b, p. 153).

With the retirement of Luns as Minister of Foreign Affairs in 1971, the Dutch role as America's small but staunch ally abruptly came to an end. Over strong objections by the USA, the Dutch government supported acceptance of the People's Republic of China as a member of the UN in 1971. Luns's successors as Foreign Secretary had fewer misgivings about decrying US overt and covert involvement in Latin America, and particularly in Vietnam. One of them, Max van der Stoel, took pride in labelling the Netherlands a 'critical ally'. In 1975 the Dutch even targeted Cuba as one of the countries on which to concentrate its development aid. Within NATO the change in Dutch policy is evidenced by an increased emphasis on arms control negotiations, and in particular on reduction of nuclear weapons. The proposed deployment in 1977–8 of the 'neutron bomb', or the 'enhanced radiation, reduced blast' weapon as it was called officially, met with strong public opposition in the Netherlands. More than 1.2 million citizens signed petitions against the neutron bomb, which probably contributed to the vote in the Dutch Parliament not to accept the proposals by the Carter administration. The episode of the neutron bomb is important, because the issue ('a bomb that kills people, but saves property') served to mobilise a large portion of the population into what became known as 'the peace movement': a loose coalition of Left-wing political parties, trade unions, fringe groups, and individuals, dominated by two organisations linked to the churches in the Netherlands, the Catholic Pax Christi and the ecumenical Interchurch Peace Council (IKV). The fact that President Carter eventually decided to shelve plans for the production and the deployment of the neutron bomb was interpreted by the peace movement as a victory, and reinforced its resolve.

Only one year later, in December 1979, NATO took its so-called dual-track decision: the pursuit of multilateral arms reduction coupled to the modernisation of the Alliance's long-range theatre nuclear weapons. As part of the deployment of 572 new nuclear delivery systems, the Dutch were to accept the stationing of 48 cruise and Pershing II missiles on Dutch territory. The Dutch government made formal reservations to these plans in what became known as 'the Dutch footnote' to the protocol of the NATO meeting. Despite these reservations the government narrowly escaped a vote of no confidence in the following parliamentary debate. Actually, the Dutch footnote was the first step of what was to become one of the classic examples of 'depoliticisation' in Dutch politics (see Chapter 2).

Domestic opposition to the cruise missiles was fierce. More and more people rallied around IKV's slogan, 'Rid the world of nuclear weapons; starting with the Netherlands' (surveys showed that more than half the population agreed with the catch phrase). In 1981 about 400 000 people participated in a demonstration against the missiles in Amsterdam; the following year 550 000 people marched through The Hague in a similar demonstration; and in 1983 3.2 million Dutch citizens petitioned the government to reject NATO's nuclear modernisation. Of the major parties, the Labour Party was adamantly opposed to the missiles (but one third of its voters favoured accepting the weapons on Dutch territory) and made its position a major plank in its platform. The Liberal Party welcomed the NATO plans (but one third of its voters rejected the missiles), and the CDA was divided. For the Christian Democrats the issue was particularly threatening: we have already mentioned the involvement of the churches in the peace movement. The Dutch Reformed Church had already rejected the use of nuclear weapons as un-Christian in 1962. Moreover, the NATO decision came at a particularly awkward moment for the Christian Democrats. The CDA had only just been formed (see Chapter 3) and had not really amalgamated yet. A group of MPs and party activists, especially from the former ARP, feared (correctly, as it later turned out) that the new party would shift to the right. They opposed the formation of a governing coalition with the VVD in 1977, and they now used the issue of the cruise missiles to strengthen their position within the party. Following its reservations in the Dutch footnote, the government sought to depoliticise the issue by postponing a decision: each year it announced to its NATO partners that a decision would be taken next year. Eventually, in 1984, this position became untenable within the Alliance. Prime Minister Lubbers then came up with one of the most ingenious depoliticisation ploys in the history of consociationalism: a final decision to accept the American missiles was to be postponed one more year. If, by 1 November 1985, the Soviets had not increased the number of their SS-20 missiles, the Dutch would refuse to accept the missiles, whereas an increase in the number of Soviet missiles would lead to automatic acceptance of the cruise and Pershing II missiles. In practice this clever manoeuvre shifted responsibility for Dutch foreign policy to the Kremlin! After a year the Soviets appeared to have added to the number of their missiles, and without any significant protest it was decided to accept the American weapons. Shortly thereafter Gorbachev and Reagan reached an arms reduction agreement, making the Netherlands the only NATO country that had accepted the Pershing II and cruise missiles, but where they never arrived.

The Dutch opposition to the neutron bomb, and the subsequent reluctance to accept their share of the cruise missiles, have led to the diagnosis of 'Hollanditis', a supposedly contagious Dutch disease. Laqueur and others have speculated about a re-emergence of the tradition of neutralist abstentionism, now that both gratitude for American aid and fear of Soviet expansionism have waned. Such a diagnosis can be valid only if it is accepted that the penchant for neutralism disappeared when the Netherlands joined the Atlantic Alliance. Neutralism can then be said to have been pushed to the background by the exceptional circumstances of the first post-war decades. Now that things are returning to normal, the Dutch return to neutralism. If, on the other hand, we agree with the view that NATO only provided the security umbrella under which the Dutch could continue to foster their aloofness from power politics, the Dutch misgivings about nuclear weapons cannot be interpreted in this way. In this respect it is interesting to note that, whilst the percentage of the population agreeing that NATO contributes to *détente* in Europe dropped from 65 in 1968 to 39 in 1978, the proportion of the population in favour of continued membership of NATO did not decrease significantly (Van Staden, 1989b, p. 354).

Most observers disagree with the Hollanditis diagnosis, whether they think that neutralism was abandoned when the Dutch joined NATO or not. There are three major counter-arguments to the Hollanditis thesis. Some argue that the shift from staunch to critical, or even reluctant, ally should not be interpreted as a sign of neutralist abstentionism, but as a development towards a less submissive attitude, and a more activist role of the Dutch government in international affairs. If there is a return to old traditions at all, the Dutch opposition to NATO's nuclear deterrent fits in with the moralist or idealist orientation of Dutch foreign policy. That is why the churches are involved; that is why opposition to the missiles was closely related to a stronger emphasis on human rights and development aid (see below). One author even speculates that the changes in foreign policy are caused by post-colonial guilt, felt in particular by Social Democratic Cabinet Ministers (Pijpers, 1991, pp. 66–8).

It is also argued that the more critical posture of the Dutch government within the Alliance should not be explained in terms of Dutch foreign policy traditions. If they are traditions at all, they are traditions of the foreign policy elite, not of the general public. More than other policy areas, foreign policy has always been in the hands of a small, close-knit establishment. In general, foreign policy was not the subject of conflicts between the political parties, with few notable exceptions (such as rows over a Dutch embassy at the Holy See in the 1920s). Foreign policy-making was also not embedded in a neo-corporatist network of interest groups and advisory councils. In many respects foreign policy making was the last remnant of a nineteenth-century style in politics: elitist and non-partisan. This changed abruptly in the late 1960s and early 1970s. In Chapter 2 we have seen how depillarisation at first seemed to change the policy-making style: politicisation, polarisation, and a call for democratic reform. Foreign policy-making did not escape this change. As a result of politicisation and polarisation the political parties, and in particular the Labour Party, developed and emphasised their own partisan proposals for the Netherlands' external relations. In the population at large 'action groups' became more vocal and visible, and some of them sought to change the country's foreign policy. Popular disenchant-ment with the Dutch role as America's staunch ally is thought to have resulted from factors such as the coming of age of a new generation that had not itself experienced the Second World War, the revulsion arising from the widely televised atrocities of the Vietnam war, and exasperation with the ongoing arms race (Van Staden, 1989b).

It is this 'domesticisation of foreign policy' (Van Staden, 1989a, p. 103; Everts, 1983) that is often held responsible for the change in Dutch foreign policy. Support for this view can be found in the fact that the return from politicisation and polarisation to the original 'rules of the game', as discussed in Chapter 2, was followed by a less 'deviant' position of the Netherlands within NATO. It can also be argued, however, that the removal of the nuclear missiles from the international agenda made such a return to the mainstream of NATO possible, and the collapse of the Warsaw Pact since Gorbachev came to power in 1985 may even have brought the mainstream of NATO closer to the Dutch position. The position of the Netherlands within the Alliance in the late 1980s and early 1990s is best illustrated by the opposition, on the one hand, to President Reagan's Strategic Defense Initiative, and the reversal, on the other hand, of an earlier decision to scrap the nuclear capabilities of the F-16 jet-fighters and Orion anti-submarine planes.

Both these counter-arguments accept that a change in Dutch foreign policy has taken place, but disagree with interpreting the change as a return to neutralist abstentionism. However, the strongest argument against the Hollanditis diagnosis comes from those observers who argue that, in practice, the changes in the foreign policy of the Dutch government have been only marginal. They argue that, pressured by domestic critique of NATO's nuclear strategy, the Dutch government paid lip service to the ideal of nuclear disarmament, while continuing its support of NATO. Perhaps the only difference with other member states was the impact of public opinion on the Dutch government (Eichenberg 1983, p. 158). But if this resulted in the official rhetoric being neutralist, so the argument goes, the reality was not so affected. Voorhoeve, for one, does not concur with the popular description of Dutch security policy after 1970 as that of a critical or reluctant ally. Himself a member of the opposition at the time, he writes of the Cabinet that is held most responsible for the changes in the country's foreign policy: 'They left not only staunch NATO supporters, but also the disarmament lobby highly dissatisfied. By steering in-between these extremes, the Den-Uyl Government had simply changed the country from a "super-loyal" into a "normal" ally' (Voorhoeve, 1979, p. 130). In support of this analysis he points to the cuts in the Dutch defence budget in the mid-1970s which have often been used as evidence of Hollanditis. Whilst such cuts may have been important in absolute terms, they were not greater than in many other NATO countries. On the contrary, the relative contribution of the Dutch to NATO's defence expenditure increased slightly during the 1970s, whereas that of countries such as the US or the UK decreased at the time.

## European Integration versus Atlantic Orientation?

The Dutch have the reputation of being enthusiastic subscribers to the ideal of an integrated Europe. The practice of European integration, however, is not always as wholeheartedly embraced: the Netherlands has been one of the slowest member states in implementing measures under the single market. But Europe is not an issue on the political agenda: no major political party questions EC membership, and surveys consistently show higher than average popular support for European unification in the Netherlands. From the Dutch point of view the EC has fulfilled its two main promises. It has been almost too successful in cementing Germany not only militarily (through NATO) but also economically into Western alliances, and the Dutch are now wary of a French–German directorate within the Community. The second promise, of fostering Dutch economic growth by demolishing obstacles to trade (two-thirds of Dutch industrial exports is to other member states), has also been a success, and the Netherlands has, until 1992, always been a net earner from the EC.

Interestingly enough, the Dutch had to overcome initial hesitations before developing their pro-Europe attitude. When the European Coal and Steel Community was set up, the Dutch objected to a supranational authority, whereas supranationality was later to become one of the characteristic Dutch desires in Brussels. Another source of hesitation was even more curious: fear (by all major parties except the KVP), of a papist Europe. This fear even had an impact on the composition of the 1952–6 Cabinet. In Chapter 2 we noted that in 1952 the portfolio of Foreign Affairs fell to the KVP, but that the other parties balked at the prospect of all the Foreign Secretaries in the EC being Catholics. As a compromise a non-partisan Minister of Foreign Affairs, the banker Beyen, was appointed, in addition to whom the Catholic diplomat Joseph Luns became minister without portfolio, with the right to call himself Foreign Secretary when abroad. When asked why the Netherlands had *two* Ministers of Foreign Affairs, his stock reply was that, the Netherlands being such a small country, the rest of the world was too large an area to be covered by just one minister. Ironically, it was the Catholic Luns who turned out to be a staunch Atlanticist, and it was Beyen who became one of the founding fathers of the Community. The latter succeeded, together with Belgium's Foreign Secretary, Spaak, in laying the foundations of the EC Treaty after attempts at a European Defence Community and a European Political Community had foundered in 1954.

Once these initial hesitations were overcome, two important obstacles to European integration remained: a fear of domination by one or more of the larger member states, and an emphasis on Atlantic cooperation in the areas of defence and foreign policy. Because of these reservations it has been argued that the Dutch Foreign Office sought to model 'Europe as a greater Holland' (Heldring, 1978). The fear of a directorate of larger countries, France, or a Franco-German coalition, made the Dutch into proponents of widening the Community by including more countries, but it was primarily translated into proposals to strengthen the EC's supranational institutions, the Commission and the European Parliament.

Countries such as the Netherlands, it is felt, are too small to exert influence in an intergovernmental power game. Supranational bodies, on the other hand, are likely to pursue pan-European interests, and such interests are deemed more compatible with Dutch interests than are specific French or German interests. Thus supranationalism became a preoccupation of the Dutch within Europe, from the near unanimous motion in the Second Chamber to transfer powers to supranationalist institutions in 1948, to the conflict in 1991 between the Netherlands as temporary chairman of the EC and the British government about supranationalist tendencies in a Dutch draft for the Maastricht treaty. The Dutch insistence, since 1964, on a directly elected European Parliament with real powers should also be interpreted in this light.

Officially, the Dutch have always worried about the 'European democratic deficit': decision-making increasingly shifts to Brussels, where it is outside the purview of national parliaments. This gap in democratic accountability should be filled by a competent European Parliament. The introduction of direct elections to the European Parliament, first held in 1979, was celebrated as a Dutch victory for democracy. Turnout for these elections was low everywhere, but it was particularly disappointing in the Netherlands (see Chapter 4). This has not helped much in giving the supranational Parliament democratic legitimacy, but the low turnout has only strengthened the resolve of the Dutch government to push for more powers for the European Parliament, claiming that the low turnout is caused by a reluctance to vote for a third-rate legislature. It is difficult to ascertain to what degree this concern for European democracy is real, or whether it merely serves as a flag of convenience under which to strengthen the supranational character of the Community in defence of Dutch national interests.

Whatever explanation is the correct one, it should be emphasised that the campaign for supranationalism has always taken second place to the Atlantic orientation in Dutch European policy. It is in the interest of Dutch trade that the Netherlands has always attempted to prevent the development of a 'fortress Europe' by welcoming the accession of new member states, and by objecting to European protectionism. Yet, within that framework, the Atlantic

orientation has always been given precedence. Dutch Atlanticism is
evidenced by a reluctance to extend European cooperation to defence
and foreign policy, and by its support of British applications for
membership of the Community. The Dutch attitude is epitomised by
Foreign Secretary Luns's finest hour: his 'no' to De Gaulle's
aspirations in 1961–2. In 1960 the French President announced his
proposals for a European Political Union, which included taking over
some of NATO's military responsibilities, and in which European
institutions would be firmly controlled by intergovernmental bodies.
The circumstance that France was the only nuclear power within the
Europe of the original six member states, and De Gaulle's suggestion
that the new political union's secretariat be located in Paris, provided
sufficient fuel for fear of a Gaullist Europe. This anxiety, the lack of
supranational elements in the proposal, and the challenge to
America's leadership of the Alliance by the formation of a French-
led European defence bloc within NATO, all ran counter to
established Dutch foreign policy precepts. Irritation over the plans
mounted when De Gaulle secured German (and Italian) support on
the eve of the 1961 meeting where the proposals were to be discussed.
All other member states, except the Netherlands, agreed to under-
write the French plans. Much to the surprise of Europe's two most
venerable statesmen, De Gaulle and Adenauer, their proposal was
thwarted by a Minister of Foreign Affairs (not even a head of state or
government) from a small country. Luns demanded that the political
union should not affect NATO, and that it should develop
supranational institutions. He was willing to drop these conditions,
however, provided that the UK was included.

This last element, which became known as the Dutch *préalable
Anglais*, is interesting since it shows that for the Netherlands
Atlanticism took priority over supranationalism. Because of Britain's
special relationship with the USA, its accession to the Community
would provide the Dutch with a powerful ally in promoting an
Atlantic orientation within the EC. At the same time it was well
known that the British were, (and still are) excessively wary of
transferring some of their national sovereignty to a supranational
organisation. The Dutch could not hope to get support for their plans
in that direction from British membership of the Community. After
the inconclusive 1961 summit the Dutch were gradually forced to
accept compromise proposals, and they might have lost their struggle
had not De Gaulle 'snatched defeat from the jaws of victory' by

rejecting the compromises, reverting to his original plan, and vetoing British membership. In 1962 the Netherlands, now joined by Belgium, once again (and this time definitely) vetoed the proposals.

It is only in the late 1980s and early 1990s that the Atlantic orientation seems gradually to have been pushed into the background. The causes of this change – it is still little more than a shift in emphasis – are to be found on both sides of the Atlantic. The USA is perceived to be less focused on Europe than it was in the past. In the 1970s there were already growing doubts about the American guarantee of European security, and subsequently there were calls to develop a European defence option within the context of the Western European Union (WEU). Now that the Soviet threat has collapsed, the USA need no longer give priority to Europe's defence. A new, more globally-oriented, USA foreign policy is reflected in President Bush's 'new world order'. In economic terms, the US is forced more and more to look westward. This Pacific economic orientation of the USA has also weakened America's cross-Atlantic ties. At the same time, the international situation has changed for the Dutch, too. The Europe of the Six has become the Europe of the Twelve. From the Dutch point of view the most important of the new member states has been the UK. There is less need for an Atlantic reservation to European integration now that the Community includes a large extra-continental power to counter-balance Franco–German aspirations.

The Dutch are also less opposed to European political cooperation because they have learned from the 1973 Arab oil embargo that it can be risky to stand alone. Before 1973 the Netherlands had a strongly pro-Israel reputation, perhaps not always warranted by its actual policies (Soetendorp, 1989). The Arab countries took particular offence at the Dutch adherence to the English version of resolution 242 of the UN Security Council, calling for Israeli withdrawal from 'occupied territories', rather than '*the* occupied territories' mentioned in some other versions. When war broke out in the Middle East in 1973, the Dutch government unequivocally condemned the Arab countries, just as it had done in 1967. It refused to join the other EC member states in a common reaction because of the more pro-Arab attitude of the French in particular. For these reasons, in October 1973, the Arab countries imposed an oil embargo not only on the USA, but also on the Netherlands. The embargo of the Netherlands was even kept in place four months longer than that of the USA.

Despite panicky reactions at first – 'car-free Sundays' were declared to save oil – the economic effect of the embargo was insignificant because oil was diverted from other EC countries to the Netherlands, despite their irritation over the Dutch obstinacy. The political effect has been more important. Not only have the Dutch distanced themselves more and more from Israel, but they have also come to see the advantages of a common European foreign policy.

Now that the renewed momentum of European integration leading up to '1992' has spilled over into closer military cooperation within the WEU, and in renewed proposals for a European Political Union, the Dutch take a less deviant stance than they did in the 1960s. Yet, when the Netherlands took over the EC presidency in July 1991, it attempted to redraft the existing Luxemburg proposal for the treaty to establish a European Political Union to include more supranationalist elements, and to allow a common security policy only as a complement to NATO, much to the annoyance of several other member states. Apparently the traditional reservations have not yet been completely abandoned.

## Interests versus Idealism?

In the past the third constant of Dutch foreign policy, 'internationalist idealism' primarily took the form of the promotion of international law. More recently it has also surfaced in foreign policy statements and documents in the form of role-conceptions such as 'example' and 'developer': protecting human rights abroad and providing aid to developing countries (Van Staden, 1978a). These activities are pursued primarily, but not exclusively, within the context of the UN. The peace-keeping missions of that organisation have also been supported either financially or militarily (as most recently in what was formerly Yugoslavia), but that has not been the most conspicuous Dutch contribution to the UN.

As a result of its historical links to the Boers in South Africa, the Netherlands voted in 1961 against expelling the country from the UN for its policy of apartheid, but subsequently the Dutch have become ever more critical of South Africa. Since 1963 the Netherlands has complied with a non-mandatory embargo on military supplies to South Africa, and as a temporary member of the Security Council from 1983 to 1985 it took the initiative for a resolution boycotting weapons made in South Africa. The Dutch have also offered financial assistance to victims of apartheid. The Netherlands has similarly sought to put pressure on South Africa through the EC.

It is not only in South Africa that the Netherlands has supported the cause of human rights. The Dutch have always advocated the appointment of a UN High Commissioner for Human Rights. In terms of governmental policy, this support is to a degree symbolised in the person of the Foreign Secretary, Max van der Stoel (1973–7, 1981–2). Streets have been named after him in Greece and Eastern Europe because of his support for democrats and dissidents when these countries were still ruled autocratically.

In the absence of objective and quantifiable indicators it is, however, difficult to gauge the importance of human rights in Dutch foreign policy compared with that of other countries. The Dutch preoccupation with development aid lends itself more readily to cross-national comparisons. Whether out of a sense of guilt about its colonial past, or as a modern extension of the churches' missionary work, the Dutch attitude towards developing countries borders on *tiers-mondisme*. The importance of development aid is probably the one aspect of foreign policy on which all major parties are most in agreement. Political disagreement is largely confined to which criteria should be used to select countries for bilateral aid. Constant among these criteria are the degree of poverty, the degree to which the indigenous government puts in an effort of its own, and the existence of an historic responsibility (i.e., to former colonies such as Indonesia and Surinam). More controversial are criteria such as respect for human rights (especially when it conflicts with the historic responsibility for former colonies turned dictatorial), or the degree to which Dutch exporting companies can profit from the aid. In 1992 such conflicting criteria led to an ironic episode in which the Indonesian government retaliated against Dutch criticism of its human rights' record by suddenly announcing that it would no longer accept Dutch development assistance.

Bilateral aid is not the only element in the Dutch development programme. Multilateral aid constitutes about one third of the total outlays for development assistance and, officially, is preferred to bilateral aid. The Dutch minister without portfolio in charge of these matters is therefore called the Minister for Development Cooperation, rather than Development Aid. For the same reason the Netherlands is an active defender of Third World interests within various UN organisations in this field. As chairman of a UN commission, the Dutch Nobel prize-winning economist, Tinbergen, was instrumental in setting as a target for the 1970s that all rich countries spend at least 0.7 per cent of their national income on development aid. Only Sweden and the Netherlands met this target before the 1975 deadline. In absolute terms, the Netherlands spends as much on development aid as the UK.

Too much should not be made of the idealism in Dutch foreign policy. It is striking that references to Dutch vital national interests are extremely rare in documents and debates devoted to the country's foreign policy. However, this should not be mistaken for political altruism. Interests and ideals are often compatible, or the ideals are formulated as 'aims that are as vague as they are pious' (cited in Rozemond, 1987, p. 32), leaving sufficient leeway for an interpretation that does no harm to national interests. When interests and ideals do clash, it is fair to say that, generally speaking, the Dutch merchant carries more weight than the Calvinist minister. The example of how the Netherlands adjusted its Middle East policy after the 1973 oil embargo has already been mentioned. On the other hand, the idealism is more than mere rhetoric. In 1976 the government refused to give export guarantees for the sale of nuclear reactor parts to South Africa; in 1981 the government narrowly escaped being censured for its rejection of an oil boycott of that country. Most significantly, development aid, now at over 1.5 per cent of the national income, is the only chapter of the government's budget that has escaped unscathed in budget cutbacks until the early 1990s.

## Foreign Policy Constants Re-examined

We began this chapter with Voorhoeve's list of three clusters of traditions or tendencies in the foreign policy of the Netherlands: maritime commercialism, neutralist abstentionism, and internationalist idealism. Together these three themes cover so wide a range of policies that it has been argued that anything the Dutch Foreign Office does can always be construed as evidence of at least one of the three traditions (Van Staden, 1989a, p. 103). If one avoids that particular pitfall, however, these tendencies provide a useful framework for an analysis of developments in Dutch foreign policy. They can still be detected in the Dutch position in the international arena.

If the neutralist attitude has been forsaken, it was already abandoned when the Dutch joined the Atlantic Alliance in 1949, but the abstention from international power politics remained. With the benefit of hindsight we were also able to conclude that it is at least an exaggeration to interpret the somewhat less submissive attitude *vis-à-vis* the USA in the 1970s as a return to neutralism. The emphasis on internationalist idealism received a new impetus from the domestication of Dutch foreign policy since the 1960s, and was broadened to include the protection of human rights and development cooperation. The only potential change lies in an incipient decline of the Atlantic orientation, but it is more a gradual (even reluctant) adaptation to changing international circumstances (i.e., weakening American interest in Europe, and a renewed momentum of European integration) than a conscious change of course. The Dutch may have too little sense of history to maintain traditions, but they are also too conservative to throw them overboard.

# 10

# The Capability of a Fragmented System

## Decision by Negotiation

Only in the Dutch language itself is the country known by the singular label *Nederland*: elsewhere it is the plural Netherlands, *Pays Bas*, or *Niederlande*. Despite Napoleon's successful territorial centralisation, the overwhelming first impression foreign students of the Dutch political system are bound to develop is still one of remarkable fragmentation. Indeed, this book has no doubt contributed to that impression.

We started our exploration with the source of fragmentation that has put the Dutch polity on the map of comparative politics: pillarisation, or *'verzuiling'* (see Chapter 2). According to authors on pillarisation, Dutch society was 'deeply divided', 'highly segmented' by the social cleavages of religion and class. Since the late 1960s, however, pillarisation has given way to depillarisation. In Lijphart's classification, societies are either segmented (pillarised) or homogeneous, and depillarisation can thus be expected to have rendered Dutch political culture more homogeneous. In reality depillarisation has probably resulted in more fragmentation. The pillars of the past at least divided society into only 3–5 (depending on the definition used) easily recognisable homogeneous segments. Within these segments political and social activities were highly integrated. Depillarisation has broken up these social segments into numerous smaller fragments, without replacing the former intrapillar integrating mechanisms with some functional equivalent. Political parties are criticised for having lost their function of interest aggregation (see

229

Chapter 3). Single issue 'action groups' are playing a more prominent role.

Depillarisation has also done little to simplify the Dutch party system. The number of parties that contest parliamentary elections has gone up and down, but without a clear underlying downward trend. Although we have argued that the Dutch electoral system of extreme PR cannot be held responsible for the development of the multi-party system, it certainly has done nothing to scare off smaller parties or to reduce artificially the number of parties achieving representation in Parliament (see Chapters 4 and 5). Despite even the relatively recent mergers of three parties into the CDA, and four parties into Green Left, the number of parties that have overcome the low electoral threshold has hardly declined. More importantly, all the parties are minorities, both in the electorate and in Parliament. In order to secure parliamentary majorities for the government, the Cabinet is based on a coalition of several political parties, usually arching over at least one of the two social cleavages. The cultural and political fragmentation is thus carried over into the heart of the decision-making system itself (see Chapter 6).

In addition to cultural and political fragmentation, our exploration has identified a second major source of fragmentation, which is often analysed under the label of neo-corporatism. Consociationalism and neo-corporatism are sometimes confused in descriptions of Dutch politics (e.g., Smith, 1988). They are certainly interlinked in many ways but, other than in pillarisation (and consociationalism), however, the source of neo-corporatist fragmentation is functional. Functional decentralisation (see Chapter 7) in the Dutch political system starts with the incorporation of relatively strong, cohesive interest groups into the decision-making process through a dense network of formal and informal bipartite and tripartite consultations. The bureaucracy contributes to functional fragmentation through its high degree of departmental specialisation. The recruitment pattern of Cabinet Ministers also favours specialised expertise (see Chapter 5), and Parliament does little to counter-balance the fragmentation because of its committee system based on policy sectors (see Chapter 6).

It is only in the Cabinet and in Parliament that political and functional fragmentation both play a role: the Cabinet is both a coalition of parties and a board of departmental chiefs; Parliament has been defined as (among other metaphors) both a political arena and a market place for trading social interests (see Chapters 5 and 6). Sometimes the two sources of fragmentation may counter-balance each other, but they may also reinforce each other. It is rare to see them reconciled into one integrated policy. In this fragmented political system, decision is by negotiation or, as Prime Minister Drees put it to Parliament in 1957, coordination is through consultation.

Observers who are accustomed to political systems less plagued by fragmentation may well wonder how the Dutch system can work at all. Lijphart and other authors on consociational democracy may have convinced the community of political scientists that divided countries can be stable democracies, but stable at what cost? In Chapter 2 we argued that the most fundamental principle of the politics of accommodation is the avoidance of clear-cut, zero-sum game, yes/no decisions. Is the price paid for the fragmentation not one of immobilism, stalemate, and non-decision-making? How can decisive action be taken in a political system in which the buck seems to stop nowhere? It is to these questions that the remainder of this chapter is devoted, in a search for the centripetal forces and the integrating mechanisms that compensate for at least some of the fragmentation.

## The Constraints of Consensus

*An Underlying Consensus*

All the descriptions of pillarisation and functional decentralisation should not blind us to the fact that underlying the fragmentation that is so characteristic of Dutch politics is a consensus that considerably constrains the scope of political conflict. The social cleavages of the past, for example, were deep, but they were not very wide. First of all, the polity itself has never been subject to political strife. In Brian Barry's words, the conflicts are about how the country is to be run, not about whether it should be a country at all (Barry, 1975, p. 503). Although many Dutchmen seem to take pride in disclaiming any nationalist sentiments, their collective hysteria on those occasions when the Dutch national football team manages to defeat its German rival indicates something rather different. Surprisingly little is known about Dutch attachment to national symbols and rituals. The monarchy undoubtedly plays an important role in this respect.

During the Second World War, Queen Wilhelmina became a symbol of Dutch resistance to the German occupation. She was said to have been 'the only man' in the Dutch government in exile in London. After the war, therefore, the monarchy was a popular and unifying factor, rather than the source of division it had become in Belgium at that time. If there had been any republican sentiments before the war, they have since evaporated; surveys have found little more than 6 or 7 per cent of the population in favour of abolishing the monarchy.

In addition to a common national identity, the underlying consensus may also include some agreement on how the country is to be run. Scholten even goes as far as to argue that the fragmentation is only organisational, and does not extend to the level of substantive values (Scholten, 1980). Scholten writes about pillarisation from a social control perspective, and his claim that Dutch social and political organisations are more oriented to internal control than to outward combat rests on his subjective judgment. The same applies to his thesis that the party system did not freeze around the areas of greatest political conflict, as it assumes the religious cleavage to be less conflictual than the class cleavage. He is, however, on much firmer ground when he argues that the pillars of the past need not have had incompatible ideologies on some of the most fundamental issues: 'No one would argue that separated goat-breeders associations reflect ideological incompatibility about functional activities' (p. 342). All major parties did share in a 'corporatist consensus' on how policy was to be made. The need to rebuild the country after the war also provided common ground. There was hardly any disagreement on such important decisions as joining NATO and the EC. Nowhere is the existence of an underlying consensus as clear as in the exaggerated claim of one author that, ideologically, the Netherlands has evolved into a one-party state (Oerlemans, 1990).

### The Crucial Role of Experts

An important part of the underlying consensus is the regard in which experts, facts, and figures are held. The role of independent experts is sometimes described as crucial in neo-corporatist policy-making, as Katzenstein asserts: 'experts matter because they provide a common framework and acceptable data, evidence of a pervasive ideology of

social partnership. This ideology incorporates a continuous reaffirma-
tion of political differences with political cooperation' (Katzenstein,
1985, p. 88). This certainly holds true for the Netherlands. The role of
experts goes beyond keeping the debate between opposing parties or
interest groups honest. They are often instrumental in forging a
consensus where none previously existed, as technocratic findings
seem to take precedence over ideological values. Indeed, without this
respect for experts, depoliticisation could not have become such an
important device in the politics of accommodation. Illustrating its
importance, Daalder has equated pillarisation to pragmatisation
(*'verzuiling is verzakelijking'*: Daalder, 1965). In Chapter 7 we
discussed the technocratic flavour of Dutch politics, and the
recruitment of specialists into the civil service. Experts are found as
Crown Members of the SER, the pinnacle of the PBO, and in
numerous advisory councils and Royal Commissions. The Government has surrounded itself with forecasting and fact-finding agencies,
inappropriately called planning services: the Central Bureau of
Statistics (CBS), the Central Planning Bureau (CPB) for economic
forecasting, the Town and Country Planning Agency (RPD), the
Scientific Council for Government Policy (WRR), and even a Social
and Cultural Planning Bureau (SCP). Not only the government
makes use of these agencies; their reports are customarily published
and play an important role in public debate. Political parties submit
their election manifestos to the Central Planning Bureau to have
them tested for their economic effects. When it can be demonstrated
that a policy has clearly failed, or that a proposal cannot work,
parties or interest groups tend to accept this and swallow their
dogmas. This is an explanation of the Dutch approach to the drugs
problem (free methadone, clean needles, and condoms) that so often
amazes tourists in Amsterdam.

The underlying consensus and the role of experts in forging
additional consensus both make it less difficult to arrive at
compromises and decisions than could otherwise be expected in
such a fragmented political system.

## Accepted Tie-Breakers

The fragmentation of the system has hampered the development of
hierarchical mechanisms of integration. This is most evident in the

position of the Dutch Prime Minister, whose power is limited by both political and departmental jealousies. This relative lack of arbitral authorities may lead to immobilism, but this is occasionally prevented by the existence of generally accepted tie-breakers.

## The Political Role of the Judiciary

Most prominent among these tie-breakers is the judiciary. For the purposes of this Chapter we use the term 'judiciary' to include not only the regular courts, with the Supreme Court at the top, but also the various bodies of administrative appeal and of administrative justice, with two chambers of the Council of State at the top. Determining which system applies in a particular case is a science in itself and need not concern us here. Although litigation in the Netherlands is still not as popular as in the USA, the case-load of the courts is increasing rapidly. In 1950 the courts decided 90 365 civil law cases, 360 488 criminal cases, and 12 977 administrative cases. By 1986 these numbers had more than doubled for civil law cases (182 539), risen to 468 715 for criminal cases, and nearly quadrupled for administrative cases (46 204). The number of judges nearly doubled from 453 in 1960 to 833 in 1987 (Cohen, Dittrich and Flinterman 1989, p. 306). The particularly rapid rise in the number of administrative cases points to a growing political importance of the courts, but the number of civil and criminal law cases with political significance is also increasing.

Dutch constitutional law, however, is unequivocal in its rejection of any political role for the judiciary. Its independence is protected by appointments for life. In practice, appointment is by cooptation, even though the Second Chamber formally draws up a short-list of candidates for the Supreme Court. Just as politics is not supposed to interfere with the judiciary, however, the judiciary is expected to stay out of politics. Article 120 of the Constitution explicitly denies the courts the power to review the constitutionality of laws and treaties. Judges are also not allowed to pass judgments on the 'inner value or fairness' of laws, and their decisions are to have no wider application than the particular case before them. It is thus ironic that the gap between the constitutional 'ought' and the political 'is' is nowhere wider than in the case of the judiciary. The absence of judicial review has not prevented the courts from playing a political role for several reasons.

First of all, the Constitution does give treaties and resolutions by international institutions (such as the EC) precedence over domestic legislation (Article 94). Thus the courts can annul Acts of Parliament that infringe upon human rights, not with reference to the section on fundamental rights in the Dutch Constitution but on the basis of, for example, the European Convention on Human Rights. Many Dutch social insurance laws, for instance, contained provisions for lower benefits to women, on the premise that women are married to a bread-winner. The courts have struck down such provisions on the basis of anti-discrimination articles in European treaties and subsequent EC directives, resulting in considerable financial costs to the government.

Second, judicial review is only prohibited for Acts of Parliament. All other forms of regulation – Orders in Council, ministerial resolutions, legislation by provincial and municipal councils – are not affected. The courts have, for example, declared government measures to reduce the incomes of medical specialists to be *ultra vires*; the law on which these measures were based did not mention incomes policy as a ground for government interference. Faced with such a court decision, the government can either comply or seek to have the law changed by Parliament. The latter course of action is not guaranteed success because Parliament may let the court's opinion prevail. When the courts ordered the government to stop adding fluoride to drinking water on the grounds that the Water Supply Act contained no provision for the prevention of tooth decay, the government introduced emergency legislation to remedy this omission, only to be turned down by a parliamentary majority.

Third, and most important, political non-decision-making sometimes forces the courts to take on politically controversial issues. The clearest cases are where no legislation exists. A European Treaty obliges the government to introduce legislation recognising the general right of workers, even government employees, to strike, and specifying when strikes are not allowed. Such a law has never reached the statute books because of political differences. In the meantime, employers have been asking the courts to order the trade unions to end particular strike actions, and the judges have developed their own criteria for the acceptability of strikes. In one celebrated case the government itself asked the court to condemn a strike by civil service unions, only to be ordered by the court to return to the negotiating table with more realistic proposals. On the whole, the unions and the employers are quite happy with the way the judiciary handles industrial disputes, and no one is pressing for legislation any more.

Sometimes laws exist, but their wording is vague (often as the result of a political compromise), or the provisions are no longer in touch with prevailing feelings of justice. In such cases the courts often modernise their interpretation of the law. What is, or is not, pornography, for example, has changed over the years as the courts interpreted terms such as public indecency.

One of the most controversial issues that the courts have dealt with concerns euthanasia. Dating back to the nineteenth century, the penal code does not mention euthanasia, but anyone who abets a suicide is threatened with long jail sentences. With the current advanced state of medical technology euthanasia has become a moral problem for the doctors and relatives of many patients. Since all governing coalitions include the CDA, which is vehemently opposed to allowing euthanasia, attempts to liberalise euthanasia have been deadlocked. As we have seen in Chapter 2, it was once even recommended that legislation should await the development of jurisprudence on euthanasia, even though this turns the Dutch constitution upside down. In the 1980s, the courts did in fact develop guidelines for doctors, specifying the conditions under which euthanasia is permitted (incurable disease, unbearable suffering, a clear expression of the will to die by the patient, etc.). If legislation on this issue is ever passed, it will do little more than codify what is already legal practice.

As a consequence of such cases, the Dutch judiciary has been accused of acting as a deputy legislature. Sometimes, however, the courts refuse to be drawn into political territory. In 1984 groups of concerned citizens appealed to the court to prohibit the stationing of cruise missiles in the Netherlands. The judge refused, arguing that this was a matter for the government and Parliament into which he had no right to intervene. But the borderline between judicial restraint and judicial activism is constantly changing. When a controversial law was passed reducing student grants to six years, retroactively affecting some students who were already enrolled, a lower court judge decided that not even an Act of Parliament is allowed to be retroactive by citing a provision in the little known Charter that regulates the relations between the Netherlands and the Dutch Antilles. In 1989, the Supreme Court eventually quashed this imaginative decision, but in wording that hinted at regret over the absence of judicial review and which explicitly opened the door for a different decision in future. It is quite clear, however, that the courts are playing an important role in political decision-making with or without judicial review, and that secretly politicians may not be all that unhappy with the existence of this tie-breaker.

*'Brussels' as a Scapegoat*

'It may be argued an advantage that Community politics works against the fragmentation of the Dutch party system and Dutch society at large' (Peijnenburg and Sloot, 1990, p. 113). The EC has this effect in part because the precedence of Community law over Dutch law strengthens the position of the judiciary, as we have just seen. Second, to some extent Community decision-making has also led to improved internal coordination, although it is a wild exaggeration to claim that 'Interdepartmental coordination ... seems to flourish under EC pressure' (Peijnenburg and Sloot, 1990, p. 112: see also Exhibit 7.1). As Brussels sets the timetable for Community decision-making, there is, however, more pressure to arrive at a common negotiating position (Van den Bos, 1991), and non-decision-making is less easy to afford. And if the Prime Minister's role at EC summits has not already strengthened his position at home, it has certainly resulted in demands for such a stronger premiership (see Chapter 5).

Third, 'the Community may enable the Dutch government to endorse policies against the wishes of the majority of the Dutch electorate' (Wolters, 1990, p. 221). In the Netherlands, the EC is regarded as an inevitability; like the weather, sometimes it is fine and sometimes it is inclement, but little can be done to change it. This provides the Dutch government with an opportunity to hide behind 'Brussels'. Unpopular measures may be taken, deadlocks can be broken, because 'we shall otherwise be out of step with the rest of the Community'. The government has been able to defy even strong and well-integrated interest groups, such as those for fisheries and arable farming, by pointing to EC policies as if they were forces of nature (see Chapter 7). Proposals to reduce social insurance benefits are sometimes defended by claiming that Dutch welfare state pro- grammes must be brought into line with those in the rest of the Community. After the Arab oil embargo, efforts to formulate a common EC foreign policy 'provided successive Dutch governments with a useful instrument to legitimise the shift in its position with respect to the Palestinian issue' (Soetendorp, 1990, p. 141). The EC may even design its policies for this purpose: 'One of the ancillary reasons for the ambitious targets of the common energy programme was to help member-states such as the Netherlands in overcoming their internal opposition [to nuclear energy]' (Van der Doelen and De Jong, 1990, p. 66).

Such examples indicate that, contrary to what is generally assumed, European integration does not necessarily weaken national executives. In the Dutch case at least, 'Brussels' may have strengthened the decision-making capability of the national political system.

## Capability and Legitimacy

Finally, it should be emphasised that the capability of the Dutch political system is enhanced by its legitimacy. If, eventually, a controversial or unpopular decision is taken, it is accepted, although grudgingly. In his book on Dutch decolonisation policy, Lijphart cites survey evidence that only a small minority of the population supported the agreement to grant independence to Indonesia, yet when a two-thirds majority of Parliament voted in favour of decolonisation there were no protests or demonstrations (Lijphart, 1966, pp. 114–24, 247–9, 283–4). In 1964, a pirate commercial television station started broadcasting from a converted oil-rig just outside territorial waters. Although a special aerial was needed to receive the broadcasts, they became very popular, and surveys showed that 70 per cent of the population felt that the government should do nothing to hinder the broadcasts. However, after the government nevertheless silenced the television station, only 33 per cent of the population disagreed with the measures (Lijphart, 1975, pp. 159–61). Lijphart believes this passive acceptance of elite decisions to have by and large decreased since the late 1960s; however, more recent examples are not difficult to find. The issue of the cruise missiles mobilised millions of Dutchmen, but when the decision to allow them to be stationed in the Netherlands was final, there was no significant protest (see Chapter 9). As soon as Parliament had accepted the reductions in disability benefits in

1991 (see Chapter 8), all opposition similarly faded away. Those who oppose the liberalisation of abortion cannot be satisfied by the legislation that was the outcome of the long fight, but 'pro life' activists seem to have given up completely.

Such evaporation of opposition once a decision has been taken can sometimes be observed in other political systems as well, but it seems considerably more marked in Dutch political culture. Although there is no ready explanation for this phenomenon, it is tempting to relate it to the considerable legitimacy of Dutch politics. Dutch politicians and commentators always talk of a widening credibility gap between citizens and the political system, and they see evidence of such a gap in the declining membership of political parties, in the low turnout for European and provincial elections, or in votes for extreme right-wing parties. Such developments are certainly not without risk for the political system, but they have little to do with a decline of trust in politics (see Table 10.1).

Survey questions that are customarily used to tap feelings of political efficacy and political cynicism show relatively low levels of mistrust as Table 10.1 shows, especially if we take into account that only very few people express mistrust on more than one or two questions. Over the past 20 years the level of trust has hardly changed, and if there has been any trend, it is in the direction of increased rather than decreased political legitimacy. Data from other West European countries show that the legitimacy of Dutch politics is high from a comparative as well as from a longitudinal perspective. Since the early 1970s, the Eurobarometer surveys held twice yearly in all EC member states have regularly included the question 'On the whole, are you very satisfied, fairly satisfied, not very satisfied or not at all satisfied with the way democracy works in the Netherlands (or in France, Britain, etc.)?' The Dutch are consistently among the most satisfied with the way democracy works in their own country, with more than 70 per cent very or fairly satisfied. In 1990 Dutch levels of democratic satisfaction were 20 per cent higher than in France, 25 per cent higher than in the UK, and surpassed only by Denmark and Germany. It is clear that government and politics are not exempt from the general satisfaction with life that characterises the Dutch (see Chapter 1). Whether the high legitimacy enjoyed by the Dutch political system as we have described it in this book is warranted, or a sign of incredible Dutch credulity, is now up to the reader to judge.

**TABLE 10.1**
**Trust in Dutch politics, 1971–89***

| Statements | Agree/ disagree | 1971 | 1972 | 1977 | 1981 | 1982 | 1986 | 1989 |
|---|---|---|---|---|---|---|---|---|
| 1. MPs do not care about the opinions of people like me. | Agree | 48 | 48 | 41 | 34 | 45 | 38 | 38 |
| | Disagree | 37 | 33 | 45 | 58 | 41 | 54 | 59 |
| 2. The political parties are only interested in my vote and not in my opinion. | Agree | 59 | 55 | 48 | 40 | 50 | 45 | 43 |
| | Disagree | 29 | 31 | 43 | 54 | 40 | 49 | 56 |
| 3. People like me do not have any say about what the government does. | Agree | 56 | 58 | 46 | 38 | 52 | 48 | 46 |
| | Disagree | 34 | 32 | 45 | 56 | 41 | 47 | 53 |
| 4. So many people vote in the elections that my vote does not matter. | Agree | 15 | 12 | 11 | 6 | 10 | 9 | 8 |
| | Disagree | 77 | 81 | 85 | 90 | 87 | 89 | 92 |
| 5. Politicians consciously promise more than they can deliver. | Agree | | | 75 | 78 | 78 | 85 | 84 |
| | Disagree | | | 21 | 17 | 18 | 13 | 15 |
| 6. Cabinet ministers and junior ministers are primarily working for their own interests. | Agree | | | 27 | 26 | 29 | 32 | 30 |
| | Disagree | | | 65 | 65 | 60 | 62 | 68 |
| 7. One becomes MP because of one's political friends, rather than because of skills and ability. | Agree | | | 38 | 32 | 34 | 37 | 36 |
| | Disagree | 47 | 49 | 47 | 50 | 59 | | |

* Percentages for 'don't know' have not been included in the table.
*Source*: Dutch National Election Study.

# Further Reading

Below we confine our suggestions to a selection of English-language books and articles. Those readers searching for more extensive reading lists in English are referred to Daalder (1989b). To those who read Dutch, we recommend Daalder and Nauta (1986): as a regularly updated loose leaf compendium of both factual and bibliographical information, it is an excellent starting point for the study of almost any aspect of Dutch politics and society. It contains the same English language reading list mentioned as Daalder (1989b), and also incorporates a list of sources on Dutch politics in German.

## 1 The Country and the People

There is no shortage of material on Dutch history. The quickest overview can be found in Schöffer (1973). For more extended treatments see, e.g., Vlekke (1945) or Kossmann (1978) who takes a combined look at Dutch and Belgian history. Interesting, if somewhat controversial, accounts of the beginning and the end of the Dutch Republic are to be found in Schama (1987, 1978). Daalder (1966) analyses Dutch political history from the days of the Republic to twentieth-century pillarisation. On Dutch society see Hugget (1971) or the excellent (if dated) Goudsblom (1967). Information on the Dutch economy can be found in De Vries (1978) and several chapters of Griffiths (1980).

## 2 A Country of Minorities

Lijphart's classic book remains required reading for anyone studying Dutch pillarisation and consociational democracy. In English the latest (second) edition is Lijphart (1975) but in Dutch there is a fifth edition: Lijphart (1984). Daalder (1966) gives a detailed historical analysis of the roots of consociational democracy. Bakvis (1981) provides a fascinating account of the Catholic pillar. For criticism of Lijphart's approach see Kieve (1981), Scholten (1980), and some of the authors in Van Schendelen (1984). Lijphart considerably modifies his view of the consequences of depillarisation in Lijphart (1989).

## 3  Political Parties and the Party System

Because of the origins of most of the major parties in one of the pillars, the reading suggested for Chapter 2 is also relevant here. For individual parties we suggest Daalder and Koole (1988) on the Liberals; Wolinetz (1977) on the Social Democrats; and Bakvis (1981) and Kuiper (1979) on the Christian Democratic parties. On party finance see Koole (1989, 1990). The party system is discussed in Irwin (1980), Daalder (1987), and Wolinetz (1988). Some of the suggestions listed for Chapter 4 also give information on developments in the Dutch party system.

## 4  Elections

The Dutch electoral system, and attempts to reform it, are discussed in Daalder (1975) and Lijphart (1978). Irwin (1974) studies the impact of the abolition of compulsory voting. How parties nominate their candidates is the topic of Koole and Leijenaar (1988). Electoral behaviour is probably the one aspect of Dutch politics on which most has been published in English. Andeweg (1982) analyses various explanations of electoral change in the Netherlands. Irwin and Van Holsteyn (1989a, 1989b) give an overview of the explanatory power of various models of voting behaviour. Van der Eijk and Niemöller (1982) emphasise the importance of Left–Right ideological positions for party choice. Thomassen (1976) dismisses the concept of party identification in the Netherlands. Middendorp (1991) presents an alternative model of voting behaviour.

## 5  The Cabinet

For studies of the Dutch experience with coalition formation, see Andeweg, Van der Tak and Dittrich (1980), Gladdish (1983), Vis (1983) and Daalder (1986). Attempts at democratic reform are discussed by Gladdish (1972) and Andeweg (1989). Theoretical explanations of the outcome of coalition formations are to be found in De Swaan (1982), Daudt (1982), and Van Deemen (1990). For the recruitment of Dutch government ministers, see Bakema and Secker (1988). Various aspects of Dutch cabinet decision-making are described in Andeweg (1985, 1988a, 1988c, 1991).

## 6  Parliament

Van Raalte (1959) is a general text on the Dutch Parliament, but some of it is outdated. The recently revised Dutch edition, Van Raalte (1991), is excellent. On the recruitment of MPs see Daalder and Van den Berg (1982), Fairlie, Budge and Irwin (1977), and Irwin, Budge and Fairlie (1979). Van Schendelen (1976), Gladdish (1990), and Andeweg (1992) discuss various aspects of parliamentary behaviour. Wolters (1984) provides a

quantitative analysis of voting patterns in the Second Chamber. The Second
Chamber itself publishes an English-language brochure on its role in Dutch
politics.

## 7 The Policy-Making Process: Territorial Centralisation and Functional Decentralisation

On the relations between the central government and provincial or
municipal governments, see Toonen (1987, 1992). Andeweg and Derksen
(1978) discuss the appointed mayor. That, and other aspects of local
government, are the subject of Morlan (1962, 1964). Neo-corporatist
arrangements are analysed in Akkermans and Grootings (1978), Wassenberg
(1982), Scholten (1987), and Wolinetz (1989). Singh (1972) analyses the role
of the SER. Windmuller (1969) is an excellent source on Dutch labour
relations until its year of publication. In Dutch it has been updated as
Windmuller, De Galan and Van Zweeden (1983). Van Schendelen (1987)
discusses relations between government and private companies. Information
on the Dutch bureaucracy is to found in MacMullen (1979) and Eldersveld,
Kooiman and Van der Tak (1981).

## 8 Socio-Economic Policy

De Vries (1978) and several chapters of Griffiths (1980) discuss social and
economic policies. Roebroek and Berben (1987) present information on rules
and regulations and growth of the Dutch welfare state in the book edited by
Flora. Various aspects of the government's attempts to deal with the 'crisis' in
the welfare state are explored in Van Schendelen (1983), Snellen (1985),
Andeweg (1988), and Goudzwaard (1990). The state of the Dutch economy
is analysed in annual English-language reports by the Central Planning
Bureau, the Dutch Bank, and the OECD.

## 9 Foreign Policy

Leurdijk (1978), Voorhoeve (1979) and Wels (1982) provide general surveys
of Dutch foreign policy. 'Hollanditis' and other purported changes in the
Dutch role in NATO are analysed by Van Staden (1989). Recent
developments in various aspects of foreign policy are discussed in a special
English-language issue of the Dutch journal, *Internationale Spectator* (1989).

## 10 The Capability of a Fragmented System

Scholten (1980) argues the case for an existing underlying consensus in the
Netherlands. The importance of technocratic expertise is epitomised in
studies of Dutch planning, such as Griffiths (1980) and Dutt and Costa

(1985). Polak and Polak (1986) analyse the growing political role of the judiciary. The impact of 'Brussels' on various Dutch policy fields is evaluated in Wolters and Coffey (1990). Thomassen (1990) demonstrates that in the Netherlands deprivation produces apathy rather than protest. Van Schendelen (1981) provides data on political efficacy, trust in politics, etc.

# Main Data Sources

The Dutch National Election Studies are a joint project by all universities in the Netherlands carrying out research in political science. Surveys have been carried out at the parliamentary elections of 1971, 1972, 1977, 1981, 1982, 1986, and 1989. Principal funding has come from the Netherlands Organisation for the Advancement of Pure Research (ZWO) and its successor, the Netherlands Organisation for Scientific Research (NWO). Additional funding for specific surveys has been provided by the Department of Internal Affairs, the Social and Cultural Planning Office, the University of Amsterdam, and Leyden University. All data are made available to researchers through the Steinmetz Archives in Amsterdam.

The Dutch Parliamentary Studies are surveys of Members of Parliament carried out in 1968, 1972, 1979, and 1990. These studies were financed by the Netherlands Organisation for the Advancement of Pure Research (ZWO) and its successor, the Netherlands Organisation for Scientific Research (NWO). Enquires concerning these studies may be directed to the Department of Political Science, Leyden University.

# Bibliography

Akkermans, T. and P. Grootings (1978) 'From Corporatism to Polarisation: Elements of the Development of Dutch Industrial Relations' in C. Crouch and A. Pizzorno (eds), *The Resurgence of Class Conflict in Western Europe since 1968*, vol. I (London: Macmillan), pp. 159–89.

Alberda, W. (1990) 'Werkloosheid' in J. W. Van Deth and S. C. P. M. Vis (eds), *Politieke Problemen* (Leiden: Stenfert Kroese BV), pp. 73–90.

Andeweg, R. B. (1982) *Dutch Voters: Adrift on Explanations of Electoral Change (1963–1979)*, doctoral dissertation, Leyden University.

Andeweg, R. B. (1985) 'The Netherlands: Cabinet Committees in a Coalition Cabinet' in T. T. Mackie and B. W. Hogwood (eds), *Unlocking the Cabinet: Cabinet Structures in Comparative Perspective* (London: Sage), pp. 138–54.

Andeweg, R. B. (1988a) 'Centrifugal Forces and Collective Decision-Making: the Case of the Dutch Cabinet', *European Journal of Political Research*, 16, pp. 125–51.

Andeweg, R. B. (1988b) 'Less than Nothing? Hidden Privatisation of the Pseudo-Private Sector: the Dutch Case' in J. Vickers and V. Wright (eds), *The Politics of Privatisation in Western Europe* (London: Cass), pp. 117–28.

Andeweg, R. B. (1988c) 'The Netherlands: Coalition Cabinets in Changing Circumstances' in J. Blondel and F. Muller-Romme (eds), *Cabinets in Western Europe* (London: Macmillan), pp. 47–67.

Andeweg, R. B.(1989) 'Institutional Conservatism in the Netherlands: Proposals for and Resistance to Change' in Daalder and Irwin (eds), *Politics in the Netherlands: How Much Change?* (London: Cass), pp. 42–60.

Andeweg, R. B.(1991) 'The Dutch Prime Minister: Not just Chairman, not yet Chief?' in G. W. Jones (ed.), *West European Prime Ministers* (London: Cass), pp. 116–32.

Andeweg, R. B.(1992) 'Executive–Legislative Relations in the Netherlands: Consecutive and Coexisting Patterns', *Legislative Studies Quarterly*, 17, pp. 161–82.

Andeweg, R. B. and W. Derksen (1978) 'The Appointed Burgomaster: Appointments and Careers of Burgomasters in the Netherlands', *Netherlands Journal of Sociology*, 14, pp. 41–57.

Andeweg, R. B., Th. Van der Tak and K. Dittrich (1980) 'Government Formation in the Netherlands' in R. T. Griffiths (ed.), *The Economy and Politics of the Netherlands since 1945* (The Hague: Martinus Nijhoff), pp. 223–49.

Bakema, W. E. and I. P. Secker (1988) 'Ministerial Expertise and the Dutch Case', *European Journal of Political Research*, 16, pp. 153–70.

Bakvis, H. (1981) *Catholic Power in the Netherlands* (Kingston: McGill-Queen's University Press).

Barry, B. (1975) 'Political Accommodation and Consociational Democracy', *British Journal of Political Science*, 5, pp. 477–505.

Baylis, Th. A. (1989) *Governing by Committee: Collegial Leadership in Advanced Society* (Albany, New York: SUNY Press).

Bodenheimer, S. (1978) 'The Denial of Grandeur: the Dutch context', in J. H. Leurdijk (1978), pp. 235–84.

Braam, G. P. A. (1973) *Invloed van Bedrijven op de Overheid* (Meppel: Boom).

Brants, K., W. Kok and Ph. Van Praag, Jr. (1982) *De Strijd om de kiezersgunst: Verkiezingscampagnes in Nederland* (Amsterdam: Uitgeverij Kobra).

Centraal Planbureau (1989) *Macro-Economische Verkenningen* (Den Haag: SDU).

Central Planning Bureau (1991) *Central Economic Plan The Netherlands* (The Hague: Central Planning Bureau).

Cohen, M. J., K. Dittrich and C. Flinterman, (1989) 'Rechter en Politiek' in R. B. Andeweg, A. Hoogerwerf and J. J. A. Thomaassen (eds), *Politiek in Nederland* (Alphen aan den Rijn: Samsom), pp. 303–22.

Commissie subsidiering politieke partijen (1991) *Waarborg van Kwaliteit* ('s-Gravenhage).

Daalder, H. (1965) 'Politiek in Nederlands Kader' in H. Daalder *et al.*, *Mensen en Machten* (Utrecht), pp. 99–122.

Daalder, H. (1966) 'The Netherlands: Opposition in a Segmented Society' in R. A. Dahl (ed.), *Political Oppositions in Western Democracies* (New Haven: Yale University Press), pp. 188–236.

Daalder, H. (1974) *Politisering en Lijdelijkheid in de Nederlandse Politiek* (Assen: Van Gorcum).

Daalder, H. (1975) 'Extreme Proportional Representation: The Dutch Experience' in S. E. Finer (ed.), *Adversary Politics and Electoral Reform* (London: Wigram).

Daalder, H. (1987) 'The Dutch Party System: From Segmentation to Polarization – And Then?' in H. Daalder (ed.) *Party Systems in Denmark, Austria, Switzerland, The Netherlands and Belgium* (London: Pinter), pp. 193–284.

Daalder, H. (1986) 'Changing Procedures and Changing Strategies in Dutch Coalition Building', *Legislative Studies Quarterly*, 11, pp. 507–31.

Daalder, H. (1989a) *Ancient and Modern Pluralism in the Netherlands*, the 1989 Erasmus Lectures at Harvard University (Center for European Studies Working Paper Series).

Daalder, H. (1989b) 'English Language Sources for the Study of Dutch Politics' in Daalder and Irwin (eds), *Politics in the Netherlands: How Much Change?* (London: Cass), pp. 162–85.

Daalder, H. and S. Hubée-Boonzaaijer (1976) 'Parliament and the Budget: Procedures and Politics in the Netherlands' in D. Coombes (ed.), *The Power of the Purse: The Role of European Parliaments in Budgetary Decisions* (London: Allen & Unwin), pp. 268–312.

Daalder, H. and G. A. Irwin (eds) (1989) *Politics in the Netherlands: How Much Change?* (London: Cass). First published as a Special Issue of West European Politics, 12, 1 (January 1989).

Daalder, H. and R. Koole (1988) 'Liberal parties in the Netherlands' in E. Kirchner (ed.), *Liberal Parties in Western Europe* (Cambridge: Cambridge University Press).

Daalder, H. and A. P. N. Nauta (eds) (1986) *Compendium voor Politiek en Samenleving in Nederland* (Houten/Deurne: Bohn Stafleu Van Loghum.

Daalder, H. and J. Th. J. Van den Berg (1982) 'Members of the Dutch Lower House: Pluralism and Democratization, 1848–1967' in M. M. Czudnowski, *Does Who Governs Matter? Elite Circulation in Contemporary Societies* (De Kalb, Ill: Northern Illionois University Press).

Daudt, H. (1982) 'Political Parties and Government Coalitions in the Netherlands since 1945', *The Netherlands Journal of Sociology*, 18, pp. 1–24.

De Jong, J. and B. Pijnenburg (1986) 'The Dutch Christian Democratic Party and Coalitional Behaviour in the Netherlands: A Pivotal Party in the Face of Depillarisation' in G. Pridham (ed.), *Coalitional Behaviour in Theory and Practice* (Cambridge University Press).

De Kam, C. A. and J. De Haan (1991) *Terugtredende overheid: realiteit of retoriek? een evaluatie van de grote operaties* (Schoonhoven: Academic Service).

De Swaan, A. (1982) 'The Netherlands: Coalitions in a Segmented Polity' in E. C. Browne and J. Dreijmanis (eds), *Government Coalitions in Western Democracies* (New York: Longman).

De Vrankrijker, A. C. J. (1946) *De grenzen van Nederland: Overzicht van wording en politieke tendenzen* (Amsterdam: Contact).

De Vries, J. (1978) *The Netherlands Economy in the Twentieth Century* (Assen: Van Gorcum).

De Vries, J. (1990) 'De Vis Bleef Zwart Betaald' in J. A. M. Hufen and A. B. Ringeling (eds), *Beleidsnetwerken; overheids- semi-overheids- en particuliere organisaties in wisselwerking* (The Hague: Vuga), pp. 39–54.

De Wolff, P. and W. Driehuis (1980) 'A Description of Post War Economic Developments and Economic Policy in the Netherlands' in R. T. Griffiths (ed.), *The Economy and Politics of the Netherlands since 1945* (The Hague: Martinus Nijhoff), pp. 13–60.

Dutt, A. K. and F. J. Costa (eds) (1985) *Public Planning in the Netherlands* (Oxford University Press).

Eichenberg, R. C. (1983) 'The Myth of Hollanditis', *International Security*, 8, pp. 43–159.

Eldersveld, S. J., J. Kooiman and Th. Van der Tak (1981) *Elite Images of Dutch Politics, Accommodation and Conflict* (Ann Arbor: University of Michigan Press).

Everts, Ph. P. (1983) *Public Opinion, the Churches and Foreign Policy; Studies of Domestic Factors in the Making of Dutch Foreign Policy*, doctoral dissertation, Leyden University.

Everts, Ph. P. (1989) 'Recent and current research on international affairs in the Netherlands', *Internationale Spectator*, 43, pp. 646–53.

Fairlie, D., I. Budge and G. A. Irwin (1977) 'Political Recruitment and Drop-Out: The Netherlands and the United States', *British Journal of Political Science*, 7, pp. 465–92.

Fernhout, R. (1980) 'Incorporatie van Belangengroeperingen in de Sociale en Economische Wetgeving' in H. J. G. Verhallen, R. Fernhout and P. E. Visser (eds), *Corporatisme in Nederland* (Alphen aan den Rijn: Samsom), pp. 119–228.

Fuchs, D. and H.-D. Klingemann (1989) 'The Left-Right Schema' in M. Kent Jennings, J. W. van Deth *et al.* (eds), *Continuities in Political Action* (Berlin/New York: Walter de Gruyter), pp. 203–34.

Gladdish, K. R. (1972) 'Two-Party vs. Multi-Party, the Netherlands and Britain', *Acta Politica*, 7 (3), pp. 342–61.

Gladdish, K. R. (1983) 'Coalition Government and Policy Outputs in the Netherlands' in V. Bogdanor (ed.), *Coalition Government in Western Europe* (London: Heinemann), pp. 169–86.

Gladdish, K. (1990) 'Parliamentary Activism and Legitimacy in the Netherlands', *West European Politics*, 13, pp. 103–19.

Gladdish, K. (1991) *Governing from the Centre; Policy and Policy-Making in the Netherlands* (London: Hurst).

Glastra Van Loon, J. F. (1964) 'Kiezen of Delen', *Nederlands Juristenblad*, pp. 1133–42 and 1161–7.

Goudsblom, J. (1967) *Dutch Society* (New York: Random House)

Goudswaard, K. P. (1990) 'Budgetary Policies in the Netherlands: 1982–1990' in *Finanzarchiv* (Tübingen: J. C. B. Mohr), pp. 271–84.

Goudswaard, K. P. and V. Halberstadt (1982) 'Het belang van het financieringstekort voor het financieel-economisch beleid', Report 82. 27 (Center for Research in Public Economics: Leyden University).

Griffiths, R. T. (1980) 'The Netherlands Central Planning Bureau' and 'The Netherlands and the European Communities' in R. T. Griffiths (ed.), *The Economy and Politics of the Netherlands since 1945* (The Hague: Nijhoff), pp. 135–61, 277–303.

Griffiths, R. T. (ed.) (1980) *The Economy and Politics of the Netherlands since 1945* (The Hague: Nijhoff).

Heldring, J. L. (1978) 'De Nederlandse buitenlandse politiek na 1945' in E. van den Beugel *et al.*, *Nederlandse Buitenlandse Politiek: heden en verleden* (Baarn: Anthos).

Hillebrand, R. (1992) '*De Antichambre van het Parlement*' doctoral dissertation, Leyden University.

Hoogendijk, F. A. (1971) *Partijpropaganda in Nederland* (Amsterdam: Agon Elsevier).

Houska, J. J. (1985) *Influencing Mass Political Behavior: Elites and Political Subcultures in the Netherlands and Austria* (Berkeley: University of California Press).

Huggett, F. (1971) *The Modern Netherlands* (London: Pall Mall Press).

Inglehart, R. (1990) *Culture Shift in Advanced Industrial Society* (Princeton, NJ: Princeton University Press).

*Internationale Spectator*, 43 (1989) 'Changing profile of a Low Country; The Netherlands from Colonial Power to International partners'.

250    *Bibliography*

Irwin, G. A. (1974), 'Compulsory Voting Legislation: Impact on Voter Turnout in the Netherlands', *Comparative Political Studies*, 7, pp. 292–315.

Irwin, G. A. (1980) 'The Dutch Party System', in P. Merkl (ed.), *Western European Party Systems* (New York: Free Press), pp. 161–84.

Irwin, G. A., I. Budge and D. Fairlie (1979), 'Social Background v. Motivational Determinants of Legislative Careers in the Netherlands', *Legislative Studies Quarterly*, 9, pp. 447–65.

Irwin, G. A., C. Van der Eijk, J. J. M. Van Holsteyn, and B. Niemöller (1987) 'Verzuiling, issues, kandidaten en ideologie in de verkiezingen van 1986', *Acta Politica*, 22 (2), pp. 129–80.

Irwin, G. A. and J. J. M. Van Holsteyn (1989a) 'Decline of the structured model of electoral competition' in Daalder and Irwin (eds), *Politics in the Netherlands: How Much Change?* (London: Cass), pp. 21–41.

Irwin, G. A. and J. J. M. Van Holsteyn (1989b) 'Towards a more open model of competition' in Daalder and Irwin (eds), *Politics in the Netherlands: How Much Change?* (London: Cass), pp. 112–38.

Katz, R. S. and P. Mair (1992) 'Changing Models of Party Organization: The Emergence of the Cartel Party', paper presented to the Workshop on Democracies and the Organization of Political Parties, ECPR Joint Sessions, University of Limerick.

Katzenstein, P. J. (1985) *Small States in World Markets; Industrial Policy in Europe* (Ithaca, NY: Cornell University Press).

Keuning, H. J. (1965) *Het Nederlandse volk in zijn woongebied* (Den Haag: H. P. Leopolds Uitgeversmij NV).

Kieve, R. (1981) 'Pillars of Sand: A Marxist Critique of Consociational Democracy in the Netherlands', *Comparative Politics*, 16, pp. 315–34.

Klamer, A. (1990) *Verzuilde Dromen: 40 jaar* SER (Amsterdam: Balans).

Kleinnijenhuis, J. and O. Scholten (1989) 'Veranderende verhoudingen tussen dagbladen en politieke partijen', *Acta Politica*, 24 (4), pp. 433–61.

Klingemann, H.-D. (1979) 'Measuring Ideological Conceptualizations' in S. H. Barnes, M. Kaase et al., *Political Action* (Beverly Hills/London: Sage Publications), pp. 215–54.

Koole, R. (1986) 'Politieke Partijen' in H. Daalder and A. Nauta (eds), *Compendium voor politiek en samenleving in Nederland* (Alphen aan den Rijn/Brussels: Samsom Uitgeverij), pp. A1100–1–132.

Koole, R. (1989) 'The 'Modesty' of Dutch party finance' in H. E. Alexander (ed.), *Comparative Political Finance in the 1980s*, (Cambridge University Press), pp. 209–19.

Koole, R. (1990) 'Political Parties Going Dutch: Party Finance in the Netherlands', *Acta Politica*, 25, pp. 37–65.

Koole, R. (1992) *De opkomst van de moderne kaderpartij: Veranderende partijorganisaties in Nederland 1960–1990* (Utrecht: Het Spectrum).

Koole, R. A. and M. Leijenaar (1988) 'The Netherlands: The Predominance of Regionalism' in M. Gallagher and M. Marsh (eds), *Candidate Selection in Comparative Perspective: The Secret Garden of Politics* (London: Sage).

Kossmann, E. H. (1978) *The Low Countries: 1780–1940* (Oxford: Clarendon Press).

Kruyt, J. P. (1959) *Verzuiling* (Zaandijk: Heijnis).
Kuiper, D. Th. (1990) 'Historical and Sociological Development of ARP and CDA' in C. Den Hollander (ed.), *Christian Political Options* (The Hague: Kuyperstichting), pp. 10–32.
Laqueur, W. (1981) 'Hollanditis: a new stage in European neutralism', *Commentary*, 19–26 August.
LeDuc, L. (1981) 'The Dynamic Properties of Party Identification: A Four-Nation Comparison', *European Journal of Political Research*, 9, p. 257–68.
Leurdijk, J. H. (1978) *The Foreign Policy of the Netherlands* (Alphen aan den Rijn: Sijthoff & Noordhof).
Lijphart, A. (1966) *The Trauma of Decolonization* (New Haven: Yale University Press)
Lijphart, A. (1971) 'Verzuiling' in A. Hoogerwerf (ed.), *Verkenningen in de Politiek* (Alphen aan den Rijn: Samsom), pp. 24–37.
Lijphart, A. (1974) 'The Netherlands: Continuity and Change in Voting Behaviour', in R. Rose (ed.), *Electoral Behaviour: A Comparative Handbook* (The Free Press: New York).
Lijphart, A. (1975) *The Politics of Accommodation: Pluralism and Democracy in the Netherlands* (Berkeley: University of California Press, 2nd edn; 1st edn, 1968)
Lijphart, A. (1977) *Democracy in Plural Societies: A Comparative Exploration* (New Haven: Yale University Press)
Lijphart, A. (1978) 'The Dutch Electoral System in Comparative Respective', *The Netherlands Journal of Sociology*, 14, pp. 115–33.
Lijphart, A. (1984a) *Democracies: Patterns of Majoritarian and Consensus Government in Twenty-one Countries* (New Haven: Yale University Press).
Lijphart, A. (1984b) *Verzuiling, Pacificatie en kentering in de Nederlands Politiek*, 5th edn (Amsterdam: de Bussy).
Lijphart, A. (1989) 'From the Politics of Accommodation to Adversarial Politics in the Netherlands: A Reassessment' in Daalder and Irwin (eds), *Politics in the Netherlands: How Much Change?* (London: Cass), pp. 139–53.
Lipschits, I. (1969) *Links en rechts in de politiek* (Meppel: Boom en Zoon).
Lubbers, R. F. M. and C. Lemckert (1980) 'The Influence of Natural Gas on the Dutch Economy' in R. T. Griffiths (ed.) *The Economy and Politics of the Netherlands since 1945* (The Hague: Martinus Nijhoff), pp. 87–114.
Luyten, J. W. and Middendorp, C. P. (1990) 'Links, Rechts en politieke strijdpunten', *Sociale Wetenschappen*, pp. 113–39.
MacMullen, A. L. (1979) 'The Netherlands', in F. F. Ridley (ed.) *Government and Administration in Western Europe* (Oxford: Martin Robertson), pp. 227–39.
Metcalfe, L. (1988) *Institutional Inertia versus Organizational Design: European Policy Coordination in the Member States of the European Community*, paper presented at the ECPR joint sessions in Rimini.
Metze, M. (1990) *Intermediair rapport: Hoe flexibel is de bv nederland?* (Amsterdam: Het Spectrum).
Middendorp, C. P. (1991) *Ideology in Dutch Politics* (Assen/Maastricht: Van Gorcum).
*Miljoenennota 1992* (1992) (The Hague: SDU).

Morlan, R. L. (1953) 'Local Government in the Netherlands', *American Political Science Review*, 52, pp. 103–16.

Morlan, R. L. (1959) 'Central Government Control of Municipalities in the Netherlands', *Western Political Quarterly*, 12, pp. 64–70.

Morlan, R. L. (1962) 'City Manager Contrasts: The Netherlands Experience', *Public Administration Review*, 22, pp. 65–70.

Morlan, R. L. (1964) 'Cabinet Government at the Municapal Level', *Western Political Quarterly*, 17, pp. 317–24.

*OECD in Figures: Supplement to the OECD Observer*, no. 164, June/July 1990.

Oerlemans, J. (1990), *NRC/Handelsblad*, 14 February.

Parris, H., P. Pestieau and P. Saynor (1987) *Public Enterprise in Western Europe* (London: Croom Helm).

Peijnenburg, L. J. T. and T. Sloot (1990), 'Democratic and Administrative Performance' in M. Wolters and P. Coffey (eds), *The Netherlands and EC Membership Evaluated* (London: Pinter), pp. 62–9.

Pijpers, A. E. (1991) 'Dekolonisatie, compensatiedrang en de normalisering van de Nederlandse buitenlandse politiek', *Internationale Spectator*, 45, pp. 62–70.

Polak, J..M. and M. V. Polak (1986) 'Faux Pas ou Pas de Deux? Recent Developments in the Relationship between the Legislature and the Judiciary in the Netherlands', *Netherlands International Review*, vol. 33, pp. 371–411.

Polsby, N. W. (1975) 'Legislatures' in F. I. Greenstein and N. W. Polsby (eds), *Handbook of Political Science* (Reading, Mass.: Addison Wesley), pp. 277–96 .

Robinson, A. D. (1961) *Dutch Organized Agriculture in International Politics 1945–1960* (The Hague: Nijhoff).

Roebroek, J. and T. Berben (1987) 'Netherlands', in P. Flora, *Growth to Limits* (Berlin/New York: Walter de Gruyter).

Rose, R. (1980) 'Government against Sub-Governments: a European Perspective on Washington' in R. Rose and E. Suleiman (eds) *Presidents and Prime Ministers* (Washington, DC: American Enterprise Institute), pp. 284–347.

Rose, R. and I. McAllister (1986) *Voters Begin to Choose. From Closed–Class to Open Elections in Britain* (London: Sage).

Rosenthal, U. and R. Roborgh (1992) 'Administrative trends in the Netherlands', paper presented at the conference on Administrative Modernisation in Europe, Perugia.

Rozemond, S. (1987) *Nederland in West-Europa: een plaatsbepaling* (The Hague: Clingendael).

Sartori, G. (1976) *Parties and Party Systems* (Cambridge University Press).

Schama, S. (1977) *Patriots and Liberators: Revolution in the Netherlands 1780–1813* (New York: Alfred Knopf).

Schama, S. (1989) *The Embarrassment of Riches: An Interpretation of Dutch Culture in the Golden Age* (New York: Alfred Knopf).

Scheffer, P. (1988) *Een Tevreden Natie; Nederland en het wederkerend geloof in de Europese status quo* (Amsterdam: Bakker).

Schöffer, I. (1973) *A short history of the Netherlands* (Amsterdam: Allert de Lange).

Scholten, I. (1980) 'Does Consociationalism Exist? A Critique of the Dutch Experience' in R. Rose (ed.), *Electoral Participation, A Comparative Analysis* (London: Sage), pp. 329–54.

Scholten, I. (1987) 'Corporatism and the Neo-Liberal Backlash in the Netherlands' in I. Scholten (ed.), *Political Stability and Neo-Corporatism* (London: Sage), pp. 120–52.

Schutte, G. J. (1989) 'The Dutch and South Africa: From Sympathy to Aversion', *Internationale Spectator*, 43, pp. 675–9.

Singh, R. (1972) *Policy Development: A Study of the Social and Economic Council of the Netherlands* (Rotterdam: Rotterdam University Press).

Smith, M. L. (1988) 'Some historical problems of corporatist development in the Netherlands' in A. Cox and N. O'Sullivan (eds), *The Corporate State: Corporatism and the State Tradition in Western Europe* (Aldershot: Edward Elgar), pp. 170–97.

Snellen, I. Th. M. (ed.) (1985) *Limits of Government: Dutch Experiences* (Amsterdam: Kobra).

Sociaal en Cultureel Planbureau (1990) *Sociaal en Cultureel Rapport 1990* (Rijswijk: Sociaal en Cultureel Planbureau).

Soetendorp, R. B. (1989) 'The Netherlands and Israel: From a Special to a Normal Relationship', *Internationale Spectator*, 43, pp. 697–700.

Soetendorp, R. B. (1990) 'Security Policy' in M. Wolters and P. Coffey (eds), *The Netherlands and EC Membership Evaluated* (London: Pinter), pp. 137–44.

Stuurman, S. (1983) *Verzuiling, Kapitalisme en Patriarchaat* (Nijmegen: SUN).

Taagepera, R. and M. S. Shugart (1989) *Seats and Votes: The Effects and Determinants of Electoral Systems* (New Haven and London: Yale University Press)

Thomassen, J. (1976) 'Party Identification as a Cross-National Concept: Its Meaning in the Netherlands' in I. Budge, I. Crewe, and D. Farlie (eds), *Party Identification and Beyond* (London: John Wiley), pp. 63–79.

Thomassen, J. J. A. (1990) 'Economic Crisis, Dissatisfaction and Protest' in M. K. Jennings, J. W. Van Deth *et al.*, *Continuities in Political Action* '(Berlin/ New York: Walter de Gruyter).

Thurlings, J. M. G. (1978) *De wankele zuil* (Deventer: Van Loghum Slaterus).

Toonen, Th. A. J. (1987) 'The Netherlands: A Decentralized Unitary State in a Welfare Society', *West European Politics*, 10, pp. 108–29.

Toonen, Th. A. J. (1992) 'Dutch Provinces and the Struggle for the Meso' in L. J. Sharpe (ed.), *Between Locality and Centre: the Rise of the Meso in Europe* (London: Sage).

Tops, P. W. (1990) *Afspiegeling en Afspraak; coalitietheorie en collegevorming in Nederlandse gemeenten* (1946–1986), doctoral dissertation, Leyden University.

Tromp, B. (1985) 'Het verval van politieke partijen', *Het Parool*, 20 December.

Van der Doelen, R. C. J., and J. H. de Jong (1990) 'Energy Policy', in M. Wolters and P. Coffrey (eds), *The Netherlands and EC Membership Evaluated* (London: Pinter), pp. 62–9.

254    *Bibliography*

Van Delden, A. Th. (1989) 'Externe Adviesorganen van de Centrale Overheid' in R. B. Andeweg, A. Hoogerwerf and J. J. A. Thomassen (eds), *Politiek in Nederland*, 3rd edn (Alphen aan den Rijn: Samsom), pp. 146–66.

Van den Berg, J. Th. J., D. J. Elzinga and J. J. Vis (1992) *Parlement en Politiek* (The Hague: SDU).

Van den Berg, J. Th. J. and H. A. A. Molleman (1975) *Crisis in de Nederlandse Politiek*, 2nd edn (Alphen aan den Rijn: Samsom).

Van den Bos, J. M. M. (1991) *Dutch EC Policy Making*, doctoral dissertation, University of Utrecht.

Van Deemen, A. M. A. (1990) 'Theory of Center Parties and Cabinet Formations with an Application to the Dutch Parliamentary System', *Acta Politica*, 25, pp. 187–208.

Van der Eijk, C. and B. Niemöller (1982) *Electoral Change in the Netherlands* (Amsterdam: CT Press).

Van der Eijk, C. and B. Niemöller (1987) 'Electoral Alignments in the Netherlands', *Electoral Studies*, 6, pp. 17–39.

Van Gunsteren, H. R. (1976) *The Quest for Control; A Critique of the Rational-Central-Rule Approach in Public Affairs* (London: Wiley).

Van Mierlo, H. J. G. A. (1986) 'Depillarisation and the Decline of Consociationalism in the Netherlands, 1970–85', *West European Politics*, 9, pp. 97–119.

Van Praag, Ph. (1987) 'Verkiezingscampagnes in de afdelingen' in *Jaarboek Documentatiecentrum Nederlandse Politieke Partijen* (Groningen), pp. 69–70.

Van Praag, Ph. and C. Van der Eijk (1987) 'De laatste tien dagen' in C. van der Eijk and Ph. van Praag (eds), *De Strijd om de Meerderheid* (Amsterdam: CT Press), pp. 97–123.

Van Putten, J. (1982) 'Policy Styles in the Netherlands: Negotiation and Conflict' in J. Richardson (ed.), *Policy Styles in Western Europe* (London: Allen & Unwin), pp. 168–96.

Van Raalte, E. (1959) *The Parliament of the Kingdom of the Netherlands* (London: Hansard Society).

Van Raalte, E. (1991) *Het Nederlandse Parlement* (revised by P. Bovend'Eert and H. Kummeling (The Hague: SDU).

Van Schendelen, M. P. C. M. (1976) 'Information and Decisionmaking in the Dutch Parliament', *Legislative Studies Quarterly*, 2, pp. 231–50.

Van Schendelen, M. P. C. M. (1981) 'Disaffected representation in the Netherlands: A Nonaffected Reappraisal', *Acta Politica*, vol. 16, pp. 161–97.

Van Schendelen, M. P. C. M. (1983) 'Crisis of the Dutch Welfare State', *Contemporary Crises*, 7, pp. 209–30.

Van Schendelen, M. P. C. M. (ed.) (1984) *Consociationalism, Pillarization and Conflict Management in the Low Countries*, special issue of *Acta Politica*, 19, pp. 1–178.

Van Schendelen, M. P. C. M. (1987) 'The Netherlands: from low to high politicisation' in M. P. C. M. van Schendelen and R. J. Jackson (eds), *The Politicisation of Business in Western Europe* (London: Croom Helm).

Van Staden, A. et al. (1978a) 'Role Conceptions in the Post-War Foreign Policy of the Netherlands' in Leurdijk (ed.), *The Foreign Policy of the Netherlands* (Alphen aan den Rijn: Sijthoff & Noordhof), pp. 119–35.

Van Staden, A. (1978b) 'The Role of the Netherlands in the Atlantic Alliance' in Leurdijk (ed.), *The Foreign Policy of the Netherlands* (Alphen aan den Rijn: Sijthoff & Noordhof), pp. 137–65.

Van Staden, A. (1989a) 'The Changing Role of the Netherlands in the Atlantic Alliance' in H. Daalder and G. A. Irwin (eds), *Politics in the Netherlands: How much change?* (London: Cass), pp. 99–111.

Van Staden, A. (1989b) 'Nederland in Internationale Organisaties' in R. B. Andeweg, A. Hoogerwerf and J. Thomassen (eds) *Politiek in Nederland*, 3rd edn. (Alphen aan den Rijn: Samsom).

Van Thijn, E. (1967) 'Van Partijen naar stembusaccoorden' in E. Jurgens *et al.*, *Open Brief* (Amsterdam: Arbeiderspers).

Van Valkenburg, S. (1943) 'Land and People' in B. Landheer (ed.), *The Netherlands* (Berkeley: University of California Press).

Vis, J. (1983) 'Coalition Government in a Constitutional Monarchy: The Dutch Experience' in V. Bogdanor (ed.), *Coalition Government in Western Europe* (London: Heinemann), pp. 153–68.

Visser, J. (1990) *In Search of Inclusive Unionism* (Deventer: Kluwer).

Vlekke, B. H. M. (1943) 'The Dutch Before 1581' in B. Landheer (ed.), *The Netherlands* (Berkeley: University of California Press).

Vlekke, B. H. M. (1945) *Evolution of the Dutch Nation* (New York: Roy Publishers).

Voorhoeve, J. J. C. (1979) *Peace, Profits and Principles; A Study of Dutch Foreign Policy* (The Hague: Martinus Nijhoff).

Voorhoeve, J. J. C. (1991) 'Nederland: een middelgrote mogendheid in zakformaat', *Internationale Spectator*, 45, pp. 54–61.

Wassenberg, A. F. P. (1982) 'Neo-Corporatism and the Quest for Control: the cuckoo game' in G. Lehmbruch and Ph. Schmitter (eds), *Patterns of Corporatist Policy-Making* (London: Sage), pp. 83–108.

Windmuller, J. P. (1969) *Labor Relations in the Netherlands* (Ithaca NY: Cornell University Press).

Windmuller, J. P., C. De Galan and A. F. van Zweeden (1983) *Arbeidsverhoudingen in Nederland* (Utrecht: Aula).

Woldendorp, J. J. (1985) 'Hoe Neo-Korporatistisch is Nederland Georganiseerd? een overzicht' in J. E. Keman, J. J. Woldendorp and D. Braun, *Het Neo-Korporatisme als Nieuwe Politieke Strategie: krisisbeheersing met beleid en (door) overleg?* (Amsterdam: CT Press), pp. 115–37.

Wolinetz, S. B. (1983) *Neo-Corporatism and Industrial Policy in the Netherlands*, paper presented at the Annual Meeting of the Canadian Political Science Association, Vancouver, British Columbia.

Wolinetz, S. B. (1989) 'Socio-Economic Bargaining in the Netherlands: Redefining the Post-War Policy Coalition', in Daalder and Irwin (eds), *Politics in the Netherlands* (London: Cass), pp. 79–98.

Wolters, M. (1984) *Interspace Politics*, doctoral dissertation, Leyden University.

Wolters, M. (1990) 'Political and Legal Effects' in M. Wolters and P. Coffey (eds), *The Netherlands and EC Membership Evaluated* (London: Pinter), pp. 62–9.

Wolters, M. and P. Coffey (eds) (1990) *The Netherlands and EC Membership Evaluated* (London: Pinter).

# Index